# TOWNSHIPS

# A BUR OAK ORIGINAL

# TOWNSHIPS

EDITED BY MICHAEL MARTONE

PHOTOGRAPHS BY RAYMOND BIAL

UNIVERSITY OF IOWA PRESS 〜 IOWA CITY

University of Iowa Press, Iowa City 52242

Copyright © 1992 by Michael Martone

All rights reserved

Printed in the United States of America

First edition, 1992

Design by Richard Hendel

Printed on acid-free paper

Frontispiece: Dana, Indiana, 1986, photograph by Raymond Bial

Library of Congress Cataloging-in-Publication Data

Townships/edited by Michael Martone; photographs by Raymond Bial.—1st ed.

p.      cm.—(A Bur oak original)

ISBN 0-87745-354-3, ISBN 0-87745-355-1 (pbk.)

1. City and town life—Middle West.   2. Middle West—Social life
and customs.   3. Middle West—Biography.   I. Martone, Michael.

II. Bial, Raymond.   III. Series.

F355.T68   1992          91-25925

977—dc20          CIP

# CONTENTS

# TOWNSHIPS

# CORRECTIONVILLE, IOWA:

# AN INTRODUCTION

Pelisipia, Polypotania, Saratoga, Illinoia, Assenispia, Michigania, Cherronesus, Metropotania, Sylvania. . . . Thomas Jefferson drew up a list of names for the new states northwest of the Ohio River. Since 1776, Congress had been promising land to the soldiers who fought the War of Independence and had considered the sale of land in the new region as a way to raise money for the war. Now with the war over and the land being purchased from the tribes and ceded by the states with claims, Congress appointed two committees, one to plan for the governments of the new territory, the other charged with locating them and drawing up methods of their disposal. Thomas Jefferson sat on both committees.

I think of him sitting on top of his mountain in Virginia, not in the squat fireplug mansion of Monticello with its collections and contraptions, but in the little cubic cottage out back, the honeymoon house, the first building he put up after balding the hill. Through the mullioned windows he watched his slaves tend the latticework of gardens that stretched along the ridge, square beds divided into smaller squares. Before him he had a rough map of the territory under consideration. For his purposes, it didn't matter how accurate that map was. He had never been there, though George Washington had actually toured Ohio and even surveyed a few miles there. With a ruler, Jefferson drew a straight line north from the falls near what is today Louisville. The lakes, the rivers, the hills did not deflect the line. From his original meridian, he began to lay out squares of space that would eventually add up to new states that needed naming.

Jefferson's list has a goofy classicism. He screws Latin endings on native names. Sitting in his little cottage, he is like a kid in a tree house daydreaming about the secret club he is founding where everyone holds a title and everything is ordered and embedded in ritual. Of course, Jefferson's musing isn't *like* the summer distractions of the neighborhood gangleader, it is exactly the same thing, the only difference being in the scale of the invention. It is not just a map of the backyards in the local cul-de-sac but a whole continent he is considering. I like very much the names he scribbled inside his neat squares. They contrast smartly with the severe and logical grid he generated to net up the beginnings of an empire. The names that did settle on those places are harmonics of those Jefferson toyed with. Michigan, Illinois echo the originals as if they are the final versions of copies of copies, only the main plosives picked out from the mumbling through time. But it is the chutzpah of the whole enterprise, the wicked inventiveness and brute reason that allowed him to sweep away the physical features of the West and coolly scale it down to human size.

There were compromises. Jefferson originally thought in hundreds, ten-by-ten-mile squares. And his miles were the nautical kind, I don't know why. With the Ordinance of 1785, the Congress of the Confederation created the office of the Geographer of the United States charged with surveying the new lands into six-by-six-mile squares called townships. The land ordinances of 1784, 1785, and 1787 address how the recently independent colonies would handle their own colonial expansion and were platforms for confronting the issues of expanding slavery and extending human rights. Those laws prefigured the workings of the Constitution, being written in Philadelphia while the initial ranges were being surveyed in Ohio, and its first ten amendments. But I am more interested here in the physical residue of these acts, the scoring of the land with that waffle grid of true bearings.

✽

Recently, I came across a book by Joseph W. Ernst called *With Compass and Chain: Federal Land Surveyors in the Old Northwest, 1785–1816*, published by Arno Press in 1979. In it, Ernst explores how Jefferson's abstract ideas were made real. Ernst is consumed with procedure and the practical questions of implementing theory in the field. He records the surveyors' food and pay, their measuring instruments, their letters and notes, their payoffs and politic⸱

These men walked every inch of the ground that would become the Midwest.

On September 30, 1785, Thomas Hutchins, the Geographer of the United States, sent his first survey notes to Congress:

> Based on observations made while running the E-W line from the North bank of the Ohio at point due north from Western termination of a line run as a southern boundary of Pennsylvania. 46 chains and 80 links West of this point, lands disposed for growth of vines. Variety of trees and bushes. The whole of the above described Land is too rich to produce Wheat, but is well adapted for Indian Corn, Tobacco, Hemp, Flax, Oats, etc. and every species of Garden Vegetables, it abounds with great quantities of Pea Vine, Grass, and nutrias weeds of which cattle are very fond and on which they soon grow fat.
>
> 33 Chains, 14 links, which make a mile from the Meridian, High land.
>
> 22 Chains, 37 links, the land is extrodinary [sic] good, and in some places it is too rich for Wheat, where fine Meadow may be made. Timber Locust, Black Walnut, Mulberry, Hickory, Elm.
>
> 21 Chains, crosses a ridge, land between good, in several places it is tolerably free from brush or underwood.
>
> 6 Chains, 60 links, brook running South 20 degrees West.
>
> 14 Chains, 40 links, steep narrow ridge nearly 170 feet high, perpendicular. Covered on east side with many bushes and weeds. Golden rod, the latter when timely and properly applied has been found efficacious in curing the bite of the most venomous Snake. Soil on the ridge equal parts sand and black mould
>
> 13 Chains, gradual descent, thicket with trees, the whole of this distance was cut through for the Chain carriers to pass.
>
> 5 Chains, 63 links, makes two miles.

In the first two miles of his survey, Hutchins plows through a sheer ridge face, fords a stream, and clears a straight blaze through a thicket. As the geometry of his task draws him straight on, his eye is drawn to this new, new world in his periphery. He sometimes reports what he finds, but of course he sees deeper into what he sees to what can be used and exploited. He is musing on the proper order of domesticating the wilderness. It is another act of imagination. In his mind, he imports the grain and crops. A pedestrian Adam, he names the trees he finds while at the same time he pictures the lumbering. It goes without saying the timber's sectioning, milling, and planing follow. Its metamorphosis into furniture and into the wagons to haul it to new houses is the final destination. He brings the garden to the Garden. His vision even includes the metabolism of the native weeds into the fat on cattle. He gets carried away here, a touching flourish, empathizing with the livestock. He almost breaks into narrative. This flight of fancy is made even more tender when the reader remembers that its writer is mired down in mire, swamp, and jungle, bitten by bugs and ever conscious of those venomous snakes. Linking it together is the stretching of the chain itself, inching along the ground, another snake, rattling over rocks and hollow logs and fresh-cut stumps, sizzling through the grass as it is reeled back in. Sound has come to the forest, the haunting racket of the ghosts to come trailing the forged, precise shackles of their vices. There is someone here now who will hear the trees falling.

In the geographer's notes as well, there is another story. While he suggests the cultivation of Indian corn and tobacco, his eye is peeled for the Indian himself. His survey had already been delayed by skirmishes, his stakes and corner markers would be destroyed once he moved on. The American incursion into the lands northwest of the Ohio River would proceed in its crystalline manner, square by square, but it was preceded itself by the most irregular pattern of purchase, conquest, or acquisition. In contrast to the logic woven by the patient web of townships, a Midwestern map of treaty cessations looks like the splotches of woodland camouflage. The patches of Indian territory sold or won were chewed away from the edges, eating their way toward the center. The water routes took the Europeans far inland where they struck out from the forts at Detroit, Chicago, Louisville, and St. Louis. The irregular shapes of the treaty lands, their borders fixed not by compass and chain but by the land itself, rivers, lakes, and hills, suggest the anarchy of their taking, a swipe here, a swath there.

Which is more terrifying? This random rent or the steady quilting? Perhaps they were worse taken together, the chaos so reason ably ordered and camouflaged by the brand of that order which remains cut into the land today.

No other feature so marks the Midwestern landscape as the signature of townships. The six-mile squares broke down into thirty-six sections of one square mile each, and each square mile of 640 acres reduced to those plots of recognizable dimension, the 80, the back 40. There is nothing natural about it. It is not like the Spanish moss drooping from Southern trees or the dripping ferns of the Pacific Northwest, nor is it like the rocky scrabble in the soil of the East or the dusty reaches of buttes and mesas in the West. We know the Midwest by this arbitrary and artificial pattern that has been imposed upon it.

Though most of the public lands outside the original colonies and the South were surveyed into these grids, it is this chunk of land, stretching from Ohio west to Minnesota and Iowa, where its pattern is most deeply inscribed. Here, the subtlety and variety of the region's topography and ecology cannot suppress the imposition of the grid. Farther west, the landscape becomes much more spectacular, space an identifying feature in itself. The people are fewer, and they begin to speak of the land in sections not acres. Historically, the Homestead Act of 1862 changed the focus of land claims. Individual settlement powered land acquisition west of the Missouri River rather than the communal motives that informed the original ordinances. The grid "took" in those more eastern states, and, though the townships governing structure have withered away in many places, but not in all places by any means, what survives is the network of roads and fields oriented north to south and east to west, and measured out on a human scale of rods and acres that scores this place.

The Midwest, then, began as a highly abstract work of the imagination and lingers so today. The power of the grid that overlays it often prevents us from seeing the place itself. It has been characterized from its inception in two dimensions alone, flattened by fiat. At the same time, for those of us from the Midwest, this plane geometry that enmeshes us might be the only connection we have between us. What links the autoworker in Detroit with the actuary in Des Moines, the mussel digger near Galena with the strip miner near Athens. Perhaps it is only this thin tissue of coordinates plotted a long time ago that can tie together this region's inhabitants.

We are Midwesterners because we think ourselves into the map of the place without having to fit into the place itself. We relate to each other on that mathematical plane alone.

*

I didn't know it then but the borders of my own neighborhood where I grew up in Fort Wayne, Indiana, were streets that followed the original township grid. My mother had set State Street on the north and Tyler Street on the west as the limits of my range. There was one exception. I could be ushered across those busy streets by watchful safety patrols to Price Elementary School, sited at their intersection. On the south was Spring Street where we lived. On the eastern edge was the smaller square of Hamilton Park.

But within this one-square-mile border, developers had carved out streets with asymmetrical abandon. A map of those streets looks like the burrowings in cross section of a colony of termites. Jefferson thought the grid to be the most democratic of forms. North Highlands, my neighborhood, the first suburb in town, was having nothing to do with democracy. Its larger houses, brick with droopings awnings, were perched on hills at the prows of parabolas. There were pockets of cheap ranch houses that looked like sprouting motel courts set off behind massive clapboard four-squares positioned off-center on oblong lots. The roads followed the contours of the land. The land had been bulldozed, before the subdivision, into the traps and bunkers, the roughs and fairways of a golf course. A friend of mine lived in what had been the clubhouse. Its lawn still had patches of the practice green disrupting the bluegrass like a strange weed infestation. It seemed you were meant to get lost in the winding streets as if they were a defense against invading hordes from the greater city who could then be defeated in the maze of tree-lined streets. The neighborhood was a watered-down version of vernacular villages of Greek Islands where the dice-white buildings tumble down a hillside. Its warren of alleys and doublebacks were defensive measures against pirates. Here, the houses were all detached, the only raiders the armies of children free to run wild in the yards between them.

Before the golf course, the land had been owned by the Hamilton family. Some of the street names were Edith, Alice, Ida, Jesse, names of the Hamilton children. Edith grew up to be the grea* popularizer of ancient Greek myths. We read her book, *Mythology*, in our language arts classes at school. Growing up in Fort Wayne, I read about Perseus and Medusa, Theseus in the labyrinth, Odysseus wandering home. I also marveled at the strange connection that had brought these old stories to me. I saw a picture of the ancient Miss Hamilton in the theater of Dionysus in Athens being named a citizen of the city. She wore the draping gown of the Golden Age. I'd sit on the steep banks of Hamilton Park, where we sledded in winter, and imagine it was another classical theater.

Hamilton Park had those steep hills because it had been, before it was grassed over, a trash dump. I played in a ruin. The grass covered the terraced steps of the sides where dogwoods, redbuds, and flowering crab apples had been planted. Rows of lilac outlined the square rim of its top lip. There were ball diamonds, tennis and basketball courts, and picnic tables where you could play Rook at the bottom of the pit. When it rained, water collected on the floor of the sunken park, and, sometimes, the buried trash would work its way back to the surface. Burned and broken blue glass, smashed tin cans, rusted springs, buttons, plates and cups bottle caps, nails, books with rotting pages. All the kids had collections of their finds.

I look back now and see how this little patch of ground surrendered up its history, how too it was a frame for the larger histories of the world. Somewhere along the way I realized that classical Athens was not much bigger than my own home town, and the stories I read of those golden ages, interpreted by someone from my town, were relentlessly local while they spoke to the larger human condition. I also realized that the stories of this place were just beginning to be told. Platting the landscape, subdividing the subdivisions of property would not be enough to kick-start the culture of myth. We who grew up in the Midwest would have to sit here awhile, within the borders of our own defined neighborhoods, on the banks of a natural theater and watch as the junk of our too recent past resurrected itself and appeared to us as treasure in the dust at our feet.

*

In Iowa, the idea of the township was raised to the nth degree. The squares of the sections quilt the larger squares of the townships that form the squares of the counties. It is a joke in Iowa that there is only one diagonal road. From the air, Iowa looks like a rumpled crossword puzzle. The squares spell out the season in an alphabet of three green letters—corn, beans, pasture—that alternate with the ink-black turned fields. Driving through the country on all those straight roads, I could check my odometer with the regular rotation of features. Intersecting road, cornfield, soybean field, lane, corn, bean, house, bean, corn, road. A Midwestern mantra of quarter-mile heartbeats. When you drive long enough in Iowa you've strung together a rosary of small towns as well that punctuates the rhythm of the spaces between. Cottonville leads to Garry Owen, Garry Owen to Cascade, Cascade to Monticello. The towns are like knots in the chains the surveyors used. The towns can go together to form a kind of picaresque story line. Driving through Iowa can become a kind of modern walkabout, the water towers painted with the pictographs of town names, booster slogans, and zip codes rise up to meet you like giants on the horizon.

Once, I strung together a story that drew me west. Starting from Spillville in the northeast corner of the state, I vectored to Hospers in the northwest. In between was the town of West Bend. It takes three points to draw a line, and the line I sketched followed US 18 as it stepped north or south occasionally shooting across the state. The towns were linked by an eccentric geometry. Each contained the life's work of bachelor folk artists. In Spillville, brothers had built gigantic wooden sculptures housing clocks. In West Bend, a priest had constructed a grotto dedicated to the Virgin on the lawn of the church. In Hospers, a citizen sculpted a garden of painted concrete statues for the town square. Each of these creations is amazing in itself, but I find the parallels of their creation more interesting.

You learn that the artists never traveled more than a few miles from their homes. The wood for the clocks, you hear, was shipped in. Butternut, grapefruit, mahogany, teak arrived by train whose conductors on their travels were always on the lookout for the fresh scrap of lumber, a new bark to peel. The shells and semiprecious stones that encrust the bubbling chambers of the grotto were also imported. Quartz and coal, fossils and pumice. The corals of the tropics grew on the thickening reef in West Bend. The artist in

Hospers took his models from the books he read. Sculptures of Carrara marble were copied in the other medium of cement. The worldly contributions to the art came into the hands of resolutely local artists, and yet each of them included in their elaborate schemes a piece or niche or grouping dedicated to the act of travel itself. There is a History of Transportation clock, a tower of Babel wedding cake with marching bas-reliefs of vehicles topped by the legend "Time Flies." There is also a clock commemorating Lindbergh, a globe carved up with latitudes and longitudes cutting through the swirling clouds of the wood's grain. The grotto blesses mobility. Do I remember a side altar of the flight into Egypt? In Hospers, another History of Transportation includes a green tractor in the evolution from dinosaur to rocket ship. The tractor is rendered most realistically. Its models bubbled through the town as I toured. The artist swiped the paint for his tractor, the green Deere shade, from the local machine shop.

The clocks must stay in Spillville. They were willed to the town on that condition. The grotto is rooted to its lawn in West Bend. The garden of melting statues is cemented to its square in Hospers. I like how all of these artists had recognized their own boundaries and then constructed a few more but still managed to elaborate, to the extreme, their chosen art. Once they defined their labor to such narrow tolerances they seem to have found an infinite source of freedom. The clocks, the grotto, the sculptures are amazing, literal mazes of their creators' visions. They play all the variations within those limits.

Think of the Midwest as a vast plane studded with nodes of creation where artists are making a place by staying in place, riddling it with possibilities. Some, like the artists of Spillville, West Bend, and Hospers, remain physically in the places they are creating while others take their places with them. Those who travel still worry the fragments they take with them from their given coordinates, a piece of the true cross.

You can draw another line through Iowa from Dubuque to Sioux City. That line would be the western extension of the northern border of Illinois. It also forms the northern border of a tier of counties in central Iowa. Remember that in Iowa counties are laid out in a regular pattern of squares that replicates the township squares forming those counties. Just south of the Dubuque line there is a parallel line called a correction line. The county boundaries running north and south take a little jog to the west along this line so that this tier of counties isn't exactly square but whittled down a bit as they head north. The correction allows a two-dimensional surveying system to be placed on the spherical globe. Reading *With Compass and Chain*, I learned that not only did the surveyors of the townships have to struggle with the physical burdens of their task but they also had to face the geometric paradox of their assignment. They were charged with squaring the earth. A correction line was one of their solutions.

Correctionville, Iowa, sits in the notch of correction between Ida and Woodberry counties. When I lived in Iowa, I always wanted to visit the place where theory butted up against reality. I never made the trip, but in my idle moments, I did like to speculate what the small town might be like. I imagined a main street filled with shops making minor adjustments to small engines, bicycle seats, and television sets. A town of photo retouchers, glassblowers, paint mixers, piano tuners, tree pruners, barbers, and tailors. Every house would need fixing up. In my mind, Correctionville was a kind of rheostat regulating the flow of all the forces coursing through the Midwest. The Delphi of tinkering. The epicenter of alteration. The mecca of dentists.

"We don't have the prison, that's for sure!" Maude Schemmel told me. "People usually think we have the prison here."

I had called the town clerk in Correctionville, thinking I could have a city map sent to me. I thought I could find out if there was a chamber of commerce and when the library was open. I called the clerk, but Maude Schemmel, the librarian, answered the phone.

"I answer the phone when the clerk is out of the office," she told me. "She answers the library phone when I'm not here." A cybernetic logic behind this, I thought.

I told her that I knew the town wasn't the seat of the penitentiary and that I called because I was interested in the correction line, in townships, and in mapping. We talked about the town name and its history. She would send me their Bicentennial booklet. Then we got lost while talking about geography and charts. I told her about the Greenland problem, how the island isn't as big as it looks like it is on certain maps.

"It depends upon the projection you use. Every map distorts the world some way," I said. "Iowa uses a different projection than Illinois or Indiana. They want their maps to be more accurate running north to south."

I continued. Not really knowing what I was saying. For a moment I became confused and suggested that the correction corrected something on the earth itself instead of on the map of it.

Maude said, "You mean if I started walking due north from Correctionville, the miles would get longer the farther I went?"

"Only if you were walking on a map," I said vaguely. I was distracted by the picture in my mind of the librarian striding across the map of Iowa, crushing the names and numbers, trampling the ideograms of campsites and rest stops. I also thought about Thomas Hutchins, the first Geographer of the United States, as he stepped off into Ohio dragging his chains behind him, the ones he would use to try to shackle the planet.

I had exhausted the limited expertise I had in the matters of cartography when Maude asked her final question. "But what if the map was as big as the world?"

I'd like to go to the real Correctionville someday. I have been living and working as a writer in the other Correctionville, the one in my mind. There, I am constantly tinkering with the maps of the Midwest, trying to damp the distortions as much as possible while realizing that each selected vision of the place is a map more detailed than the thing it represents.

The Midwest is unique for this framework of squares stretched across the landscape, this cage of reason that has never quite fit. It is ground that has been imprinted, literally. It comes to us with its own fractal geometry where the smallest of its parts replicates itself on ever larger scales. All the efforts of politicians and surveyors to net up the region in knowing have not begun to capture the spaces between the weave. To write about the Midwest is to cast a web in those spaces and then wait patiently for things to begin to stick.

For this volume, I invited Midwestern writers to contribute essays. I asked them first to think of their actual townships, if they knew them at all, or to extend the notion to any bordered region of their childhoods and how those places formed them and inform their writing today. I thought of the book as a kind of quilt itself, another version of the quilted landscape. It would be a kind of crazy quilt, the fabric each author brought to this book a scrap from the fabric of poems, stories, or essays he or she usually wrote.

It is hard to think of the Midwest as a distinct region. There is little agreement as to just what states make up the territory. I made an arbitrary division when I chose the states of Ohio, Indiana, Michigan, Illinois, Wisconsin, Minnesota, and Iowa to represent my Midwest. Even within the limited definition, the harder task was in finding a device to link together the disparate lives the authors recounted. The metaphor of townships provided such a device. It is a kind of portrait in pointillism, filling in a square here or there. I cannot pretend that this current volume begins to cover all the territory. Once I employed the model of township to capture the Midwest, the possibility of infinite subdivision presented itself. Perhaps the essays here will begin to cohere in some way as you read them. I am depending on finding a gestalt that will apply and then a picture will emerge.

It seems to me still that the metaphors linking us together as Midwesterners are few and flimsy. Anyone claiming to have found the common thread of regionalism here also tends to initiate its unraveling. Even the simple argument about the Midwest's location is a telling one. If that question remains unanswered, the one that follows, just what it means to be a Midwesterner, can be avoided. We are left always with the Midwest as lump, as leftover. We are always making the most of it, whatever it is.

Arbitrary as well was the one criterion I imposed on the authors to qualify them as Midwestern writers. They had to be native to one of the states in my arbitrary listing. The final list of contributors, the careful reader will note, includes a few authors born outside my boundaries who either surprised me with that fact after I saw the essay or convinced me to include them with the authority of a Midwestern childhood. And some other authors I associated with a par ticular state surprised me by writing about another area altogether. It doesn't matter to me now. I like a flaw in the carpet's pattern. The reality of townships, the things themselves and this book, never fit the relentless logic of its conception.

Think of these essays then as a collection of corrections that are not quite correct. They are minute though complex attempts at location. They are adding, bit by bit, layer by layer, to the accumulating sediments that underlie our understanding of this place.

# AT THE EDGE OF TOWN:

# DULUTH, MINN.

Like all curmudgeons I am devoted to insulting someone's emotion of a given moment in hopes they will move away from it to a germane but more ethical emotion. For example, curmudgeons know that patriotism and nostalgia are the cheapest emotions there are: bullies, especially, are much given to patriotism and nostalgia. Their eyes fill as Jimmy Stewart keeps Bedford Falls from turning into Pottersville. Their eyes fill when someone drags out the old Brownie 620 snapshots—but the weeper may in the very next hour batter his wife or work out a new legal loophole for his firm, giving it an extension on its wrecking the planet for profit. It is not uncommon for lobbyists who contrive exquisite ways to cheat the poor to have by heart several of Lincoln's bons mots. We curmudgeons don't trust people who swing into a throaty tenor to "Ich hatt' einen Kamerad." Teary memories are easy. Planning for peace, difficult. Curmudgeons fear people whose hearts cry about the past. Incidentally, a thoroughgoing nostalgia addict doesn't stop at crying over lost wilderness in Brazil or Minnesota: he or she mews over the manufactured U.C. British 1910s of Masterpiece Theatre, or the 1850s of the Dakotas, without knowing beans about either.

Patriotism is known as "the last refuge of the scoundrel," and nostalgia is one of the first demons psychotherapists relieve their clients of. But there is a third facile emotion: it is the virtuous feeling attendant upon loving natural places. People who feel it is actually *virtuous*, somehow, to love a place save themselves the pain of realizing there aren't many lovable places left. We curmudgeons worry, and then scold. We feel a sort of dread that so few people follow Wendell Berry from simple love of a particular countryside to thinking through *how* all systems connect, so we can try specif ways of amending our greed in order to preserve the patterns. For every person willing to do such thinking, there seem to be thousands simply feeling *virtuous* because they prefer woods to hotels or, say, Duluth's Lester Park Road to New York's Alphabets. They need to admit it takes money to live in beauty.

Money. The poor do not have the money of Kenneth Fearing or Louis Bromfield or Aldo Leopold or of the hundreds of people scribing logs and raising their cabins at the edges of forests. The "simple" life is a luxury. Second, nature lovers should figure out exactly who—which large groups—are ruining our planet. Then they should design conversations to have with high-up people in those organizations that would help those people identify finer feelings than conventional profit making.

Before going further, I would like to offer information that may surprise people who don't particularly cotton to the social-science approaches to ecology. In Minneapolis, the course at Central High School with the longest sign-up list is a new "interpersonal skills" course. Apparently, young people want to know how to talk to opponents so they won't feel hopeless. We lovers of place want to stop feeling hopeless, too. The social-work idea and the family-therapy idea is this: certain types of conversations serve to wake the torpid ethics even of administrators of rich organizations now wrecking human and animal and plant life. Sometimes, those people—very high-up, thoroughly middle-aged people—*change.*

A place lover of worth, then, is not a sixty-year-old noting how beautifully Duluth droops on its gigantic escarpment over Lake Superior. It is true that the foghorn's cold grunt, every three minutes of a thick summer morning, and the rocky edge and the mindless, beautiful forests running away northward, and the wind slaking down from Hudson Bay are wonderful—but a place lover of worth can't settle for rejoicing but must say, "Such love of place is simple. *Anyone* can hide in mere love of place. What is *uncomfortable* is to realize that the very rich are going to mine gold from northern Minnesota, splatting cyanide into the ground, because cyanide is a chemical used in the cleaning of gold from its coarse ore. The rich are going to sell the ancient forests of Canada (to Japan, of course, but not only to Japan), and for all the talk of reseeding, those forests will not regrow nearly so fast as they are taken."

It is so painful to think of all that the rich get away with. It is easier to rail at how the middle class manage their small holdings at the forest's edge. On the outlying roads of Duluth, for example—Arrowhead Road, Pike Lake Road, the Howard Gnesen Road—likely at the edges of anywhere, gravel driveways are flung down at short intervals across the raw culverts like little drawbridges to castles. The houses stand thirty or forty feet behind the ditchline, with pickups (while they still run) parked next to the kitchen door, and pickups (when they no longer work, and no one has picked up on the Coast-to-Coast FOR SALE signs in their windows) relegated to anywhere they will fit between the birches or Norway pines behind the house. To save a lot of money, you don't subscribe to the garbage service: you simply dump metal and glass trash farther back into the woods. You can play your rock all you like because this is the *edge*, not the center, of civilized life. There is more vandalizing of allotment gardens and toolsheds than there was during the 1930s, but there is no more disrespect for forest as such than there was then. As a child I grieved at any new building on these wild roads. It was as if the new little houses in their rows were dozens of little fists stuck into nature. Like all children who know some woods, I wanted the world to stay wild. Wild, to me and to my best friend, Arlene, was holy: city was dreamless. At nine years old, Arlene and I shook hands: when we were old, at forty, we would leave our husbands and go to the North Woods and live until we died in a log cabin. Forty years later, I visited Arlene during the week before she died of cancer. I asked her when I should come. Nights, she said: would you come at two or three in the morning? Right. That was when the drugs didn't cover well. That was when her exhausted husband was asleep. It was hard to hover by her bed, dangling one arm on her tubings stand, watching as she gathered herself from the dispersal of pain in order to say a sentence. She was spooky with drugs, too. "We had better do it," she made out to me: "We had better do it—go to the log cabin in the North Woods." I said, "That was one of the best ideas you and I ever had."

When we love our planet so much, it seems queer that we haven't talked everybody into saving it. Perhaps what stands in our way is those very feelings of virtuousness that nature lovers indulge in. I have put together three likely reasons for their holierness-than-thou.

First, perhaps nature lovers lack compassion for those who live in ugly places because they don't *know* how ugly people have made the earth. Joan Didion recently remarked in the *New York Review of Books* that "what is singular about New York, and remains virtually incomprehensible to people who live in less rigidly organized parts of the country, is the minimal level of comfort and opportunity its citizens have come to accept."

Or second, perhaps we all make a virtue out of anything we enjoy lest we otherwise feel guilty that others haven't the same blessing. I have even heard men feel virtuous because they weren't bald. Surely the unconscious chooses that attitude so it won't have to feel sorry for people who are bald. If we noticed that others haven't the same access to land that we have, we would suppose we ought to share with them—but there are so *many* of them! And the poor often have not been brought up with a taste for quiet solitude, reading, listening to Mozart. If they came to our edge of wilderness they would hound loons, otters, and philosophers with TV-ad values— rock, loud motors for the skiers shouting "Hit it!" a thousand times in an afternoon, snowmobiles to shatter the snowy woods' quiet. It is education (alas) that makes people use nature quietly.

The third reason for virtuous feeling is that it is psychologically natural to regard nature as holy. It is a necessary part of stage development to ascribe *holiness* to what lies far outside our parents. Here is how this worked in me. My father was a very high-minded, fallen-away Presbyterian. Once he discovered that good churchmen were frequently just as crooked as nonchurchmen, he left the church. My mother came from a gregarious, confident family of agnostics, every one. Both parents either growled or joked about the Sunday School pamphlets I brought home. "Color Jesus's robe blue," went the instructions, and I had happily done so. "Color his hair yellow." (Of course! This was Minnesota in the 1930s!) "Leave his gown white. Lightly shade in brown and yellow together to make the sands of Judea." Sunday Schools did not yet provide three-tiered Crayola boxes, which held so many colors we might have given a different blue each to the Sea of Galilee and the Jordan and the Red Sea. Both parents jeered at my pastel Jesus. Well—but kids are brave. I tried again: I recited for them my Memory Line: "The Lord God loves each one of us like a child." No god in his right mind, my mother allowed, would love our species with its hypocrisy, its warmongering, and its racism. We were a family where Mussolini's cruelty in Abyssinia got discussed at the table. There were often quite crispy phrases floating about our living room, such as God would be an idiot to love our species and therefore, since God is not an idiot, there is no God, all said with a lift of the chin.

That is all very well for *adults,* but a psychological fact is that if *children* are locked out of feeling loved by the gods of Duluth churches, they will go looking for a god they *can* imagine and feel loved by. It is a healthy wanting for a species with a neocortex, after all: we have to move away past our parents to what is greater, more general—the *omnium invisibilium.* As species go, the human one is partial to concepts. We love to connect unlike things by metaphor, and once we've got the taste for it, we are never satisfied with just the actual parents anymore.

So when conventional religious adoration is not allowed, the child turns pantheist, if that child has any access at all to natural landscape. I gratefully pottered about the rough paths of Hunter's Hill, the rock outbreaks between the Jean Duluth Road and the cliff edge, and with Arlene, who had a satisfying penchant for the morbid, fantasized about all the dead at the bottom of Lake Superior. Virginia Woolf said we must each live in the world of people and the world of trees: I went 87 percent for trees. As I played in the vacant dairy pastures, I was sorry each time a new road was cut through to the forest.

It has been over a century since Tolstoy remarked that adults concentrate so hard on pushing coal smoke and naphtha into the sky—and cheating one another—that they fail to enjoy this world given to us for our joy (in the first paragraph of the novel *Resurrection*). There is some good to shaming, which Tolstoy intended with that passage, but not enough. Corporations still mine and wreck the environment. Perhaps we people who so much love certain *places* and who know there is a "sense of place" that can exhilarate the mind need to think of ourselves as corporate shareholders. If we do not own stock in companies ourselves, perhaps we know relations or friends who do. At least we can imagine ourselves to be shareholders. What if we were Exxon shareholders? It is likely that thousands of us would gladly have eschewed 0.3 percent of our dividend (if that's what it would have taken) to fire a drunken captain or to mount job searches for sober captains. Corporations lie a good deal. Perhaps they lie in saying that all their shareholders want is profit. Perhaps the fee owners of mining companies do *not* want cyanide trickling or splashing into the aquifers of northern Minnesota. If keen businesspeople in fact have better ethical instincts than their groups claim they have, we need a new kind of conversation—the kind called group consciousness raising.

Growing up on the line between two opposites—town and wilderness—has disabused me of any notion that opposed ideas make restful tangents. But I have also stood on the line between literature and social psychology. Literary people look down on social psychologists and usually refuse to see how they can change attitudes in fairly rigid, grown-up people. Social scientists are more and more using literature in their training programs, but what they respect least in literati is the puling nature lover who neither in poetry nor in fiction takes on the big boys—those in extractive industries. Social scientists would like us writers to drop the vague sensitivity and learn skills like Intentional Interviewing—if we really want to save our place.

Let's give ourselves, right here, two minutes' jeering at phrases like "group consciousness raising" and "Intentional Interviewing." How revolting the jargon of the social sciences is! So turgid is it, in fact, that for every Ernest Becker and Virginia Satyr and Murray Bowen there seem to be hundreds of social workers and therapists whose prose is so abstract, given to generalities, and without particulars that their own colleagues refuse to breast through the sludge of it.

But when we are done insulting their bad writing, let's tell the social scientists that we want to learn their jargon (for its accuracy) and their new processes. Put simply, it is the therapists and social workers and group psychologists who can move a polluter from his or her laugh, "Yeah? Just try fighting profit and progress, chump!" to noticing that some part of that very polluter really doesn't want to wreck the Arctic, or the Antarctic, or the places between that we love.

We had better approach the rich shareholders of extractive industries than settle for snapping at small-scale trashers and polluters on near-the-city roads. Besides, a couple of hours a month studying how actually to *change* planet wrecking organizations will be such horrible work we can feel conscientious about it. If we did two or three *days'* worth of learning this new field—intentional interviewing—even the crossest curmudgeons of us could relax as we regard Duluth's choppy harbor—or any harbor. For we would know we had done very modern, very exacting, intelligent labor for our planet. We could relax as we hike lightly between (not on) lichen and flowers of St. Louis County—or of any county.

# THE QUIET HOUSE

The closest I've ever come to myth was that favorite game in college—
we called it Earliest Memory, my friends sprawled out in someone's
living room. *Moonlight on the bedroom floor* we'd say or *oh god, that
fall down the steep back stairs.* . . . Still, I've always been puzzled: do
we carry around stories, these old images, because we remember
them or because they have been told to us over and over, held up
like communal treasure? That river of milk, say, pouring down the
long hallway in our tiny Chicago apartment one morning when I
was four, and my mother, sitting down at the end of that white
expanse, suddenly crying in the most hopeless way—did I see that?
Or does it haunt me because my mother herself has held up this
small scene, laughing: here's our funny, luckless, cherished life.

In fact, I don't have a very good memory; everyone tells me this.
But poetry is a way of imaginative recall, bringing up detail, making
it crucial. More, it's making shape of these details, making them
mean in a way that nearly forgets the self—that sense of the poem
as mere self-expression, *I hurt* or *I love*—to discover something out
there, the first large shape, the house widening to the street, the
neighborhood, the world. How many women, then, in my mother's
weeping that day, the hallway darkened and lit by the shattered
glass, the rushing wasted milk?

If memory is a matter of *place*, then my childhood gave me two. I
was born in Chicago, spent thirteen years in its Catholic schools—
as odd and eloquent and unreal as any education might be—
moving from neighborhood to neighborhood three or four times,
finally ending those years before college at its northwest edge where
the cheap suburbs begin. The fixed point in all this was my father's
parents—the Boruchs—my Polish grandparents. I see them there
in their Old World house on Maplewood Avenue, the continual cab-
bage haze in the air, the rich rise and fall of a language my brother

and I never understood, the Virgin Mary on the wall with her pierced heart, the silk fringed pillows—"Greetings from Manila"—their American-born sons sent back in 1944, so thrilled to be soldiers, to be away. "Ma, these are American children," I remember my father saying sadly, inscrutably to them once, one of the few times I heard him speak English in that house. He stood in the doorway, restless, hands in his pockets.

As counterpoint, I held my mother's world: small-town central Illinois, the place we went most of Christmas and Easter and much of the summer. The night train took us south three hours from the city, the wheezing diesel clouds rising as the whole thing trembled, stood still, slowed by a signal light in the railroad tower—Tuscola not a stop on the regular line. I could make out my grandparents, the Taylors, there in their old wool coats to help us down the cold metal steps.

Where does imagination begin? My ordinary life was Chicago—school and afterschool and piano lessons and the predictable noisy array of Boruch cousins, aunts, and uncles at the backyard barbecue. But Tuscola was the older, secret place. No duty there but solitude and love, and history a large part of its calm—gravestones with our family names chiseled in, four generations back of Taylors and Gillses and Joneses. And my grandparents themselves—old grandparents, already in their seventies when I was born. Or perhaps, I've simply never gotten over the solemn joy of stepping down from that train into darkness, into that town, a square mile of houses and brick streets in the middle of prairie, and, of course, into those arms waiting to lift us to the ground. From the track, I could see the beat-up taxi my grandparents had hired to take us to the house, its headlights dimmed, its radio soft; though it was cold, the driver had cracked his window open so the smoke from his cigar drifted out and up and disappeared. Meanwhile we couldn't stop talking, yelling really, my grandfather even then so deaf—news of school and the people they knew from visits north, our voices the only voices in the chill night air.

It's impossible—I fear, extinct—such a catalog of riches: falling asleep later, the house of chiming ticking clocks, of pipe smoke and liniment, and the line-dried sheets, stiff and rough from the wind. Outside wonders too: the train whistle again, which—from this distance—meant both routine and adventure, and in the morning, walks past the drugstore with its gory pictures of nineteenth-century operations set up in the window, or to Gus's for a fountain coke or outside the old hotel where my grandfather stopped to talk to the ancient men leaning back in the metal chairs—the day warm enough—among them the one gassed in the First World War, Mr. Arthur who couldn't speak, who just sat there blankly. *Mustard gas*, my mother had told me, and he had stared that way, she said, since the twenties when she was a kid.

Imagination might be tied up first—perhaps always—with mystery. I wanted, of course, to walk by the old men quickly, but my grandfather, who was, after all, one of them, stood and talked happily, even sitting down for a while if there was an empty chair, while I fidgeted on the sidewalk, my eye coming back to Mr. Arthur and whatever stony secret he kept locked inside. That dark surprise, then, in the most ordinary circumstance, the slow shock of things: is this the beginning of poetry? I kept wishing for anything else—just to be playing on the porch or in the battered side yard, to be talking endlessly in the kitchen with my grandmother about all my urgent nothings. Instead, it was my grandfather's usual exchange—the weather, corn prices, and as he claimed to be the town's only Democrat, certainly politics—all of it worth repeating a million times. But under their voices, Mr. Arthur loomed. Occasionally, he'd turn his head and look at me.

I need to be careful. It isn't some awful nostalgia that pulls me back to that look, nor is it even its historical weight. I don't think I ever woke out of nightmares because of him, and it was years before I learned the gruesome facts of trench warfare. No doubt the man dropped out of my head as soon as I could drag my grandfather off, taking his hand to cut across Sales Street to Main and straight home. It's more, perhaps, how Mr. Arthur's silence spoke, how his curious isolation mirrored some underside thing in me that felt sad and true and inevitable. That this town, so wonderfully picturesque with its band shell gazebo, its Andrew Carnegie Library, its bright heroic WPA mural in the post office—that such a place carried inside it another place, badly lit, seemingly senseless: this was news, but only memorable because that delicate, puzzling design repeated, made a pattern.

The usual pattern of small towns, maybe: feuds, bad feeling as inherited as red hair, entire streets where my grandmother refused to walk for whatever reason. But against that, friends back to the 1880s, when my grandparents were children, one old lady so blind, she'd stoop and feel my face—slowly, lovingly—before saying hello. Various rituals of distress or pleasure; my brother and I were born to them, they were clear—clear enough—meaning we largely accepted their mysteries, that is, until that mystery came home, and filled the quiet house.

It was something my grandmother told us herself one summer: when our Uncle Larry went to war—not Mr. Arthur's, but the Second World War—he went crazy. We were on the high sleeping porch off my grandfather's bedroom, a tiny screened-in place overlooking the backyard smelling of dust, mothballs, and faintly, almost sweetly, of urine. My grandmother pointed to the trunk. Lawrence wrote a novel before he left, she told us, and god knows what was in it. But he locked it up, right there. Of course, he came back; we knew that much. He'd been in North Africa, the Italian campaign. But just raving by the time he got home, my grandmother was saying, shouting terrible things out the back door to Mrs. Helm, and then to the grocer, the preacher, even Tack Green, the undertaker—until he tore up the stairs and barricaded himself right here, on the porch. My brother and I sat there; I heard the neighbor's screen door bang, and a truck downshifting blocks away. My grandmother was slowing up now, but it was what came next that got me, how she found him later, standing in the cellar, feeding his novel, page by page, into the small flaming window of the coal furnace. It was dark down there, and all so private. She said nothing to him, turning back up the stairs, up and back into the bright kitchen.

Pattern is tension, the weave of opposites, imaginative engagement. Mr. Arthur's mute standstill among the arguing, wise-cracking old men was one thing, but my uncle in the cellar, furious and without hope? I tried to think—still think—of this passionate, mad flash of him against the witty, startlingly urbane uncle we knew in Chicago who drove over from Oak Park with his cool, towering wife for an occasional Sunday afternoon. I think of the containment of that trunk, and feverish pursuit and denial of what was in it. As a kid, during those afternoons of his visits, looking from the hallway, I kept eavesdropping as my uncle sipped his scotch, trying to figure some grave clue from the scene's slick surface.

I'll never get to the end of these mysteries—therefore I write poems, as Descartes surely meant to say. Of course Mr. Arthur but my uncle too, they're both dead now, and recently, since I live only ninety miles east of Tuscola these days, I drove back to that town, first finding the place the hotel was—it burned to the ground in the mid-seventies—then parking on south Main in front of my grandparents' old house. It looked far shabbier, more desolate than I remembered. The green bamboo shades had vanished from the porch, the flowering spires uprooted from the yard. I walked around to the back where the sleeping porch still hung off the second story like a thing dreamt up later, a last good idea.

It wasn't winter but spring, though I remembered one thing more about that trunk—my uncle's wool uniforms were in it, carefully folded khaki trousers and shirts, and caps narrow as envelopes. The Christmas after we learned about the novel, my brother and I opened the trunk, and put everything on, tying up the waists with string. Outside, the alley was one long frozen slick, and we slid and fell and laughed, the pants rolled up but unrolling, the big sleeves flapping. I recall it perfectly, down to the most trivial detail. Still, I have this curious vision: I'm not playing at all, but alone in the house watching us play, looking down from the high back bedroom at these kids, reeling and breathless, their clothes way too big for them.

# WATER PLANS

A visiting biologist, Mr. Reed, recently said that the country here-abouts is so flat, its soil of such compact clay, that it makes ideal wetlands terrain: water neither drains from the flat surfaces nor seeps through the clay. "Some of the water down in this soil moves so slow, it could be 8,000 years old—give or take a week," he told a reporter for the *Duluth News-Tribune*. Mr. Reed looked at home in our wetlands. He had traveled to northwestern Wisconsin to write "a management plan that protects the best of Superior's wetlands, yet leaves room for development."

In a century and a half, many planners have ventured here. Not quite that long ago, talk arose of ore and packet freighters, lumber hookers and tugs circumnavigating the city. Looking at an aerial map, one sees why. In the Superior Bay to the north and St. Louis Bay and River to the west, navigable waterways exist. The nineteenth-century plan was to dredge and widen the Pokegama Bay to the south and the Nemadji River to the east, thus allowing waterborne commerce around the city. Another nineteenth-century planner, the politician Stephen A. Douglas, envisioned a rail and port city here to rival Chicago. Still another dreamt of barge canals linking the lake with the Mississippi by way of the Bois Brule and St. Croix rivers. Their water plans fell through like so many others—the recent "bubbler system" plan, for instance, whereby Superior's and Duluth's harbor entries would be kept ice-free by means of suba-quatic bubblers moving the water.

We are left with the water once the water planners leave. It is trickling beneath us in the compact clay, flowing around us in Bluff and Newton creeks, in the Pokegama and Nemadji rivers; and prin-cipally it is in the lake, the "big north waters." Water haunts this city. It haunts the memories of those who remain and those who flee to drier places. No planners, I think, will change Superior's wetlands too much, Mr. Reed's report notwithstanding. The area is wet, cold, and low—too much so to bother with. The water below us is ancient, glacial.

Over this eight thousand–year–old water grow tag elder, low shrubs and sedges, wild rice, and Canada bluegrass. Among the "water plantain family," according to John B. and Evelyn W. Moyle's *Northland Wild Flowers*, is the broadleaved arrowhead that in late summer in marshes and along shores produces starchy tubers in the bottom mud, which the Indians called "Swan Potatoes," which they "dried . . . for winter food." In drier places grow spruce and fir, aspen, poplar, and birch. From late fall and throughout the winter, color—except for the red osier dogwood and the pines— drains from the land. The sky mirrors the gray. Even the birds that stay or that come to visit, like the snow bunting, blend in with it.

Except for the floodplain of the Nemadji, or "Left-Handed," River and a few broad creekbeds scoured into the fields by the latest glacier, the land is flat, although eight or ten miles back it rises quite dramatically and you see the forests and fields, the town, and Lake Superior, the Great Sweetwater Sea, spread below—in the distance, the gray and white buildings of Duluth, a city on a hillside of 1.1-billion-year-old rock called "the Duluth Gabbro Complex" by geologists. For all that, I prefer low, flat places. In sedge meadows, along the flat clay roads that hide the glacial waters, one's thoughts tend downward, backward in time.

My paternal great-grandfather arrived here in the 1890s. Dziaduś, "grandfather" in Polish, once tended the coach and horses of a wealthy Berliner. For several months he did such work for a wealthy Superiorite, but soon tiring of negotiating clay roads in the rain and fog, he found work sweeping the wooden floors of a flour mill on the bay. Since then, one hundred years of time—both geologic and human—have passed, and I have witnessed nearly half of them.

A kind of Coast Guardsman, I have lived in the house two blocks from Superior Bay for more than forty years. Before that we lived, appropriately, in rooms above a Coast-to-Coast store a few blocks away. From the upstairs windows of my old room in this house, I can see the mill where Dziaduś worked, Superior Bay, Wisconsin and Minnesota points, which together form "the world's longest freshwater sandbar," and Lake Superior. Ore boats glide quietly by on the bay, and once fifteen years ago, twenty-seven crewmen died when the ore carrier *Edmund Fitzgerald* sank, and once three years ago, I saw out there a three-masted schooner. On the house's opposite side—its opposite shore—lies the flat country. My mother chose the view, giving my sister and me rooms that looked out on the Sweetwater Sea while hers and my father's faced the south where my maternal grandparents lived four miles across the wetlands.

For years, young men chose the water route out of town like my father had done. It is, or was, the most practical way to leave, because the city is backed against the lake, sunk low before the distant hills and billion-year-old bedrock. When in 1924 my father went sailing at age fifteen, he walked a quarter-mile to the Northern Pacific ore dock to hire aboard, sailing fresh- and salt-water seas off and on for many years after that until, married finally, he stayed ashore. My own friends have been deckhands in the years since, one becoming the youngest mate on the lakes.

The lake at its deepest being 1,333 feet, no doubt my sailor friends' thoughts, like my father's and mine, have tended downward or across the expansive waters to the fog signal beacons and radio relay masts of distant shores. Leaving Superior by boat, you exchange one flatness for another. Putting in again at the Northern Pacific or the Allouez ore dock, you leave the water of one of the world's largest bodies of fresh water for the kind that cannot drain from a surface, or that over a thousand years has seeped an inch through the compact clay.

I have guarded this coast with my life, it seems. Even when I lived in Rhode Island and Massachusetts, I would remember the ancient water of home that seemed everywhere beneath me. Ship captains know the depths and bottom conditions of the Great Lakes, the topography of shores, the various beacons and antennae upon them. They fear November storms on the Inland Seas. "Sailing courses and limits indicated in magenta are recommended by the Lake Carriers Association," my nautical maps read. Other instructions read: "Owing to small scale, many aids to navigation, depths, contours, and topographic features have been omitted." I have my own recommended limits when I venture out, my own navigational guides. Almost daily in the afternoons I walk the expanse of the home ground where I have dwelt so long. I pass the mill on the bay, traverse the clay roads, or stand on the trestle above the Left-Handed River, trying to get to the bottom of things deep in memory.

Some days I walk to where the Coast-to-Coast stood. When we lived there, several bars, a bakery, a movie house, two drugstores, and a bank were among the neighborhood businesses. The Polish grade school I attended stood two blocks northward, everything tending toward the Sweetwater Sea. Fifth-through-eighth graders at Szkoła Wojciecha, St. Adalbert's School, we looked northward out second-floor windows. The church and the school are gone. Now overgrown fields stand there. The St. Adalbert's statue that protected the church is gone.

Other days I follow the creek through the fields to its source in the wetlands halfway to where my maternal grandparents Vincenty Fronckiewicz and Bernice Malinowska once lived. Mr. Reed, the biologist, recently called this area around Hill Avenue a "non-contributing wetland." It is "void of moving water to purify, too high to be a flood or storm plain, and having a wild-life habitat that's common in northern Wisconsin." He went on, "If we lost that area, it probably would not have a real big impact," though a true guardian of the coasts of home knows better.

Still other days I walk north to the bay, then two miles east along swamps and inlets, passing the shadow of the ore dock from which my father first sailed. I follow the high river bank south to the old C & NW trestle that runs a half-mile east and west over the swamp. In the cemetery on the far side, the west side, lie Wysinski, Bukoski, and Meyer, my own and my father's grandparents. It is where my ninety-four- and ninety-two-year-old great-aunts will someday be buried. This is the cemetery—St. Francis Cemetery—above the Nemadji River. My other grandparents lie in one above the Pokegama River in the south end of Superior. The Pokegama joins the Nemadji, and both flow to the bay and on into Lake Superior. How can anyone say, then, that Lake Superior receives no rivers of importance? Having stopped at St. Francis Cemetery, I walk through the muskeg home, and so spend my life in four-mile journeys.

There is a lighthouse crumbling on the Lake Superior shore not far away. It marks the zero point from which, as early as 1817, geodetic surveys of the lake were taken. My own surveys are emotional and psychological. Though I have never recorded the depths of these waters, I have their surfaces. In the house are other reminders of them, points of demarcation along the shore where I live: immigration papers and prayer books in Polish, photos of Dziaduś, sodality medals, my mother's rosary, my father's seaman's card. In one drawer upstairs lies a bottle of Holy Water from forty years ago when we first moved in, when my surveying began. It has kept the house safe. Someday when I pour it over the wetlands of home, it will mingle with the other water in the compact soil, blessing the years below it as it is blessed by them in return.

# PROVIDENCE

Quakers from North Carolina had been the first settlers, and what I remember bears the tinge of their formidable legacy. The last of their generation were Eli Reece, a figure so indistinct that it may be I only think I remember him, and his wife Asenath, who lived on and on in shrunken widowhood. Her biblical name belonged to another age no less than her person, which I recall as not bonneted in Quaker gray but rather encased and encrusted in a decently elaborate maroon. Aunt Asenath, as she was by then to half the neighborhood, would have been very young when a group of forty, led by the patriarchal William Reece, set out in the spring of 1851, driving their cattle alongside wagons loaded with their belongings. They were on the move all summer, most of the party walking most of the way. When they arrived at the beginning of September, the township was as yet undesignated, the undulating grassland unbroken except by streams, all flowing generally southeastward along hollows timbered with oak and hickory. The site chosen by these pioneers was a wooded slope above what came to be known as Honey Creek.

It seems to have been originally supposed that nobody would put up a house beyond the shelter of such woodlands, referred to by the newcomers as "groves." Among place-names now all but forgotten is an Illinois Grove to the south, as well as Honey Creek Grove itself. By the time one of my paternal great-grandmother's people arrived from Indiana, five years later, the Reece settlement had already spilled over into the open prairie. My great-grandfather had likewise come from Indiana, but by way of a carpentering and horse-trading itinerary that had taken him to Kansas and back, among other places. Here, having met and courted my great-grandmother, he set about acquiring land. And it is here, close to the southern boundary of what had been given the God-fearing name of Providence Township, that my earliest memories are centered.

The farm where I lived until the year I was ten belonged to my grandfather. As it was later recalled, somebody who helped put up the house asked him if he had picked the coldest place in the county to build on. In the year 1890 it was indeed, as my grandfather would later write, "as open to the winds of heaven as when the Lord first made it." He and my grandmother lost no time, their first spring on the property, in planting both seeds and seedlings of what before many years would be a "grove" of their own—silver poplar, wild plum, apple, willow, and the native red cedar, whence the name of Cedardale Farm. By the time my own memory begins, shrubbery and shade trees, neatly fenced and gated, enclosed the place with what amounted for me to a charm, in the etymological sense of a spell against harm from without; and in the sense that the word derives from *carmen*, a song, my earliest consciousness is rooted in the stuff of poetry.

Very many years later I would come upon what Gaston Bachelard has to say in *The Poetics of Space* about tracing the phenomenological germ of well-being to its shell—and would experience nothing less than a confirmation of what I had always known. Similarly, the dialectic of inside and outside amounted to a paradigm of what my grandmother had done when she dug up and brought in the native bloodroot and bluebells, columbine and Dutchman's-breeches from the banks of Honey Creek to the shady edge of her garden. These airily magical blooms came up every spring in the company of peonies and lilies of the valley whose emerging crimson horns and pallid multiple points were not native but had in their turn been uprooted from halfway around the globe. My early memory of those flower beds made no such distinction, and in the deepest sense there was none. Here, awe and delight not only intersected but converged, and the bliss of which those early years would seem in retrospect to have consisted had its apotheosis in the return, every spring, of what came out of the ground.

The first discrete recollection—its very distinctness perhaps an inkling of how infinitely fragile was the shell of seeming safety I had inhabited—can be dated exactly. It is the twenty-sixth of April, 1923; I am not yet three years old, and I have learned of the arrival that day of a baby brother—most probably from an aunt, my father's sister Edith, who is leading me past barns and through feedlots to the outermost grove. What holds these details in place is the sight, out under those trees, of a bed of violets whose hue I cannot reach except by way of a later metaphor: the contained intensity of a body of water. It is as though I became in that instant aware of edges, shores, boundaries, limitations. The shell had cracked: an exodus, an expulsion, was under way.

To be under way meant the knowledge, sooner or later, of roads. The earliest settlers had found none. Very soon, though, the township was to be unimaginable without them—more so than it would have been without those knots and clusters of woody vegetation, each overtopped by a windmill's arthritic chrysanthemum, that marked the transformation of prairie into farmland. People who come back for the annual homecoming at the country church that lingers on the original site above Honey Creek still reminisce about those roads: skidding on the hill just north of the creek, which has the steepest grade in the township; the winters when every highway drifted full, and there was no school for days or even weeks; the innumerable times somebody's car got stuck or went off into the ditch after dark. Though the paving no longer turns into a bottomless morass with each spring thaw, such adventures still occur, memorably obliging a driver to get out and walk to the nearest dwelling. Otherwise, nobody goes anywhere on foot. Farmers, so far as I know, do not jog.

The roads of my childhood, however, to some degree still functioned as footpaths, almost as an extension of domicile. Certainly that is the way I remember the stretch leading uphill from a marshy bottom, now tiled and arched by a culvert, to where Ina lived. She was my first playmate, aside from the cousins toward whom, as my parents' firstborn, I maintained a sullen rivalry. Ina's father was our hired man. The invidious tendency that lurks in any human association—a blighting ailment in the mentality of townships, where there is no getting away from being known about and, ipso facto, classified—happily failed to come between us. Perhaps it was her being a bit more than a year older that evened the balance. More probably it was the cast-iron cheerfulness and enterprise of her mother, Ethel. My father, evidently mulling over the same conundrum, would later describe Ethel as a "society woman"—a term that, however ludicrous, does suggest how fickle and insubstantial a thing it is that can weigh like iron. She was a mainstay of the WCTU (the Women's Christian Temperance Union, its mission, having to a degree been preempted because there was never a saloon or tavern in all of Providence Township, had metamorphosed into its acronym). She was an excellent cook and had a talent for entertaining bored children. She gave recitations. Ina had inherited something of her comic flair; and a likable way of passing along gossip, much of it scurrilous, meant that she never lacked for an audience. Her father appeared to have no such gifts whatever, though as a farmhand and mechanic he proved too valuable to keep. By the time I began school the family had moved to town. I sometimes stayed overnight with Ina; and through the ups and downs of an increasingly precarious sense of who I was, as my first friend she had a kind of priority.

Her successors in the hired man's house up the road were quite different. Originally a one-room school for what was called the Midland District, it represented a now all but obliterated catalog of place-names—Fairview, Highland, Hopedale, and Republic among them—into which the township was parceled before a consolidated school system and its bus routes went into effect. My grandfather, as the owner of the land it stood on, had divided it into four small rooms, a dwelling of a sort. Here my parents had begun housekeeping, and I had been delivered into the light of day, a few months before they settled into the larger house down the road. For Ina's family—she had two brothers—the place would have been cramped. The new man brought with him a brood so numerous that it was not easy to keep their names straight. Variously wild-looking, curly-haired, and more or less unavoidably grimy, they might have been gypsies, except that they stayed on as long as we did. Looked down on by practically everyone, they responded with varying degrees of obsequiousness and anger. The angriest was black-eyed, oily-ringleted Vibert, whose name, his father told my father, had been found in a book. When reports are considered of the virtual absence of such things from a well-known establishment at Kennebunkport, the mystery deepens. Who were these people? One might, in the manner of Katherine Mansfield's Kezia, ponder long without reaching a conclusion. Where, finally, did they go? I am ashamed to think how fleetingly I have supposed it even mattered.

The onetime schoolhouse occupied the southeasternmost corner of my grandfather's original 80 acres. By the time he retired to a house he had built in town, the 80 had been augmented to cover half a section, or 320 altogether. I was never clear about just where their western boundary was. Of the northern one I had a fairly accurate notion, because the adjoining farm belonged to a great-uncle, my grandfather's much younger brother. Here lived my second cousins Bruce, Mabel, and Harry, who were just enough older that I looked up to them with no taint of rivalry. They rode ponies and played tennis on a court of their own. Harry was a born wit, with perfect timing and instinctive savoir faire. I adored him. He played the clarinet, Mabel the cello, and Bruce the trombone. On the walls of my uncle's office, with its massive rolltop desk and its swivel chair upholstered in black leather, were portraits of pedigreed shorthorns, adorned with gilded ribbon cockades won at the state fair. There was of course a piano in the front room. So was there in ours—my father's honeymoon gift to my mother. It enabled us to look down on the neighbors to the south, around the corner and across the road from the hired man. Lately arrived from North Carolina, they gave away their origins by the plink and whine of a banjo that could be heard from their front porch on summer evenings. I seem to recall a sneaking fondness for that uncultivated sound; but that an assurance as to what is vulgar might in itself constitute a greater vulgarity did not occur to me until long afterward.

These neighbors would have been tenant farmers—as we ourselves were, the only difference being that the farm was in the family. To the west stood a house so funereally embowered among evergreens that its front room never admitted the sun. The owner and his wife had married late and had no children. The mystery of childlessness, regarded by some (or so I gathered) as a sort of gentility, and the half-remembered shapes of women who seemed at once to tower and to hover set the place apart in some vague realm of the legendary and the unfulfilled.

The world I have been recalling barely exceeded the space of two square miles, whose metes and bounds could be identified on a map of the township as two contiguous sections, numbered 21 and 28. The hamlet of New Providence, whose populace never rose much above two hundred, was three and a half miles to the north.

The ride over those same three and a half miles' mud, gravel, and stirred-up dust to the building of brick and concrete that had gone up when the rural school districts were consolidated became a familiar torture—exposure day after day to all the unthinking meanness of which the young are capable. On my very first day there, I struck up an ephemeral friendship with a blond boy named (he told me) Harold Nybarr. It would be some time before I learned that his surname on paper was Neubauer. Such was my introduction to linguistic diversity in Hardin County, Iowa. A platbook I recently looked at, dating to 1892, shows an ownership largely of British descent: Andrews, Lundy, Armstrong, Hobson, Ruddick, and, dynastically, Reece. Only the names Kasischke and Klemme, in the extreme northwest corner, reflect the predominance of German immigrants to the west and throughout much of the county. They were good farmers, they made money, and they stayed put. One heard such names as Engelke, Boeke, and Broer (pronounced Broor) without thinking of them as German. Nor did one think of the Lawlers, a family or two of them, as Irish. But on Sunday mornings their absence from church was uniquely conspicuous. They had to drive all the way to the county seat at Eldora, being (a word hardly pronounced except in a whisper) "Cathlick."

Church, for me, appeared to be an imposition by the likes of Eli and Asenath, a doddering relic of outmoded ways. One descendant of the patriarchal William would famously call out "Praise the Lord!" in the midst of a sermon. His pious revulsion from bad language was so extreme that in answering the telephone, it was alleged, he said not "Hello" but "Hurrah." Yes, by then there were sermons. The Great Revival in the latter part of the previous century had dislodged the Quakers of the township, as elsewhere, from their habit of silence into a pastoral and evangelical one. What had been meetinghouses were now churches. The one we attended, on the site above Honey Creek, was (and is) of brick, squarely built with a bell tower and mollified about the entrance by a growth of Virginia creeper. The woods to this day are dense behind it. During my earliest years the pastor was a Reverend Mr. Culbertson, a young man of moon-faced earnestness, who had a growing family and with whom my father carried on, directly and indirectly, a sort of running debate. His sermons being thus questionable, I could not see why we had to go to church at all. My grandfather, a lifelong skeptic, went out of deference to my grandmother. His younger brother, my Uncle Ralph, stayed away (though his wife and family went) until his later years. I believe it was the perpetuation of intolerance they both objected to. I objected to what I saw, arrogantly, as sheer compulsory nonsense.

Perhaps these circumstances had something to do with the unhappiness, amounting almost to heartbreak, that I experienced when we moved (a distance of hardly more than two miles) to what was called Pioneer Farm, on which my father had taken what would prove a very nearly ruinous mortgage. It was the plat for which, in 1852, William Reece had been the first in the township to enter a claim of ownership. The farmhouse stood on the crest of the hill above the church, in view of the graveyard where the first settlers and many of their descendants lay buried. There were no trees to break the exposure except red cedars, which gave no shade. Indoors, the place was bleak and comfortless. I never quite ceased to hate it. The one solace was the proximity of the creek, on whose timbered banks the bloodroot, Dutchman's-breeches, and columbines I had first known in cultivation grew wild. A great lakelike patch of bluebells near the water's edge became the object of an annual pilgrimage. But nothing could reconcile me then to my own uprooting, nor has anything since.

Not long ago I found my way back to the township and was pleased with what I saw: relative prosperity, young people happy to be there, middle-aged ones unmistakably descended from adults I had once known; an exact contemporary lost sight of since grade school; the hired girl with whom I had shared a room and to whom I had become, as one does, greatly attached—not to mention two aunts and any number of cousins. The one I stayed with drove me past what had been Cedardale, now owned by total strangers. There was some discussion about whether the house was or was not, after repeated remodeling, the same one I had lived in. But the question hardly mattered, because there was so clearly no going back—except possibly by writing about it, as I have just now done.

# Rummage

I did not know where I lived when I was a child. Where on earth was I?

The North Shore trails from Chicago like some glamorous embellishment—a satin train, a stole of chinchilla tails. Houses, circling golf courses and lining the lake, tend to the Tudor, grandiose and gracious. Lawns are mollycoddled. Upkeep is everything.

Tell someone you were raised here and they're likely to mention "The Big Noise from Winnetka." That allusion has always bewildered me. Winnetka is not a noisy place.

✳

When I was very small, my grandmother came to visit from Pasadena, a town that knows its gracious from its grandiose. But Belinda Hastings Mazy, who lived in a city of old money and roses, was cowed by what she saw of Illinois. "The trees," she kept saying. "I can't get over the trees!"

My grandmother bought me a Halloween costume at Marshall Field's, a powder-blue tutu edged with silver sequins. It must have been expensive. The late-summer day was warm and still. My mother, a nervous driver, kept her eyes on the road, her hands on the wheel. All the way home I watched my grandmother's speckled hands swoop and flutter, then plummet to her lap, as her eyes took in the oaks and elms that canopied Lake Avenue. A childhood in Butte, Montana, could not have prepared those eyes for such scalding shades of green.

My fingers fidgeted with the loops of twine on the shopping bag. My grandmother touched my head like a fairy godmother altering fate. "You'll be a beautiful ballerina," she said.

"Pretty extravagant," my mother said.

My grandmother, lost to the sight of the trees again, smiled. Her wonder seemed the real extravagance. The spangled blue tutu was the most beautiful thing I had ever seen.

By the time Halloween came, my grandmother had returned to her pink stucco house, and the trees in Illinois were more than half naked. Winter started early that year.

"What are you supposed to be?" My father kept to the shadows as I was interrogated from the wedge of light at each doorway. After a while I stopped bothering to unfasten the velvet-covered buttons of my maroon wool coat to reveal myself. "Margot Fonteyn," I said.

The North Shore is a place where much may be taken for granted.

✳

Wilmette, Kenilworth, Winnetka: the towns' very names seem, like Daisy Buchanan's voice, full of money. New Trier Township, stretching from a northern edge of Evanston at the south to a slice of southern Glencoe at the north, has grabbed more than its share of the lakefront. More than its share of everything, perhaps. The water of Lake Michigan was clean then, or we believed it was, and it stayed cold until July. The Wilmette beach was at least a block wide, and if you were foolish enough in the morning to go down to the shore without your sandals, the fine ginger-colored sand would scorch the soles of your feet every step of the way back to the parking lot in the afternoon.

My first college roommate was from northern California. I married someone from New England. Both of them laughed scornfully when I said that I, like them, could not imagine living anywhere but beside the water. Fresh water, they suggested, was not really *water*.

In 1985, having been away from the Midwest for twenty years, I moved to Iowa, a place so different from where I grew up as to seem a foreign country. My second day in Iowa I found a beach. The water was lukewarm and unsalted, the sand, imported, an extravagance.

"Only you," my father said, "would go looking for a beach in Iowa."

Friends back in Rhode Island seemed miffed when I admitted I didn't really miss the ocean.

"There is a beach here," I said.

"But that's fresh water. It must be."

Their discriminations rolled off my back. I had already made myself right at home.

The Wilmette beach was the first place I ever thought belonged to me. I am always making that mistake—thinking places belong to me. I did the same thing with Iowa, took it to heart.

*

When I was fourteen my family moved from Wilmette to Kenilworth, just a few blocks away. My two parents, registering to vote in our new town, promptly doubled the size of its Democratic rank and file.

Ours was a peculiar neighborhood for Democrats to settle, a part of Illinois untouched by Adlai Stevenson. Maurice Stans lived right around the corner from us, before Watergate existed, even as a building. Conservative pamphleteer Clement Stone lived just up Sheridan Road. Senator Percy's house, lording it over Kenilworth beach, was an enclave I infiltrated more than once during high school, when "pool-hopping" was the craze. I never got caught. John Kennedy had been elected president, though not by Kenilworth, and Democrats were feeling chesty.

When I was fifteen I happened to see a friend's mother, a refined Southern woman named Blanche, install the family's elderly black maid in the back seat of a Country Squire station wagon for the ride to the El station at Fourth and Linden. I remember being shocked at behavior that struck me as not cruel or bigoted so much as highly eccentric. Slightly mad.

At what age, I wonder now, does belief in harmlessness turn to disadvantage?

*

New Trier Township High School in Winnetka was famous. Each year our swimming team won the state championship, or came close. The school's music and theater departments were legendary and it had a national reputation for academic excellence: number 2 right after Scarsdale High was the popular version. But some said we had dropped to number 3. Who, if anyone, made these pronouncements? Who made them official, and how? I never knew. I simply believed in them the way I believed all people were equal: thoughtlessly, in pure comfort.

Rock Hudson went to New Trier. So did Ann Margaret and Charleton Heston. All high schools were not, evidently, created equal. New Trier was a star factory.

*

I left Illinois at eighteen to go to college in Washington, D.C., a city outside geography—our Hague, our Vatican—with slight notion where I'd been all my life. All my clothes were new and had shoes to match them. I studied myself full-length in unfamiliar mirrors, and from what I could see I might have come from anywhere: Palo Alto, Chadds Ford, Scarsdale.

By the time I returned to the Midwest, it was June. An extravagance of shade along Lake Avenue cooled the path to the beach, but not everything had stayed the same. I walked in on a home being broken down and packed to go like a touring company stage set.

I had to show for that first year away on my own: pierced ears, a becoming weight loss, and a bad case on a basketball player. Without ever setting foot outside its northwest quadrant, I had come to think of Washington as a place that belonged to me.

My mother, moving back to California after a twenty-year exile that seemed to her Siberian—raw and punitive—had given away all our books. *Ferdinand the Bull*, inscribed to me by Munro Leaf the year of my birth, was gone. I, watching the mailbox, did not note the loss. I scarcely knew where I was.

In August, at last, the basketball player wrote. The postcard came from Lake George. It showed a 1940s bathing beauty in a red swimsuit constructed like a corset. She reclined before a backdrop of electric-blue water, on a swirl of ginger-colored sand. Where was Lake George? Was it salt water, or fresh?

*Wish you were here*: my heart, as usual, did its best to create something out of nothing. By the time I saw the light, the days were growing shorter and I was, like Cheever's swimmer, looking in the windows of my own house and finding it empty.

*

I am caught unawares today by the scantiness of my memories, blindsided on the right by innocence, on the left by shame. How, having been given so much, can I recollect so little? "What are you supposed to be?"

A writer.

But a writer is not one who keeps her coat buttons fastened against the chill, is she?

I rarely go back to the North Shore anymore. Most of the people I loved there are gone. I no longer have entrée to the beach. The grand scale of the houses intimidates me and I forget to take measure of the trees.

I live with water on both sides of me now. The water is full of salt. I do not think this small Rhode Island peninsula belongs to me, but I try to keep track of its beauty. I let it imprint itself on me because I know I won't stay.

The rooms of my house are filled with other people's mementos. I have a secondhand edition of *Ferdinand the Bull* that's even older than I am. I try not to take too much for granted. I have trouble getting myself to throw anything out.

# YOU CAN'T STEP INTO THE
# SAME STREET TWICE

A time would come every summer for yet another attempt to send me to camp. The camp was in Michigan, a place called Eagle Lake that the Boys' Club ran. Nature was waiting to be discovered there—fields, forests, fish, wild creatures other than our local fauna of stray dogs, alley cats, and rats. It sounded fine and I understood that the annual attempt to ship me out was well meaning enough. That only made it that much harder to fend off.

We lived on the near–South Side of Chicago—first on 18th Street and, later, on 25th—in a neighborhood that would today be labeled "inner-city," an old, industrial area in which apartment buildings and factories coexisted, though not necessarily peacefully. It was a landscape of contrasts between the gigantic and the small, of sprawling truck docks and tightly bunched frame two-flats; of towering smokestacks, and sunken asphalt playgrounds that looked as if they had been compressed to fit into a vacant lot; of eight-lane expressways, and side streets too narrow for delivery trucks to pass.

It's an area that's called Pilsen now, but back then it wasn't graced with a name. People referred to their neighborhood by locating the streets that formed its boundaries, and those boundaries kept shifting as different ethnic groups passed through like migrating tribes. There was a constant sense of flux. What Heraclitus said about rivers applied here as well: you can't step into the same street twice. Like any borders, great or small, those between neighborhoods were sometimes open to dispute, and their invisible boundaries were often confluences of anxiety, danger, and excitement.

But there were other boundaries more immutable than those involving human beings, boundaries that established the essential character of the place, that seemed no more man-made than the

Grand Canyon—the expressway, the bridge on Western Avenue, the railroad overpasses we called viaducts, the sanitary canal we called Shit Creek, and the industrial tracts that lined its banks with rusting, scrapyard peaks.

During the years when I was growing up, the local population was mainly Eastern European and Hispanic. The Eastern Europeans—Poles and Czechs—were migrating out; the Hispanics were migrating in. Each group had its own bars; they shared the same churches. At St. Roman's, on 23rd and Washtenaw, the priests had learned to hear confession in Polish and Spanish as well as in English. It was at St. Roman's that I first noticed that people seemed to confess more loudly and pray more mournfully in a foreign tongue—it didn't matter if the language was Polish or Spanish, the emotion seemed the same. So did the old women who attended daily Mass, dressed in black.

The neighborhood was—and has remained—an area of two- and three-storied buildings. Without high rises or skyscrapers to dwarf them, the steeples of the corner churches seemed to soar toward heaven. There were taverns on every corner. We always called them taverns, rather than bars. At certain intersections, all four corners were taverns, and it seemed to me then that there was some secret relationship, some mysterious law of human nature, that governed the ratio between churches and taverns in neighborhoods such as ours.

Across the street from the three-storied apartment building in which I grew up, there was a housing project. It wasn't one of the high-rise, architectural, and social catastrophes for which Chicago is infamous: floor upon floor of poverty piled up to the sky, as if purposely concentrating the brutal weight of hopelessness. This housing project, as if in keeping with the scale of the neighborhood, consisted of two-storied row houses that stretched for blocks. A lot of my friends lived there, as well as some of the guys who terrified me. The presence of the project gave the area a great density of young people. There was always a pickup game of softball—Chicago-style softball played with a sixteen-inch ball—going on, or a basketball being pounded across the cracked court between netless hoops. It was as if besides the ethnic tribes of Slavs and Hispanics whose language and music and food smells permeated the streets, there was another tribe, one that in a way transcended nationality, a tribe of youth, of kids born to replenish the species recently depleted by World War II. It was a barbaric tribe, half-wild, already threatening to overrun the tenuous civilization of the neighborhood streets; a tribe intent on its own language, music, dress, food, rituals, and rules. By the age of twelve, I'd probably encountered every personality type—normal and deviant—that I would encounter over the rest of my life, not to mention a few types that I've never come across anywhere else. Years later, when I came upon Flannery O'Connor's remark to the effect that anyone who has survived childhood has enough material to write about for a lifetime, it made immediate, perfect sense.

With its mix of factories, truck docks, railroad tracks, and river and its various, intermingling tribes, the neighborhood was a ceaselessly fascinating place to explore, especially during the summer. It was summer when everything really came alive. Up and down 22nd, the green awnings would flop out over the sidewalks, throwing green shade over stands of produce, and commerce moved into the streets—tamale vendors, snow cones and Mexican ices, fruit peddlers. We must have been on some truck route between markets because every summer convoys of trucks filled with watermelons would ride through our neighborhood despite the fact that every summer they would be repeatedly ambushed by gangs of kids making off with watermelons, disappearing down alleys, gangways, and abandoned buildings.

You'd think a kid running with a watermelon would be easy to catch, but no one, not even cops, learns the ins and outs of a city neighborhood in quite the way that kids do. The only people with a closer kinship to the streets are the homeless, who have stepped over some invisible edge and no longer have a choice. We didn't refer to them as homeless back then; they were bums or tramps or hoboes or bag ladies or ragmen. Mostly, they were foreigners who couldn't unriddle assimilation. Summer brought them out too, or allowed us to discover where they had been hibernating. We'd find their lean-to cardboard huts in the jungle behind billboards, or the rotting boxcars where they'd lived along railroad tracks, or the caves under the sidewalks such as the place on 21st where an old guy known as the Hermit actually lived in a cell below the pavement. They seemed part of the cityscape itself, nearly invisible against the backdrop of the workaday world. But children notice outsiders. To young eyes they appear as refugees from some merciless fairy tale and become part of the overlay of legend and myth that the streets acquire for the young.

That overlay is as much a part of the neighborhood as its architecture, and in the dimension of memory where home is most truly located, it is finally the myths and legends that are most permanent. In the eyes of those who live there, the humblest streets can be transformed by myths, memories, and the dreams superimposed on them. Shabby corners take on the glamour of the local starlets preening before their reflections in the plate glass windows. The narrow playgrounds and ball fields appear magnified by the feats of local heroes. And there are haunted places as well—the alley where Stash the wino was found frozen, the Cyclone-fenced parking lot on Rockwell illuminated by mercury vapor lights where Peanuts Biando dropped to his knees after being shot in the stomach by a rival gang.

News of these places, real and imagined, can be heard blasting every summer out of boom boxes and car radios. Pop music, like no other medium, is obsessed with formulating the legendary life of American streets—"Downtown," "Summer in the City," "Up on the Roof," "Under the Boardwalk"—all cityscape songs, anthems in which American streets, much like the American West, are actually more of a vision, an idea, an attitude, than a place. In America, one does not always need real streets in order to go walking. Throughout suburbs and small towns, teenagers cruise down a single avenue composed of legend, yearning, nostalgia, and cheap romance.

If there was a dangerous illusion in that, it wasn't something we worried about down on 25th Street. We knew the real places as well—viaducts where we could hitch rides on the freight trains as they clattered over, enormous water tanks in which it was possible to swim behind the factories where our fathers worked, a jackknife bridge spanning the canal where we could swing Tarzanlike between girders on a network of ropes that generations of kids had strung, turning the bridge into the world's most enormous jungle gym.

The standard reason for wanting to send kids from that kind of environment to camp is "to get them off the streets." Of course, that was precisely why I didn't want to go. The streets seemed at once both home and as much as an escape from home as one needed for the summer. Stepping into them offered an alternative life—alternative to school, alternative to family, alternative to the world according to television. The streets could make one feel free. But in return they exacted a certain allegiance, a loyalty that could be riskier than any of the dares we took if, on some level, one failed to recognize the limitations that came with that circumscribed few blocks.

If there were risks, there were also thrills. As Henry Miller observed, writing about the Fourteenth Ward of Brooklyn, where he was raised: "Nothing of what is called *adventure* ever approaches the flavor of the street. It doesn't matter whether you fly to the pole . . . or whether, like Kurtz, you sail up the river and go mad."

Back then I'd never heard of Henry Miller, or Kurtz, and nothing but barges loaded with gravel ever sailed up the greasy slick of a river we called Shit Creek; still, I had my reasons for not wanting to be transported for that couple of weeks in July to the boys' camp on Eagle Lake.

# BLOOMINGTON, INDIANA, IN
# CONRAD'S LIGHT

I might have glimpsed the university on rare occasions, if my mother had to venture on an errand to the east side of town. The limestone turrets of the WPA Memorial Union building or the gargoyles on Maxwell Hall would have caught my eye, but I wouldn't have known what I was seeing. Indiana University was on the other side of the railroad tracks and on the other side of my parents' minds.

My father worked in the Radio Corporation of America factory, a few miles from our home on the southwest side of Bloomington. In 1965, the factory was booming. A special railroad spur brought custom-painted RCA cars to the loading dock. I watched for those beautiful black-and-white cars whenever the train stopped us at the tracks. I loved the trademark dog, Nipper, who peered quizzically into a Victrola, mesmerized by the sound of "His Master's Voice." Ignorant of corporate advertising, I took pleasure in the fact that my father worked for a dog named Nipper.

For a while, the Bloomington plant shipped more televisions than any other in the world. It punched out sophisticated electronic stuff for NASA. It was the high temple of work for the entire county. When the whistle blew at noon, I could hear it from my backyard or my schoolroom a few blocks away and know my dad was hurrying home for lunch. When it blew at four, it meant that I should have the table set for supper. Anyone who didn't work there was trying to get hired, except my mother, who hated working the line. She quit shortly after I was born and went to work cleaning other people's houses, mostly across the tracks.

I was in high school before I ever actually heard the phrase "on the wrong side of the tracks," before I understood that the tracks were a border defining my existence as much as any township or county or state. It was on my first date that I realized it, a few weeks after my freshman English teacher, Mrs. Delkin, taught Joseph Conrad's *Heart of Darkness*.

But that was later. In 1965, I was ten, and there were other borders to heed. There was a border beyond which ten-year-olds did not venture, because their safety could not be guaranteed. I was allowed to walk east all the way to the end of our road, where it met with a dangerously busy street, only because it helped my mother for me to be able to run errands to Mutz's store. Mutz's had a Coke machine with a lid, the kind that allowed you to admire the frosted rows of Coke and NeHi, and shelves of Wonderbread and Jubilee and Peter Pan and other joyful products, and a hundred kinds of penny candy and trading cards. The Mutzes knew their clientele. A quarter would get you a candy necklace, three striped grape straws, and two little paraffin bottles filled with gooey-sweet colored water.

There was no way to walk south without cutting through people's yards and incurring all the trouble with dogs that such a foray could bring. West, more than a block or so, was out of the question because of Rockport Road, where bad young men with greasy hair and tattoos went to drive drunk in their souped-up Chevys. On Rockport, they could roar straight out of the county without encountering a stop sign. North was good for three blocks to Broadview School, where I spent my elementary years.

My increasing mobility prompted the mutilation sessions. Once or twice a month, my mother sat down to read me clippings from newspapers—detailed stories of horrific things done to children who had somehow weakened when offered a treat and ended up in the cars of psychotic criminals. Some were never found. Others were buried in shallow graves and dug up, accidentally, by bulldozers. Some crawled about for days in drainage ditches with their hands cut off. I listened in a sweat, imagining what kind of candy might tempt me unto death. I feared the day when the dark Ford or Buick sidled up to me and a leering man presented the bait. I prayed that it wouldn't be a six-pack of Hershey bars or an enormous Kit Kat.

The neighborhood was decent, despite my mother's fears. Everyone worked all the time. In 1965, life in general had a sense of propulsion. Jets left their trails in the blue skies above. Sonic booms rattled our windows. A few miles away, our parents were making little electric gadgets for the astronauts.

Despite all the motion, there was a drag on our neighborhood. A lot of our neighbors still had combines and tractors rusting down in their backyards. The Deckards, directly to the west of us, were factory workers too, but they had a grazing pasture and kept a mule named Texas. Every few blocks, the neighborhood collapsed back into open pasture.

The presence of Indians was always tangible, perhaps because the sumac and little indigo berries that they used to boil for dye grew crazily in every untended field and along the fencerows between houses. I had the persistent sense that there were still a few Shawnee camped up on the ridges beyond Rockport Road.

My parents were busy, but they somehow kept a truck garden that yielded bushels of knotty Beefsteak tomatoes and pole beans and bumpy cucumbers and sweet corn for us and whomever we could beg it off on—everyone we knew had such a garden. We hoed and weeded and picked all summer. I shucked and snapped in the cool basement on August afternoons, while my mother canned upstairs, sometimes until midnight. Those nights, we kept all the doors and windows open, and I lay on top of the sheets, a sweltering insomniac, waiting for the pings that signaled the jars had sealed.

We had a huge old barn at the back of our property, full of wasps and a few of my grandfather's rusting tools. Like everyone else's grandfather, he had been a stonecutter in the nearby limestone quarries and a farmer. I never knew him, and I almost never went in the barn because of the bats that I imagined living in the rafters. The few times I forced myself to enter and let the tall door shudder and slam behind me, my eyes adjusted quickly to the dark. I could see the rotting harnesses slung over the rafters like spiders and smell the animals in the walls. I never stayed more than a minute or two. Outside in the sunshine, it was clear that we were hurtling away from everything about that barn. It was dropping off behind us and we were going up and up, beyond animals and rusting tractors and bad winters when kids walked along the tops of fencerows to keep from drowning in snow.

Almost everyone kept their houses and front yards neat. My father set the neighborhood standard. He was making good money for a man with an eighth-grade education and had his eye on a sparkling two-tone future. My parents drove a light green–dark green '57 Chevy and kept the house scrupulously painted and trimmed in black and white. Black pots on the front porch were strictly reserved for flouncy white petunias. Dad clipped the shrubs into military attention, giving them flattops not unlike his own.

I felt sorry for him, because our neighbor to the east was a widowed farm wife whose house grew more dilapidated every year. The paint finally curled and fell off. Chickens and barefoot grandkids wore most of the grass off the yard, and the old outhouse down the path was still in use. She was a sweet, frazzled old woman, but it was scary to talk to her. She apparently had no teeth. My father called her Milly the Hillbilly and raved about her pack of lazy sons, who were always either in or recently out of prison. They came around only to freeload and to abandon their little children for Milly to raise. He was maddest of all about the infestation of cats around her place—between twenty and thirty on a regular day—that slunk over to dig and relieve themselves in my mother's prettiest flower beds.

It was Milly the Hillbilly and her cats who finally destroyed my father's dream of color-coordinated luxury on Ralston Drive and forced him to look for a house in a more established suburb. After that, we never had a barn or a garden again.

But that was later. At ten, the concept of moving was beyond the borders of my imagination, although more fantastic things were not. I have a perfect memory of watching three or four large copperhead snakes sun themselves on the fence that separated the back of our property from a wooded gulch that dipped down and up again at the edge of a new subdivision. They draped their fat bodies languorously along the fence, oh, maybe two or three times a summer. I had the good sense not to go near them or to tell my parents what I had seen, which is why it is fruitless now to ask them to corroborate this memory.

I also remember being the first to inspect a load of good black topsoil that had been delivered in a heap at one end of our garden one early spring. A scoopful brought something sharp into my palm, a small arrowhead, precisely wrought out of some kind of pinkish stone. The dirt pile was riddled with arrowheads of different sizes and materials and with bits of clay. I took a handful inside to show my parents. But they were only casually interested, probably because they also sensed that the Indians had only just been here. Why shouldn't their things still be strewn around the garden, just as my grandfather's were in the barn? The next morning, my mother and I picked out the biggest, most interesting arrowheads and shards, and my father plowed under the rest. My parents have no recollection of such a thing ever happening, no matter how insistently I describe it.

I must have acquired the ability to remember things that did not necessarily happen from my Aunt Esther, to whom the Lord sent many memorable images. She received each one with eerie composure. Once, a small red devil danced on her fully laid dinner table. A few years later, she caught an angel folding sheets and towels into neat stacks in her laundry room. The houses of Aunt Esther and her sisters Dory and Fiona formed a protective constellation around our house in three directions. I spent countless afterschool and summer hours with them, examining what, in the early sixties, seemed to me the very surreal borders of womanhood.

None of my aunts ever learned to drive. This and other major adaptations to the twentieth century they never made, but lived instead in a more or less Victorian wonderland, where the things that traditionally occupied a lady could be observed. Like the barn, I was drawn to them by their anachronisms, more so, because my mother—a modern woman who drove and held a job—found them mostly silly and exasperating.

The year I was ten, Aunt Dory Sayres lived in a modern split-level on Sayres Drive. A few years before, Uncle John had bought a parcel of land a half mile from our house, built a little subdivision of pink limestone houses, and moved into one and named the street after himself. Compared to my parents, they had big money. Aunt Dory collected carnival glass animals, which I begged permission to dust, because it was the only way to touch them legally. From Dory, I learned how a woman should clean. I learned how not just to vacuum a floor, but its four walls, the ceiling, the curtains. I learned how the little metal registers in the floor could be pulled up and the ducts suctioned out. I learned how to gently rock a refrigerator or a stove forward without marring the linoleum and how to mop and wax behind them. I followed her from room to room, laden with rags and a pail of ammonia water. All the while she drank sweet iced tea and smoked Winstons at regular intervals and with such intensity that I believed smoking was part of her housekeeping genius, that it somehow kept the curtains straight and the throw rugs from flipping up at the corners.

Later, two things happened. Her heart began to fail, and linen companies came out with brilliantly colored towels—solids, stripes, and florals. After that, Aunt Dory denounced housekeeping and took to sewing most of her clothes out of large bath towels—shifts mostly, and beach cover-ups—and sunbathed compulsively through the unbearably humid Indiana summers on a chaise lounge behind her house.

Aunt Fiona took life easier, but she was no slouch. She fixed a farm lunch every day of her adult life, though there hadn't been a family farm since the forties and, thus, no farmers to feed. A farm lunch was something like a ham or maybe a meatloaf, a bubbling two-quart casserole of macaroni swimming in one entire box of Velveeta, a plate of sliced tomatoes and peppers, a bowl of mashed potatoes, and pie. She fixed it whether or not there was anyone at all to eat it, on the presumption that someone might visit, I guess.

Things had happened to her, my parents told me when I was finally grown up. There was a baby, out of wedlock, that died of a heart defect soon after birth. Later, she was married and wanted another child, but couldn't have one. Her first husband, whom I never met, was fine one day and then he wasn't. He had a psychotic break on a Friday, at work, and spent the rest of his life in an insane asylum. Then a gentleman companion who looked after her died suddenly of a heart attack. It seemed a lot of trouble for a deeply kind woman who wanted to settle down and have children.

But Aunt Fiona's life circumstances pleased me immensely. She was comfortably matronly, with no brats of her own to distract her from the task of fussing over me. Her shelves were full of racy romance novels and her dresser drawers stuffed with Avon and outrageous chiffon scarves. There was no such thing as a visit to Aunt Fiona's that did not include a gift of talc and moisturizer.

When I was ten, it never occurred to me that the lives and fates of my aunts, or of my parents, might have any relationship to mine. I was fourteen by the time my kooky aunts were capable of embarrassing me. By then, I was surly at home, because the universe had shifted, and the center was, officially, at school. I excelled in certain subjects, enough to be told that I was staring a college scholarship in the face, if I kept it up. No one in my family knew anything about college. No one had ever been. My friends at school seemed to know all about colleges, particularly Indiana University, where it seemed everyone but me had an older brother or sister. I was most surprised when a friend told me she used the IU library for her reports, because it was only a short walk from her house.

That was the year Mrs. Delkin, the only black teacher at Bloomington High, taught *Heart of Darkness*. She did not mess around.

"This book is about evil," she said. "And it applies to you."

We sat up and listened.

"Is Conrad talking about a river, or is he talking about the nature of objects and the human imagination?"

We stared at her, most stupefied.

"What could Conrad's river represent?"

No one knew.

"Come on," she said, "a river is never only a river."

"It could be a snake," someone said, "like, from above."

"Like an artery that flows through the land."

There was a long silence.

"A stream of thought. You can float on it in your mind," a girl said.

Hands went up around the room. Mrs. Delkin smiled. We were a class full of Helen Kellers, learning the language that could lift us out of the darkness. Infused with literary light, the ordinary shimmered with multiple meanings. A fence, a barn, a factory would never again be only what they were.

Because of Mrs. Delkin, I understood fairly quickly what a cute, popular boy named Clark meant on our first date, over breadsticks at Pizza Hut, when he explained that he and his best friend, Bret— the class president—had discussed whether it would be okay to ask me out, because I lived on the wrong side of the tracks.

"Does your father work on the line?" Clark asked.

"No," I said, insulted. Anyone knew that only women and hopeless losers worked the lines.

When I asked him how he arrived at his decision, Clark grinned reassuringly and punched my shoulder.

"You're smart," he said. "And you have great hair."

I've always wondered how hereditary gifts of reasonable intelligence and wavy hair, alone, made me eligible for the invisible visa that allows me to cross back and forth across the tracks—that allowed me access to the university for four years, to graduate school, to life in an eastern city and beyond—though traveling back across is never quite as simple as it should be.

Cast in Conrad's light, the place where I grew up would never again hold the sense of destiny it had when I was ten. Like the continent where Conrad's river ran, my side of the tracks had "ceased to be a blank space of delightful mystery. It had become a place of darkness."

One day in the early seventies, all the windows in the RCA plant disappeared and were replaced by solid panels—to protect the workers, plant officials said, from any trouble brought to town by student war protesters. I grew to dread watching my silent father stare into his morning coffee, as though nothing was visible beyond the cup, as though he were already fixed on something inside those windowless walls. In Conrad's light, I saw the green work shirt and pants and steel-toed shoes he wore every day for thirty-five years for the prison uniform they were. And the pure sensation of hurtling up and out of the past that used to thrill me disconcerts me now, with its sheer speed and the unsettling sense that something important is always dropping away.

# WHERE I'M FROM—

# ORIGINALLY

"You're not from around here, are you."

The man puts it like a statement, but I recognize the question that's being implied. Having lived "around here" for nearly a dozen years, I also know that if I don't answer as expected, I'll be leaving the door open for the outright questions that are certain to follow: *"Where are you from?"* and *"No, but I mean, where originally?"* Asked openly, I ought to add, in a friendly spirit. Even so, I'm still not used to it. I try a smile.

"That's right," I say, and volunteer nothing more. I'm just asking for trouble, of course.

"So, where are you from?"

I turn and face the man fully, now. "Toledo," I tell him. Which I know perfectly well isn't at all what he's asking. He looks to be a nice sort, a youngish grandfather. Why am I being so contrary? All he's doing is making small talk. It's a sunny autumn day and here we've found ourselves, two adults among children—my daughters, his grandkids—in line at a county fair carousel in Iowa. The white crispness of the short-sleeved shirt he has on, along with his hairless arms and clean, pink-tipped fingers, makes me think he's maybe a dentist. That, and his no-nonsense persistent manner.

"Originally?" he says, as if to specify.

I answer, "Ohio. Toledo, *Ohio*," pretending to specify, too, since there's a Toledo, Iowa, not far from here. I'm behaving badly. Is it my fear of dentists? My frayed nerves from being with the kids all day? It's not as if this man's curiosity isn't understandable. After all, I don't look like I'm from around here; "here" being a part of the country that is more familiar with a blond Scandinavian/Irish/

German mix than with the olive skin and black curly hair common to people from Lebanon.

Nor does he know that I hear the question a lot "around here," the last time only a few days ago. I'd taken my daughters swimming, and a little girl they'd made friends with at the pool kept glancing at me out of the corner of her eye. I was in a bathing suit, and I'm fairly certain it was the body hair. "Your dad's not from around here, is he," she stated just as I dove under water. Surfacing, I heard, "No, I mean *originally*."

In '71, before the war in Lebanon, I visited Zahle, the town where I'm from—originally. Although I'd bought my clothes locally, I was easily recognized (from my manner? my gait?) for an Americanized Lebanese. Even so, I still felt I fit in. The people looked as if they all could be members of my family. I could see where my sister got her classic dark beauty, the black hair and almond eyes. The men looked like my brother, my father, me. I saw hair that grew in the same curly whorled patterns as mine. (Zahle remains the only place on earth where I ever got a decent haircut.) I remember one small boy in particular, dashing past me and glancing behind in a familiar lopsided, just-got-in-trouble grin that instantly brought to mind my own face as a child shortly after we came to America: me grinning and saluting for the camera on the pavement in front of my father's newly opened grocery store in Toledo.

It's the same grin I can feel forming on my face now as "the dentist," having helped his smallest grandchild onto a pastel pony, steps down off the carousel and joins me once more.

"No," he says, taking up where he'd left off, "no, I mean *originally*." He squints a pale eye at me as if to underscore his persistence.

"Ah, you mean *originally*. The country of my origin, you mean!" I'm taking it too far, and I consider relenting. Back in Toledo in the sixties I used to save bus money by hitchhiking to classes at the university. I didn't find it strange that on the basis of my looks the driver might begin talking to me in a foreign language (I eventually learned to identify Greek, Yiddish, Italian, and Spanish). In Toledo, with its ethnic mix, this wasn't unusual. My parents used to do it, calling out *Ibn Arab intah?* to any olive-complected fellow on the corner or in the car next to us at a stoplight, while my brother and sister and I slid groaning to the backseat floor, out of sight of the stranger's puzzled shrug.

My grin widens. The dentist responds with a grandfatherly smile, his eye unsquinting for my answer.

Which I deliver straight, deadpan: "Norway."

He doesn't call me a liar. Instead, he simply nods his head. This is Iowa—"heaven" in the movies—and not only are the people nice, they have a hard time believing anyone else is not nice.

But, being an Iowan myself after all these years, I can't leave him like this. For one thing, Iowa's a small world; what if I need dental work someday? (I picture myself in the chair, helpless, and him in his business whites, pliers in hand: "Norway? I'll give you Norway!") So I take it all back, beginning with, "Not really."

What I don't tell him is that most of my life, child and adult, has been an attempted escape from my Arab roots, and that these innocent questions—from dentists, from my daughters' playmates—were reminders that I hadn't yet blended into the Great American Melting Pot.

My family left Lebanon and came to America at the end of World War II, when I was still a toddler. I didn't begin to speak English until I started first grade. So I remember feeling different at an early age, and not liking the feeling; I was teased for my accent, for the garlicky-smelling food in my lunch box. I remember schoolmates calling me "Dirty Syrian," chasing me and yelling at me to go back where I came from. (They didn't know any better; being kids, they were slow to extend to humans the empathy they lavished on puppies and goldfish.) When they eventually did know better, many of them would become the first friends I ever made. I remember, too, how American women made a fuss over my thick curls, pausing in department store aisles to pat them fondly with their white-gloved palms. Of course, I was fully aware of how cute those curls were. But I also remember wanting those curls to be blond. Because Americans, real through-and-through Americans, were blond. They had blue eyes. And nobody'd ever think to tell a blond-haired, blue-eyed American to go back where he came from.

During the first couple years of school, my accent faded, but I remember working at it too, mouthing Peter Piper and his peck of pickled peppers over and over on the long walks home. (More than a tongue twister for Arabic speakers, since the language has no *P* sound.) Perversely, this accomplishment seemed only to make me all that much more aware of my parents' heavy accents. Fixing a self-conscious gaze on my mother and father, I was ashamed at the way they haltingly massacred English in front of Americans (who, from my view, were an impatient, finger-drumming lot), but I was mortified whenever they back-slid into Arabic. They couldn't open their mouths around me, in Arabic or English. Either way, they couldn't win, those two.

As Arabic faded in my determination to become "American," along with it went the two remaining sources of pride for Lebanese immigrants: the music of their heritage, and the ethnic food.

Refusing to partake in Arabic dancing, I sulked my way through wedding receptions and family reunions and those hall-sized festive gatherings called *haflis*, making faces at my sister to scorn the atonal repetitive singsong of the music she loved. (At thirteen and fourteen, what pains in the neck little brothers can be!)

After school, I wanted to eat only American food. I insisted that my mother make hamburger for dinner; and she—being a good sport—not only gave it a try, she figured to do hamburger one better. And so, what I ended up getting was more like lamb-burger, with garlic and parsley and vinegary onions ground into it. Couldn't she see that I didn't want better than hamburger? What I wanted was not to be different.

My newfound friends weren't much consolation in this; they never seemed to notice the differences as much as me, or if they did, they invariably took my mother's side. For reasons that are obvious enough to me now but that I couldn't at the time fathom, my mother's cooking was famous among my friends. They loved being asked to stay for supper, even though this meant being served something as strange as lemon chicken stuffed with pine nuts and pilaf and ground cinnamon lamb; sweet greens cooked down in olive oil and garlic, then mashed and rolled into well-salted, paper-thin bread; almond butter cookies or baklava for dessert.

In high school I downplayed the Arab business. Bookish and nonathletic by nature, I nevertheless tried to develop an interest in All-American sports. No luck. Especially since I'd grown up not knowing how to throw, hit, dribble, or catch a ball. I found baseball so slow, and myself such a daydreamer, that I risked getting hurt out there; in football I did get hurt, dislocating my hip in the first scrimmage of practice. Some years later I tried golf, only nine holes, but my attitude was all wrong. I kept remembering a Saturday in my childhood when I was sick with the flu. Our TV picture tube had been on the blink and the only sounds that came in on all three Toledo stations that entire cold, rainy, endless afternoon were the hushed voices of three different golf announcers.

As I finished high school, my family's financial situation began to decline steadily, along with my father's health; it was to prove to be his last illness. As a result, I stayed at home far longer than was good for me—right through my early twenties, working nights in the stockroom at Sears Roebuck while attending the University of Toledo on partial scholarship.

There, I had begun writing fiction. Luckily, the first teacher I showed any of it to—Gregory Ziegelmaier, a young playwright who was new to the English faculty—proved to be both kind and generous. From my first course with him, he urged me to begin taking my writing seriously. More and more, as I composed my latest poem or story or play, he became the audience I wrote to; there was a commonsensical, intuitive wisdom to his advice that I trusted. Always, it seemed, his critiques went straight for the heart, but gently, and with good-natured humor.

Sometimes I used to drop by during his office hours just to chat— about writing, usually, or the advantages of one program of study over another. And because he seemed interested, I also found myself telling about my family, how both my parents had less than three years' schooling between them; how my father was so superstitious he kept a piece of what he called the True Cross wrapped in a bandage under his armpit, claiming that if he lost it he would lose all his luck (years later, standing by his hospital bed, I'd remember the bandaged silver, long lost by then, and wish to God I'd taken the thing and sealed it in a vault for him); how my mother used to utter startled blessings whenever I chuckled over something funny in a book—she never understood how, outside of demonic possession, anyone staring at an inanimate object, a book, could suddenly be moved to laugh out loud.

I remember once how Mr. Ziegelmaier had smiled when I paused, nodding his head and saying "yes . . . yes," because he got it, he could picture what I was telling him. Meanwhile, I was sort of taken aback: he was an American and he was getting it?

Another time I told him the story of how my father had tricked the steamship officials when my sister came down with typhoid the day before we were scheduled to sail from Beirut, rouging her fever-yellow face and tickling her to alertness as we ascended the gangplank; and about how my whole family got stuck on an escalator in our first days here—the stairs in America just wouldn't stay still! And the childless Jewish couple who "adopted" our family; the trip to the art museum ("where they have pictures on the walls and music") that ended up with all of us listening to piped music on the lawn of a gas station that was celebrating its grand opening, its plate-glass windows painted with cartoon characters.

Mr. Ziegelmaier enjoyed these stories, and I had to admit that I liked telling them. "Okay, Joe," he said once, pausing to fix me with one of his famous do-I-have-to-hit-you-over-the-head-with-the-obvious looks, "so why is it you're not writing any of this?" (At the time he hadn't been too happy with my fiction, which was taking an artsy turn in the direction of film noir, complete with smoky wet city streets and a vague—no doubt borrowed—sense of angst.) He wanted me to understand, he continued, that taking my writing seriously meant, after all, taking my experience seriously, too, including my immigrant heritage.

What he didn't understand, of course, was that to include such material would be to identify myself with exactly what I'd been avoiding all my life. So, I tried to put him off by appearing to agree. Sure, I told him, that certainly was something I really ought to think about. In a way I meant it, too; back then I was nothing if I wasn't earnest. He laughed anyway. He could tell I wasn't ready. And so, although my writing skill improved under his guidance, even my better stories remained imitations, mostly, in the mode of whatever writer I currently admired, peopled by characters with bland phonebook names, no pasts, no crazy uncles, and who lived, invariably, in "a large American city."

My teacher recognized all this in my writing, of course. But he ~o saw how important readiness was to me, and never tried to ral" my work (as he put it) to his way of seeing things. Better to let me make my own discoveries. Meanwhile, he continued to trust in me—something that he must have sensed I needed far more than I needed to write a good story. He seemed to know things about me that I hadn't even started to learn, and yet, paradoxically, he began encouraging me to respect my own opinions above his. A part of me understood, agreed; another part, like a beginning swimmer, felt the need for a firmer sense of readiness before letting go.

But in this world, readiness is often a luxury. I had just moved away to start teaching at my first faculty position when I learned that this man, who seemed able to read my own heart better than I ever could, had been diagnosed as having cancer. The news of his death came only a few months after that. There was a selfishness to my grief: for years afterward my dreams would be haunted by the sense of his actual presence, benevolent, promising to tell me more, only to turn a corner or leave a room and disappear, dream after dream, in silence.

My first teaching job was more than seven hundred miles away from the Toledo-Lebanese neighborhood, at a college in Springfield, Missouri. The people there were friendly, welcoming—in fact, they were downright sunny. Strangers trimming hedges chirruped hellos as I bicycled past their tidy yards. The mailboxes all bore standard American names like Anderson, Stone, Douglas, Brady; if I looked hard enough I'd probably find Cleaver, too. Word had it that the wife of Gene Autry—the cowboy hero of my childhood (after Red Ryder)—had once attended school here. The campus itself, like the town, was a sea of freckled good looks. Who'd have thought that this country had such a concentration of blond-haired adults? (I hadn't yet been to Iowa.)

I'd located the real America, as only television of the fifties could have imagined it, and I was determined to belong.

So why, after a few weeks, did I find myself giving in to the urge to grow back the beard that I'd shaved off months before for my job interview? Sure, beards were common enough then, then being 1968 and the dawning of the Age of Aquarius. But this was also the Deep Midwest, where college men still wore crew cuts and flattops Growing a black curly beard was certainly no way to blend in.

Nor was wearing the suspenders I'd bought at the Army Surp

Stove, or the wide-brimmed brown fedora hat from Goodwill. I loved the hat; my father used to wear one just like it. But, as this was not the late 1940s, the hat looked goofy, frankly. What was I up to? Well, this much was clear: I was engaged in self-sabotage. If blending in was my aim, I seemed to be having second thoughts.

I was having a whole chain reaction of second thoughts, in fact, all triggered by the most minor incidents. For example, one day in my first month I remember standing at a supermarket counter and waiting while the checkout clerk searched for an item on her produce price list. Finally, she indicated the item, a bulb of garlic, and asked me in her soft Missouri twang, "Whatcha call this?"

"You mean garlic?" I asked.

She nodded and thanked me. A small thing, memorable only because at a different grocery less than a week before another clerk had asked me the same question about a bunch of parsley. "This is parsley—right?" she'd said.

I was amazed. How could somebody not know parsley? Cilantro I could understand. Endive. Even watercress. But ordinary parsley? And garlic! What sort of pot was I melting into here? Instead of being eager to blend right in, I found myself holding back, as if afraid of disappearing altogether.

Next trip to the store I bought more garlic, along with some turnips and vinegar and a can of beets. In my tiny kitchenette, I sliced the turnips, salted and set them in a bowl, as I'd watched my mother do countless times, checking on them throughout the evening to pour off water that the salt drew out. In the morning I placed the turnips in jars with vinegar and garlic and beet juice; I sealed the lids and arranged the jars on my counter to wait the three to five days it would take to pickle the turnips properly. The very sight of them heartened me. three jars filled with deep red liquid. Every time I passed the kitchen I glanced at them, and I felt better. If just seeing them had such an effect, I couldn't wait to taste them. This was more than second thoughts. There was a change coming, and I had been making myself ready for it.

Session after session at my writing table—an unfinished door balanced on concrete blocks—I tried to summon that old dependable angst, vaguely set in American film noir. But, instead of nighttime on wet city streets with a muted trumpet wailing in the background, my mind kept straying to images of streets I really had walked, Jefferson and Michigan and Erie. I saw Monroe Street in morning sunlight, and myself a small boy on its pavement sweeping wine bottles from the entrance to my father's store; hearing the mutter and coo of pigeons and looking up at the flat tarred roofs for the arrival of the bum we called the Pigeonman who used a fishing rod to snag pigeons and sell them to my father for food. I saw the apartment above the store, and myself, dark-eyed and olive-skinned, looking like exactly what I was, an Arab boy in a cowboy hat, peeking from behind the blue velvet armchair at the window, watching my mother serve Turkish coffee to visitors, hearing them murmur "*Daimi,*" before the first sip, "*May we always be together like this,*" the aunt who wore two pairs of glasses on her nose at once, the uncle who was so simple that even my brother and sister and I used to look at one another and wink.

Now in Missouri, living far from those streets, and as if freed by the distance, I found available to me the landscapes of my past—people, situations, places—all that I'd rejected while breathing the actual air of those landscapes. Eyes closed, I could finally see them again, and hear them again, whole neighborhoods in Toledo, in Detroit and Cleveland, all speaking Arabic and the broken English of my childhood.

But if I'm making it sound easy, let me quickly add that along with the good memories come the bad ones. When portraying your own people there is the temptation to gloss over hangups and short-comings and meanness of spirit, especially when those people are basically so appealing anyway, with that Mediterranean emotional range that could surpass high opera's; my father, for example, who could be genuine in his passion one minute and disarming you the next with his canny, self-directed humor.

A year or so after my father died, the movie *Zorba the Greek* came out, and I was struck by a curious resemblance between my father and Anthony Quinn in the role of Zorba. And I wasn't alone. One after another, friends of mine who'd known my father saw the movie and seemed equally amazed; the correspondence was not only in attitude and spirit, but in physical looks and mannerisms, as well. I couldn't deny feeling some pride to hear my friends detail the similarities between my grocer father and Kazantzakis' earthy passionate, mad-for-life hero. Nor could I deny my private observation: poor Mrs. Zorba and the kids.

Fiction, as I tell my students, presents us with the opportunity to walk in someone else's shoes; and picturing the other guy—in this case the Arab-American immigrant—as a complex person with human frailties as well as human virtues defeats the possibility for sentimental simplifying: good or bad, black or white, us or them.

Such a lesson is especially important today, when the politically hot Middle East has been made even hotter by the Gulf War, when Arab-American businesses are fired upon and torched in Toledo and Detroit, and college-educated students in Ames, Iowa, chant "Death to all Arabs!" out their dorm windows.

These feelings are understandable; it's difficult not to get carried away at the sight of classmates and neighbors marching off in desert camouflage. And yet, "All Arabs" includes me, includes my daughters; the words alone do damage.

To say that gunmen and arsonists don't know any better may or may not be stating the obvious. But the chanting students? As understandable as their feelings are, and despite their college educations, I must conclude that they, too, simply don't know any better. Just as I had to conclude years ago when I was mocked for speaking with an accent and thinking my thoughts in another language. Those students, smart as they are, need to get out of their own shoes for a while. Reading stories can help them to do that. And I don't mean political fiction, necessarily. Most stories of any kind, if they're any good at all, ask that the reader use at least a little empathy—that particularly human faculty whereby one can appreciate what an experience must feel like for someone else. The reluctance to feel empathy can express itself in intolerance for the unfamiliar, in self-preoccupation, and narcissism. At the very least it hinders maturation; children stomp on anthills, the emotionally stunted douse cats in gasoline. Empathy, on the other hand, has a maturing effect and leads us into the world.

Last fall I was invited to read my stories at a bookstore in St. Paul, Minnesota. I'd never been to the Twin Cities before and knew no one from there, so I was quite surprised when a total stranger, an older woman from the audience, approached me afterward with a familiar "Hello, Mr. Jeha," giving my last name its Arabic pronunciation. What really floored me, though, was her adding, "You're one of Elias' boys aren't you, the littler one they called Zuzu."

I hadn't heard myself called Zuzu—the Arabic diminutive for Yousef—since I was five years old. (Entering first grade, I remember how I'd insisted that even at home I be called Joe, an American nickname.) It was a shock, hearing the first name of my childhood pronounced by a total stranger.

Who, of course, turned out not to be a stranger at all, but a distant cousin who used to visit Toledo regularly years ago, and she remembered my family when we first arrived in America. (Her memory wasn't perfect, however: she recalled *me* as the wild one, noisy and getting into everything, and *my brother* as the quietly behaved one, which is, take my word for it, laughably backward.) Her smile, especially the sidelong glance of her eyes, I recognized as the frank look that appears whenever my father's side of the family smiles. So now, in a city where I knew no one, I found it was, ironically, my turn to ask the question: "Where did you come from?"

"Here."

"No, I mean originally."

"Originally," she replied. "I was born in St. Paul, a mile from this spot. I've lived here all my life."

Here? Here looked blonder than Iowa and Missouri put together! And the odd thing was, the more we chatted, the more it began to make sense; why couldn't she be one of my people as well as from around here—*originally*? Why not, indeed? After all, who said America must be a melting pot into which we drain and disappear? The nineteenth century, that's who. The Great Melting Pot has always been a nineteenth-century notion, and I'd just as soon it stayed there, along with the Whigs and Manifest Destiny. I prefer instead an image I've come across more and more lately—that of the mosaic. The American Mosaic. Common sense (or, as in my case, years of head-butting trial and error) tells us that the American immigrant experience resulted not from melting down the uniqueness in each separate one of us, but from arranging those pieces and joining them together toward a larger, more complex picture, one that makes use of differences to create richness and power and harmony. The achievement of which is the promise of Ellis Island. And in the stories I write, the struggle for which is what America is all abou'

# ROSEWOOD TOWNSHIP

Paul DeWayne Gruchow, Ed Will's Farm, Section 28, Rosewood Township, Chippewa County, Minnesota, USA, North America, Western Hemisphere, Earth, Milky Way, Universe. I wrote the words over and over. I printed them, inscribed them in my best Palmer-method penmanship, listed them like the lines of a poem. They held for me a terrible fascination, stirring the same feeling that I had one Sunday morning when the preacher pronounced something to be "as far as the east is from the west," a phrase so magnificent and expansive, so unfathomable, that it caused me literally to shudder.

Rosewood Township was a small, out-of-the-way place. It was too small and too far away ever to be quite so parochial as some great capital; its people never imagined that they were being watched or admired from afar; in a billion years it would never have occurred to anyone in Rosewood Township to refer to it as the Big Apple. There were people who were born in Rosewood Township and never intended to leave it, who had no desire to live anywhere else, perhaps had no curiosity about what it might be like to settle elsewhere. They may have felt that Bostonians or Parisians or Afghans, given the chance to try Rosewood Township, might like it equally well, but they never troubled themselves with the presumption that such an experiment was *likely*. The most rosy-eyed inhabitant of Rosewood Township understood its importance and its appeal to be limited, and even at that obscure. If it was a parochial place, it was benignly so. One could not grow up in Rosewood Township without understanding that its significance lay not so much in its qualities per se as in the astonishing and wonderful connections that might be drawn from it to every corner of the wide universe.

As a reminder, as a talisman, perhaps as an incantation, I wrote it on the inside cover of every Big Chief tablet I carried to school, the place where the connections might be made plain: Paul DeWayne Gruchow, Ed Will's Farm, Section 28, Rosewood Township, Chippewa County, Minnesota, USA, Western Hemisphere, Earth, Milky Way, Universe.

School was conducted in a white wooden frame building two hundred yards east along the township gravel road from our house. It had a big front porch. Inside were a cloak room, a library, and a classroom. A row of tall windows on the south wall admitted an amplitude of light. The wooden desks with fold-up seats were bolted together on cast-iron runners, smaller ones forward, bigger ones to the rear. They faced east toward the rising sun and the fonts of learning. Each had a ledge, grooved to hold a pen and fitted with a round hole, into which ink pots were once secured. We lived, however, in the enlightened age of pencils.

In the beginning, I occupied the front desk in the row farthest from the windows, the one nearest the library door. From the ledge of the desk, a writing cover slanted downward. It was as rugged as the surface of the moon, pockmarked and deeply inscribed with the names and dates of its previous squatters. The carvings had been ornamented over the years in inks of many colors and etched with scrolls and filigrees of many kinds, until the whole surface had taken on the ecstatic tone of a medieval illuminated manuscript. The writing cover was attached by hinges, and when lifted, revealed a storage space where secret messages as well as the tools of scholarship might be safely kept. Along the edges of the bottom surface of the storage box, little mountain ranges of chewing gum had been deposited and had hardened into a kind of amber, a salivary record of scholars past, something to chip at when the work stymied or the days grew long and dull.

At the rear of the room there was a tall tan oil burner, which emitted heat from the top. In the winter, you put a potato wrapped in tinfoil on the grate, and by noon it was baked. A long blackboard ran along the east wall. Just in front of it, there were, from north to south, an upright piano, never tuned; a round table and a set of miniature chairs, at which recitations were said; the teacher's desk, into one of the drawers of which it was repeatedly amusing to slip a garter snake or a frog; and the water cooler and its dispenser of cone-shaped paper cups.

Filling the water jar every morning was second from the top in the hierarchy of daily chores. It required two children—one to hold the bucket, the other to work the pump handle—and it was attractive because it could be made to last for several minutes, minutes free from the discipline of the classroom; because it was outside work; and because it required bravery and fortitude, bravery in the fall, when the wasps that nested in the chambers of the pump were still active, and fortitude in the winter, exposed as the well was to the fierce blasts of arctic wind that seemed always to be raging. Pounding out the erasers over the porch railing at the end of the day was the next most desirable chore. After that came the sweeping and the dusting. Washing the blackboard was the humblest of the duties. The highest—a solemn responsibility—was raising and lowering the American flag, the only task explicitly assigned as a reward.

Along the north wall of the classroom were the door to the library, a big Regulator wall clock, the door to the cloakroom, and a bookcase. The spare texts were stored in the bookcase, along with canned provisions, in case a blizzard should strand everyone for the night, an event we children prayed for, in vain. We had crossed one of those minor divides in history: being snowbound was already pretty much a thing of the past.

The library contained a single case of books that might be borrowed—the piece of furniture was actually, I think, an old buffet cabinet—and a *Webster's International Dictionary*, forty years out of date, on a reading stand. To me, the library was a room of great mystery and enchantment. I wanted more than anything to learn to read, and when I had, I wanted to read everything. Books were not an item in the households I knew; there was something illicit and unattainable about them; they were in a category with palaces, naked women, and fast cars. (The only exception was the Gilbertson house, which not only had a bathroom, but a floor-to-ceiling case in the living room with books underneath and a display of the latest magazines on slanted shelves above; and a piano, on which my cousin Steven played "Old Black Joe"; and a mantel clock that chimed the hours. It seemed to me the most luxurious place imaginable.)

The mysteriousness of the library was greatly enhanced by the ɔlash that Mark, a new second grader, made on the day that my twin sister and I enrolled in the first grade. Sometime that first day he went into the library alone and carved into the floor a word so shocking that Mrs. Weckwerth locked the door, summoned the school board, and refused the rest of us entry until the floor could be sanded and refinished. Words, it seemed—even quite short ones—had unimaginably vast powers.

Out back, in full view of the classroom's south windows, beyond the swings, sat two privys, two-holers, one for the girls, one for the boys, each equipped with a picket privacy fence, but airy enough to invite peeking games when teacher's back was turned. Her back wasn't turned, unfortunately, the day we took a tour of the toilets, girls conducting an inspection of their facility, we of ours, which, by virtue of its tin urinal, held the greater novelty. Our field trip, it seemed, was an outrage, for which we paid with several lost recesses.

There is no quality more dangerous in a child, to a certain kind of teacher, than curiosity. I've luckily forgotten the name of this one, but in her case the system (the system being a small school diligently supervised by its constituent parents) worked: she was inspired to retire after a single year of teaching, moved north, and became a bank clerk, an occupation to which she was, no doubt, better suited. Still, she wept over us at least twice. The first tears came when our failure to make satisfactory progress in the memorization of the mathematical tables had induced her to detain us all after school. While we waited, there was a hushed conference, which she did not arrange, with our parents in the cloakroom; she returned, abruptly dismissed us, and cried into her hands as we left. At home, after chores, however, we rehearsed our tables, *or else,* until we knew them as well in sleep as in waking. The other tears were shed after school one bitterly cold February afternoon. A ground blizzard had reduced the visibility to nearly zero. The teacher had enlisted a couple of us to direct her while she backed her car out of the schoolyard driveway. We were hardhearted and could recognize an opportunity: we waved her on and on until she had backed across the township road and into the ditch on the other side. She crawled out through a window, stood in the howling wind, and bawled. One of our dads came with a tractor and pulled her out. She did not tell what had happened. That made us feel almost sorry.

There was a softball diamond and a field of mown grass. Softball was the sport of spring and fall; the talent for it was so slender among the thirteen of us, grades one through six, who attended the school that I—short-sighted, gangly with premature pubescence, as coordinated as a box of rocks—was often in the last years called upon to pitch. After the snow fell, so that proper lines could be marked out, we played Pom-Pom-Pullaway and Fox and Goose, which required stamina but no particular athletic skill.

These, in sum, were the resources on which our formal educations were built. They were Dick-and-Jane basic. We never, I think, saw a movie, took a field trip, conducted a science experiment, played a game that required more equipment than a bat and ball, were never instructed by any machine, never were subjected to any new educational panacea. We learned to read, to write, and to do sums. Every Christmas we put on a program. We sang songs, sketched, colored, and pasted, eating a dab of the wonderfully salty paste for every one we applied to paper. Once in a great while we did something exotic enough to be memorable. One year we had a rhythm band, in which I played the triangle, a grisly ordeal—a triangle sounds so horribly wrong when it is wrong. One year we practiced walking on a two-by-four. One year we learned to braid round and square ropes. I worked in strands of pale blue and yellow, a combination of colors that had suddenly come to me as the highest expression of heavenly beauty.

But mainly we sat in our seats and studied. The classes were called, one at a time, to the front of the room to recite, and recitation was what happened; these were not chatty little exercises in esteem-building; they were daily oral examinations. Those of us in our seats could always listen in when we got bored with our own work. A virtue of the one-room school was that every pupil heard every lesson at least six times before matriculating. One year we had a teacher who liked art and was so professional at it that she worked from an easel, and so we painted away the days. By and large, we taught ourselves, and each other. It was the only way one person could manage six classes at a time. It was not a bad system: our Iowa Basics scores were entirely respectable; if they weren't, children could and did fail (in that time and culture, children were thought to be strong enough to endure failure, even to profit by it); and we acquired a healthy measure of intellectual independence, never having been introduced, until it was too late, to the idea that learning is some kind of inoculant, transmitted via the mouths of teachers.

Rural School District 18, Rosewood Township, was one of forty-five in operation in Chippewa County when I started school in 1953. A decade later, they were all gone. The school pump still stands, an odd obstacle in a plowed field, and I have the dictionary still in my library. But the institution itself, the only one Rosewood Township ever had, is long dead.

Our farm was across the road from the school. We rented it from Ed Will, a retired farmer. I have been told how infatuated we children were with him, how we would follow him everywhere when he came to visit, peppering him with questions that always began with his name. "Ed Will, how long are you going to stay?" "Ed Will, did you bring us any pennies?" (He always had.) "Ed Will, where do rabbits sleep?" "Ed Will, can snails sing?" But I can't remember anything about his physical presence. The only image that comes to mind is of a visit to him after he had gone to a nursing home. Father and Mother went up to his room while we children waited on the porch, where half a dozen old men were slumped morosely in wheelchairs. One of them suddenly let out a tremendous bellow, making me jump, and a nurse came running with a long-necked urinal, and he peed into it while my sister and I stared, more in awe of the man's apparent lack of embarrassment than of anything else. That is all I remember about Ed Will.

His land was at the southeast corner of Section 28 of Rosewood Township. There were two eighties, one running east and west from the southeast section corner, and the other running north and south through the middle of the section. They made an L in the classic shape of a farmhouse. One hundred sixty acres, a quarter of a square mile, was the standard size for a farm in the early 1950s. The east-west eighty was generally level, running slightly uphill at the east end. The north-south eighty was flat for a quarter of a mile and then dipped into a rather large cattail marsh, which was at a sufficiently low elevation so that the farmstead could not be seen from it. The topsoil was a rich black prairie loam, fertile and generally friable, but with a tendency to harden into something like concrete if worked when too wet.

My father rented this land on shares. He supplied the tools, t' labor, and perhaps the seeds, and kept two-thirds of the crop. Land, in the early 1950s, still passed mainly from generation to generation, but my grandfather, the son of a German immigrant, had never owned land, and Ed Will's children, if he had any, were not farmers. So we were part of the underclass of tenant-farmers in the larger underclass of rural society, at a time when farmers still thought of themselves as the salt of the earth, but after the Jeffersonian ideal of the yeoman farmer had lost its universal savor.

Our farm was, if anything, less diverse than average. We raised corn, wheat, oats, soybeans, and flax and kept goats, sheep, and chickens, but many farms also had pigs and beef cows or dairy cows and, in consequence, alfalfa and more pasture than we did. My father was more interested in horticulture than in livestock—he was a gardener at heart—and I think, too, that sharecropping discouraged investments in pasture and hay, which worked to the disadvantage of the landowner.

A popular feature of the county weekly, the *Montevideo American*, in the early 1950s was "Mystery Farm." An aerial photograph of a farmstead was published, readers telephoned to identify its occupants, and the first reader with the correct answer won a small prize. A story about the farm followed in the next edition.

It is striking how diversified farming still was then, in what one thinks of now as the first stage in the industrialization of American farming. There does not appear to have been any farm that did not have four or five kinds of crops and two or three kinds of livestock. Because the average farm was a quarter the size of one today, this meant that the typical field was comparatively tiny. Twenty-five acres of something was a huge spread, and there were lots of fields of fewer than ten acres. I am struck, too, by how much land was not under active cultivation. Typically, in the "Mystery Farm" stories, a quarter of the land on a farm is described as in pasture or is unaccounted for. Even if the pastures were closely grazed, as they often were, there was still, in the 1950s, a tremendous amount of space in Rosewood Township where birds might nest and wild animals might roam. There were fencerows then, too. Corn hybrids, in particular, were less sturdy—genetic resistance to the corn borer was still in the offing—and corn pickers were less efficient than today's combines, so after the harvest, a lot of corn remained in the fields. The common practice was to turn the livestock loose in them to fatten on the gleanings. This required that fields be fenced; fences hemmed in the plows; so every farm was ringed by a little greenway, in which prairie grasses and flowers grew, and mice nested, and ground squirrels, pocket gophers, and badgers burrowed, supporting populations of predators—foxes, skunks, weasels, feral cats, owls, hawks. It was still a landscape that was, in a modest way, hospitable to natural as well as domesticated life. My father supplemented his income in those days by trapping. Reading the old files of the *Montevideo American*, I suddenly saw how that was possible.

Such a contest as "Mystery Farm" had reader appeal then. There was a reliable chance that the occupants of a farmstead chosen at random and pictured from the air might be identified, and that the people who lived in the buildings were farmers and were, in fact, connected to the surrounding land. Farming and farm people, quite aside from this particular contest, were once big news in Montevideo, the seat of Chippewa County. The progress of the rains, the arrival of the corn borers, the annual egg show, the annual meeting of the Rural Electrification Administration (which drew more than three thousand participants), the corn-picking contest, the yields at harvesttime: all these were front-page news in 1952, the year my family moved to Rosewood Township from a seven-acre vegetable and berry farm in an adjoining township. There was a weekly column of social news from Rosewood Township. I read in it that we had Christmas Eve dinner that year with my grandmother, an aunt and uncle, and my cousins, and that after dinner we all attended services at St. John's Lutheran Church. (Afterward, I remember, each child received a bag of treats, including an apple, some peanuts in the shell, chocolate stars, pillow-shaped peppermints, ribbons of hard candy.)

I have in front of me an issue of the same newspaper from December of 1990. It is fat and apparently prosperous. Farming doesn't exist in it, except on the agriculture page, page 2C. There one finds a (moderate) column from the extension director:

> Animal rights group,
> agricutlural [sic] industry
> must 'meat' halfway

There is an article about choosing the right commercial mix of bird food, one about the importance of snow as an insulator of gardens one about a planned study of nonpoint pollution of the Minnesota River. There is nothing wrong with these stories. They contain useful and even important information. But two of them aren't about farming at all (except as one might argue that buying bird seed is a poor substitute for farming in such a way as to accommodate wild birds). And the other two are really stories about the failures of farming. These failures are all too real, and the farmers I know acknowledge them. But where is there report of the struggles and successes of those farmers who are trying to adopt better methods in a hostile economic environment? (A standard item in the "Mystery Farm" reports was a paragraph on the farm's conservation practices.) Where are farmers as human beings? As members of the community?

The newspaper is not edited without sympathy. Elsewhere there is an account of a suicide that is not reported as one, and a story about the loneliness single pastors can feel at Christmastime, and a pep talk about supporting local merchants instead of stealing away to shop in the bigger towns nearby, and a piece about how local insurance salesmen seek only to serve the best interests of their "clients." The only tilt of this kind toward farmers occurs in the story on page 2A about the legislative priorities of the newly elected state representative, and it is not only boosterish, but pandering, and ultimately destructive. Declaring that "ethanol is definitely a key to our national energy independence," the new representative promises to push for legislation promoting ethanol sales. Perhaps he does not know that it costs more energy to produce a gallon of ethanol than is contained in the end product, and that an overemphasis on the production of corn is one of the things that has devastated the farmers in his district.

Chippewa County is among the most rural counties in the nation, one of the few where agriculture still accounts for at least half of the gross production. Farming is still economically important to Chippewa County—and it is all there is in Rosewood Township—but the newspaper is right to see farmers themselves as socially insignificant. There may be lots of farming in the county, but there aren't many farmers anymore, and most of those who remain prefer to call themselves agribusinessmen. They are producers and marketers. Farming once entailed something more than production and marketing. It was a culture. It was more than a livelihood. It was a vocation. Vocational agriculture was the subject taught in high schools, although in my experience of it, there was a good deal more talk about pig rations and eradication methods for common weeds than about farming as a work with moral purpose. Something profoundly accurate happened when people stopped talking about agriculture and started talking about agribusiness; the death of the culture in farming really did happen.

Another striking thing about the "Mystery Farm" stories is that almost all of them are about farmers with families. In 1952, there were still children everywhere in the countryside. Today, the median age of farmers is fifty-four, and children are as scarce in Rosewood Township as barns.

Our farm was across the road from the schoolhouse. The farmstead was sheltered on the west and north by a grove of maples. There was a little house, and next to it a summer kitchen. There were also a hip-roofed barn, a chicken house, a hog house, a machine shed, and a granary. Next to the barn there was a windmill, still in working order when we lived there. One of Father's annual chores was to climb the windmill and grease the gears at the top. The granary had two bins, one with slanted sides for corn, and the other, across a covered alley, with solid walls for small grains. The barn had a big haymow and was fitted for dairy cows, although we didn't keep any.

The house had two main rooms below, a living room and a bedroom, and a porch, which had been enclosed to serve as a kitchen-dining room. Up a steep staircase, two tiny slant-roofed rooms had been fashioned out of the attic crawl space, high enough for a child to stand in, but not everywhere, and just barely. My twin sister and I occupied these rooms when we were old enough to leave the common bedroom; when our younger sister came along, I moved to the summer kitchen, which was essentially unfinished; it had no insulation and no interior walls—just bare studs. It was open enough so that I found myself sharing it one summer night with a skunk, visible in the moonlight, that padded about, sniffing and poking into every cranny while I cowed in my bed, afraid to move lest I startle it and provoke a shower of scent; and climbing out from under the mountain of quilts on winter mornings and getting dressed in a room where the temperature was below freezing was always a stiff test of character. But I loved that place for the privacy and independence it afforded me. It was my Walden; like Thoreau, I spent my nights there, but a hot meal, laundry service, and companionship always waited in the big house when I needed them.

The main house was sparsely furnished. It could hardly have been otherwise, given its minuscule size. The kitchen had a cupboard, a chrome dinette set of the kind fashionable in the 1950s, and a cookstove fueled with wood and corncobs. In the living room there were a couch, several chairs, and an oil burner that sat on a metal fire pad. The living room was adorned with the only piece of art that I remember, a rendering of the Last Supper in an oval painted metal frame. In the bedroom: a bed, a dresser, and vanity table with a big mirror, the only one in the house. You can measure fairly accurately the economic status of any household by counting the mirrors in it. Upstairs, two beds, two dressers. The floors were covered with patterned linoleums, the walls with print wallpapers with ornamental borders; the whole place was a pastel riot of plaids, paisleys, and floral stripes.

Food was stored in a root cellar, a dugout with fieldstone walls and a floor that was muddy in the spring and dusty the rest of the year. It was reached through a slanted trap door just to the right of the front door of the house. It smelled dank and was lit by a bare bulb, whose string you had to grope in the dark to find. There were shelves for the canned goods. Mother put up about seven hundred quarts of produce a year: fruits, vegetables, sauces, jams, jellies, pickles, fruit butters, krauts, meats. There was also a big bin in which the root vegetables were stored, and there were tin cannisters in which apples, wrapped individually in paper, would keep until the middle of the winter.

In the springtime, the root bin presented a gauntlet to us children. You would be told to run down to the cellar and fetch a bucket of potatoes. This meant going outside; raising the trap door; descending into the dark through a curtain of spiderwebs that tangled in your hair; standing in the mud; groping for the light switch, which, when it had been engaged, made you feel better, although the bulb didn't, in fact, illuminate the potato bin; and plunging your hand in, knowing the odds were even that you would find your fingers impaled in a rotten tuber, or that you would scare up one of the tiger salamanders that had wintered there in the warmth and that would scamper across your toes, giving you the bejeebecs.

The only thing worse was fetching the eggs from under a tempera-mental hen in the mood to brood.

Ours was largely a subsistence farm. The chickens, when they were not moulting, provided eggs. Occasionally one of them sub-mitted its neck to the chopping block and, after a final headless romp around the yard, its wings beating desperately, it would be scalded in a pot of boiling water. Its feathers would be plucked (the little pin feathers stuck to your fingers as if begging still for mercy), it would be boiled to tenderize it, and then it would be pan-fried and served with gravy made from the drippings and mashed po-tatoes. The onions in the pan came from our garden; the flour to thicken the gravy was ground from wheat raised on the farm; the goats manufactured the milk; the potatoes were raised separately from the garden in a field plot. The potatoes were grown on a grander scale because they—and bread baked in the kitchen range—were the staples of our diet, served twice a day. To accompany the po-tatoes and the chicken, there might be string beans, or peas, or beets, grown also in the garden, or some asparagus gleaned from the fencerows; and with the bread there would be a strawberry jam, perhaps, or some apple butter, or honey from our own hive of bees. For dessert there might be, in summer, a fresh-baked fruit pie or, in winter, a sauce—plum, or apple, or groundcherry. The yeast, the salt, the butter, the sugar were bought in town. Breakfasts were also imported: the menu was the same every day—oatmeal with raisins and an orange or grapefruit, depending on what we could get by Railway Express from Florida. But what the farm, and our own la-bors, could provide, they did.

The work went round and round: spring plowing, disking, plant-ing, harrowing, cultivating, the first hay harvest, canning, the small grain harvest, the second hay harvest, soybeans out, corn out, corn-stalks chopped, potato digging, fall plowing, woodcutting, butcher-ing, boiling and blueing traps, running the trap lines, skinning and stretching furs, corn shelling, lambing, and then the spring rains had quit, the puddles had dried, the trees were blooming, and it was time again to start the spring plowing. It was classical work done mainly in classical ways on a classical schedule. The house schedule was weekly: Mondays, washing; Tuesdays, ironing; Wed-nesdays, baking; Thursdays, sewing, gardening, preserving; Fridays, town days; Saturdays, cleaning; Sundays, days of rest and worship.

To each day, and to each season, was dedicated a suitable labor, but no labor was ever exactly repeated. No year was ever the same as another, and each field had its own character, so farming the land was always new work; it was in the nature not of a repetition but of an experiment, always unfolding, destined never to be completed. Sometimes the experiments worked, sometimes not; sometimes an idea that succeeded once, or ten times, didn't work on the next trial, exactly why no one could say, since experiments on the farm are not like experiments in the laboratory, where the variables can be reduced to known numbers. Farmers cannot afford the luxury of Cartesian thinking; they are obliged to work in the real world, the whole world, where one thing is indivisibly connected to another.

Even in the house the work was never quite the same work. Each batch of bread, for example, was the product of a freshly ground cannister of wheat, which was not industrially milled and therefore varied from year to year, and from grinding to grinding, and with a cake of yeast that constituted a community of living organisms and multiplied, or didn't multiply, according to its own state of vigor; and each kneading was a new and individual kneading, conducted with reference to my mother's memory of the exact texture that would solicit from this lump of dough, under these conditions of heat and humidity, considering the fecundity of this yeast, and the character of this batch of flour, a fine loaf of bread, which would be baked to perfection not under the regulation of the timer, but according to its color and to the sound it made when it was tapped, each fire having been built to the occasion, its peculiar heat depending on the condition of the materials that fueled it, and on the circumstances under which it was stoked or banked, according to the judgment of the baker.

My father planted a field as my mother set out a lump of dough to rise: paying attention to experience, employing techniques acquired through long practice and varying the methods as present conditions or the impulse to experiment dictated, relying on the faith that these resources would prove adequate to meet the exigencies ahead, but knowing that the fruit would ultimately depend on the season. The work was creative; it was like making a poem, or dancing, or singing a song.

For me, the most important place on the farm was the cattail marsh at its north end. To get there, you took the farm's interior road, a grass track that ran east to the edge of the maple grove and then north as far as the waterway that drained into the slough from the east. The physical distance was not quite half a mile, but in psychological distance it might as well have been halfway around the world.

Here was a piece of Rosewood Township as it had existed for thousands of years, a surviving testament of the tallgrass prairie, and the richest and most complex representative of it. As measured by the biomass it produces, a cattail marsh is one of the earth's most abundant features. Only in a tropical rain forest is life more fertile. Rosewood Township at settlement was a great ocean of grass lapping across a level plain. It had nothing that could be called a hill; the landscape rose and fell in swells like the sea and swales. It had no trees, no river or stream, no lake. Still, it was the farthest thing from a desert, despite its modest rainfall. Because the moisture that fell had nowhere to go, it stayed on the land: the tall grasses caught and held the snow against the fierce winds in winter; in spring the thirsty sod soaked up the meltwaters, and they trickled down through the zillions of miles of roots that constitute the hidden jungle of a prairie and into the groundwater basins and channels that are its unseen lakes and rivers. The excess water that fell during the greening rains of spring drained as far as the nearest swale and collected in marshes like the one on our farm. Most of these were not permanent bodies of water. As summer wore on and the wet days of May gave way to dusty August, the ponds evaporated, exposing ovals of black mud, ringed by rank growths of cattails, grasses, and tall wetland flowers. These ovals baked and cracked, the rich alkaline deposits in them showing as a fine white powder. But the marshes persisted long enough, most years, to produce flocks of ducks and geese by the thousands, to shelter dozens of kinds of songbirds; and their waters were as thick as a primordial soup with snails, and crustaceans, and insect larvae, and with microorganisms numbering in the billions per teaspoonful; and this profusion of life attracted frogs, and snakes, and insects numbering in the tens of thousands of species; and so came the skunks and weasels, the mink and foxes, the raccoons, the mice and shrews, and on the uplands the burrowing animals, the ground squirrels, and badgers, and pocket gophers; and after them came the wolves and coyotes, and the raptors, the hawks and owls, and in the tall grasses around them grazed the great herbivores, the bison and antelope. At the edges of the larger sloughs, such as ours, a few willows and cottonwoods took root, casting a rare shade on the flowerful but severe landscape; and the water lasted from year to year, attracting muskrats and turtles, clams and small fishes. A cousin and I once caught with our bare hands a five-gallon bucket full of bullheads in the drying outlet to one of these ponds.

There were a million things to see in our marsh. I spent many days and whole nights there when I was a boy, trying in vain to catch sight of them all. I could never succeed. It was a fabulous textbook to me, and a storybook as fantastic as an *Arabian Nights*. It was my university, my theater, my refuge and strength. When I rejoiced, I went there to celebrate; when I was sad, to be consoled. In every weather, I worshiped there.

The farm survives, of course. In the midlands, land does not appear or vanish in the scale of a human lifetime. But it is now a kind of desert. The fencerows are gone. The house is gone. The marsh is gone. It was drained a long time ago. The tile inlets are marked by steel fence posts on which white plastic petroleum and chemical bottles have been hung to make them visible to the operators of the big machines that turn its soils, which are thin enough now so that the moldboards of the plows bring big yellow patches of clay to the surface. The waterfowl are gone, the raptors are gone, the burrowing animals are gone, the predators are gone. Such insects as remain are learning to become specialists in the two or three domestic crops that now grow there, and the most favored of them, like the grasshoppers, come and go in plagues. The domestic animals are gone all across the township, and the few barns that still stand are slowly imploding of their own weight. Last season, the whole 160 acres of our farm was planted to a single crop—corn.

I was wrong to say that the place has become a desert. There is hardly a desert so barren. I went walking once on a ranch in the Sonoran Desert where it takes four or five farms the size of this one to raise a single cow, and it was, in comparison, an oasis. It ought to go without saying, but doesn't, that the people are gone, too. Why are we always thinking that we can plow a piece of land to its last square inch without also uprooting ourselves? We think the world is a machine. Do we think we are machines too?

We love to flatter ourselves. We love to say that we are living through an information explosion, that our lives are complex as they never before were, that our ways are newly sophisticated. I look at Section 28, Rosewood Township, Chippewa County, Minnesota, and I don't see the evidence for this claim. What information does a cornfield convey that the cattail marsh didn't? What complexity does a cornfield hold that was missing when the farm was biologically diverse? How is a cornfield more urbane than the human family it supplanted?

If there is no one anymore to chart the way from Section 28, Rosewood Township, into the wide universe—and there isn't—does the connection still exist?

# JEFFERSON TOWNSHIP:
# THE LAND THAT MADE ME

When Thomas Jefferson threw his wide net of township grids west, and then across the Ohio, one square fell on unsettled territory north of the river in Clinton County between what is now Cincinnati and Columbus.

In that way Jefferson's obsession with the neoclassic—the grid, the white pillars of Greece and Monticello superimposed on wilderness—became a township that still bears his name.

What this township once was, or what It has become, may be attributed in part but not wholly to the Sage's vision. Two local, parallel beliefs summarize his influence on this thirty-six square miles of land: the good men do live after them; and, equally optimistic, things here *could* be one hell of a sight worse—said as one word, "hulvahsitewurs."

No matter, in this township I was born.

## Darkly the Past Is Also Here

Over centuries, in geologic time, the third Wisconsin glacier came south, stopped, then melted away. The glacier's massive debris remained, became local geography. Therefore, within Jefferson Township, farms with rich soil and farms with clay and boulders lie cheek by jowl, said, "cheakk byjuaol."

On a rocky farm of glacier debris, it was hard to raise either your hat or a cuss fight; on rich soil, weather permitting, it was said, "Any damned fool can pretty nearit break even."

Yet this must be said: Jefferson Township has no natural monuments of note or historical significance; no remembered high crimes, recorded battles, vital myths, or any save local heroes Once, briefly,

Jeff Township may have been a viable economic unit, but surrounding townships, for cause, would have denied it.

Best I mention relative importance at the onset, for in the telling, at least for the moment, Jefferson Township may seem unique. From affection and some loyalty, I would have it so.

Possibly because citizens of Jefferson Township have always seen their past through the absolute clarity of mercantile spectacles, historical awareness invariably begins with wilderness, the pioneer drive for stability, improvement, and progress, and as is nature's way, profit.

Nevertheless, in our own prehistoric times, this terrain was held by the Mound Builders.

They built the great Serpent Mound, the Circle Mound (at Circleville), and hundreds of others; most importantly, they also built the earthwork mounds at Fort Ancient, thought to be the center of their civilization.

Those pre-Indian peoples ranged to the deep South and to the far Middle West, then disappeared. Of famine, disease, war, or all three is not known. Now, park rangers guard their barrows.

Even among the Shawnee, the Miami, the Iroquois, the terrain in and around Jefferson Township had specific definition: tribal hunting grounds, but even that use was compromised.

This land was low, wet, marshy; the higher ground often clay knobs. Beneath marshes and in creek bottoms the land was rich, black. Totally wooded, a place of few trails except where creeks served, and everywhere giant oaks, walnut, sassafras, briars.

Marshland was bird land, and their flocks aloft at noon darkened the sky. Sometimes blue-on-red, yellow-beaked macaws flashed among branches.

But the Indians did not go often if ever into these dark, often flooded, low-lying woods. For reasons not known, chiefs (or their medicine men) put this territory under taboo, off limits.

There is functional superstition but not much sinister about this taboo. There were more easy—and perhaps more healthy—places to get meat.

Therefore, it was to a low, wet, not healthy place where sloughs, marsh, boulders, and scrub oak held the terrain, to a place of betrayal by flood, but not often fire, to a place of rampant fevers, mosquitoes, water moccasins, and winters of great ferocity where neither land nor men were ever equal, and to a place of a certain innocence, as by taboo, to this place, to Jefferson Township my forebears came.

## Before My Time

Even in 1800 what is now Cincinnati was only Fort Washington, an outpost in the wilderness. From that whitewashed, square enclosure of logs not far from a river landing, General Sinclair lumbered in his coach north against the Indians, was defeated; then Mad Anthony Wayne went north to victory at Fallen Timbers. In the treaties that followed, all of southern Ohio became a U.S. territory. The last white man killed by an Indian in Ohio was in about 1820.

From the Eastern seaboard, by flatboat, settlers came down the Ohio, docked in Cincinnati, took rivers then creeks inland; or they came by wagon roads across the mountains from the South, especially Virginia.

Much has been written of the ways unsurveyed lands passed from the communal ownership of Indian tribes, to the U.S. Congress, and thence by way of chartered land companies to individual purchasers. The current Savings and Loan scandal has some parallels with land sales, handled through land-sale companies. Land agents were the used-car salesmen of their day.

From wilderness and a land office to Jefferson's vision of an integrated community required more time—and lives.

In the general rush for Ohio land, the Halls came by the overland route, from Virginia.

Family legend has it that five brothers settled variously in southern, central, and northern Ohio. One had been a captain in the Continental Army and is said to have won one thousand acres in the regimental crap game, his point a four. There were other ways to get land besides through a land company. A musket, some brothers, and a military background apparently helped.

I could feel close to all of that, for the deed of one Hall farm went back to tribal hunting grounds, and I have lain in a fifty-acre woods in summer, imagined easily a huge oak's trunk was exactly here in the time of the Indians.

One immediate descendant was my great-grandfather, for whom I am named. The son of Hall pioneers, he rode horseback several days through snow to attend Ohio University (Athens), and there studied the classics. His classmates became Civil War tycoons, but Old Jim (so-called, later) returned, became a country schoolmaster, with something of a mean, managerial streak. His handwriting is steel-engraving clear; he was Southern to the core.

He taught at Second Creek and married one of his students (for whom my sister is named). Obviously a love match, for she was the daughter of the county's largest landowner.

He operated his scattered dukedom out of Midland City and is said to have given all orders early each day from his front porch, which was a hotel-restaurant he built for the accommodation of train crews.

I never knew Great-Grandfather Hall, but older women who did said he was a "land grabber" and quick with a lawsuit. I was said to be his "spitting image," and by the very old, with country irony, was sometimes called "Young Jim."

All of this was very Southern. At the time I did not notice, but later understood no black individuals or families lived or worked in Jefferson Township until sometime after World War II. But here, no slaves, even though just across the river Kentucky was a slave-holding state. Even before the War between the States, even in theory, Old Jim would have held no slaves: it was less money, long term, to hire a white man for a dollar and a dime a day and dinner, and he was off the property by sundown. Pronounced, "uh dollhe-anadimeuday un dinergh."

Call all like Old Jim in persuasion but not in stature, Midland City people.

My mother's immediate forebears were of Quaker stock, some said to have "come across" with William Penn. They arrived by flat-boat, were small farmers, given to meditation, praised always as "good neighbors," which meant they exchanged fieldwork at planting, at harvest, in sickness.

Back in Pennsylvania they had been small businesspeople as well, apparently valued a good horse, made above-average school-teachers, and betimes, an honest county commissioner.

Property and taxes being equal, they were generally for the higher things, were pillars of the church but sensible about any proposed new paint; they were forthright about education (if you deserved it).

That Quaker heritage melted away to Methodist conviction, and I am sure my mother's people did not give orders from a front porch; more likely they did the work themselves, or "neighbored it"; they drank sparingly, if at all; saw lawyers only to draw a will, and in rural Ohio lived for the day, and at the same time for the next world.

Post–Civil War line drawings show a fine horse smartly trotting, pulling high-wheeled traps, the road smooth, the fences of wood aligned, and in the background a tight, well-crafted barn, somewhat larger than the house with a cupola on a slight rise, the lane curved, leading upward to the porch—the better for horses pulling a load either down or up.

Call them Westboro people.

Between Westboro and Midland City people there were always tensions, not always creative in nature.

On the one hand there was the Westboro state of mind: several churches, the township's growing, always well tended cemetery; a woolen mill, a carding mill, a feed and grain mill, and a white, two-storied dry goods and general store of wide repute. No bank. For something that serious a man would go either to Blanchester or to the county seat in Wilmington. There were many covered bridges to shield buggy, man, and horse from hail, snow, or rainstorms.

If Westboro continued its pastoral, Quaker, conservative, ways, and if its young men went off to fight for the Union, they often came back to be buried in the overly large, very pleasant Westboro cemetery.

Only about four miles distance was Midland City, and the Midland state of mind.

Almost overnight it became a railroad town.

This transition began easily, for the first locomotives burned wood, seemed a toy in the swamps. Old Jim cut wood and sold it to the B & O, stacked track-side, and found. Every summer his own "fireman" set fire to his own pastures, and each spring Old Jim was in court for "demidgus." He cashed-cropped the B & O, and everyone knew it, pronounced, "unairone nodit."

In a second phase of expansion, trunk lines from Chillicothe and Columbus joined at Midland City, in the center of town formed a great Y, with a freight depot, cattle pens, dispatcher and telegraphers; a town with water tanks on stilts, coal chutes, and Honey

Creek damned to make a large reservoir for steam-locomotive water.

Midland City, socially, became a two-tier town: the old families in the countryside or town lived comfortably, in a rural way. In lesser houses or rental shacks, the section gang, signalmen, electricians, bridge carpenters, car hostlers, engine and boiler mechanics lived sometimes less well. The politics, the cooperation of the two tiers, was public; the difference of real or imagined class was social, private.

Even if Midland became a railroad junction town, it still had its large brick high school, but most students stopped at the eighth grade. It was well said, "There's B & O money in Midland City, and every man votes his job."

At that time, the two towns must have seemed widely separated, but the distance was only about four miles. This could seem a long way, for until after World War I, locally, these were horse-drawn communities. Even then the agents of change were present.

Jefferson Township's chief planner was always war: the War of 1812, the Civil, Spanish-American, World War I, and World War II.

New transportation brought change: the canals, railroads, and most importantly, state and interstate highways. A new industrialization brought steel, paper mills, a ceramic and a machine tool industry. Wars did not directly cause this industrialization but were often the impetus. Generally, Jefferson Township was not so much changed as surrounded by change. No mills, no factories, no super highways.

I think the dwellers of Jefferson Township at the turn of the century, people who now seem as distant from us as the Mound Builders, understood the changes, and with country stoicism accepted, knew damned well it was going to get worse, said as two words, "newtdamdwul hitwasgonnagatwus."

Understandably so.

Jefferson Township people sometimes seem obsessively protective of property, of land, in part because that land was so hard won. It was as though should a man take his eye off his land someone would make off with it, pronounced, "makhoff withed."

Secondly, death could come at any time, and there was so little defense save faith in the Good Lord.

For example, in a week, one of my grandfathers lost his mother, father, and sister to diphtheria, leaving him alone in the world at ten years of age. A neighbor took him in as a farmboy drudge. A grandmother lost mother, father, and two sisters to typhoid in one month; she was reared by an unsympathetic uncle.

There was no cure for tuberculosis, "fevers" were prevalent; midwives aided in childbirth, and once my grandmother told me that if a woman bled excessively the midwife applied handfuls of spiderwebs.

Farm injuries, especially around stables, easily "went into lockjaw"; runaway horses killed more people in the U.S., proportionately, than do automobiles today.

With so many axes, scythes, pitchforks, knives, hay hooks, gun accidents, drownings, exposure, and pneumonia, farming was a dangerous line of work.

Almost anyone who did farmwork consistently had something missing: a thumb, finger, or hand; an arm, a foot, an eye. Such things were "exterior"; otherwise, the victim would not have lived. Madness and suicide were more common than usually acknowledged.

Nor were the railroad men exempt—far from it.

At congressional levels railroad "interests" resisted the installation of the newly invented air brake and other safety devices. A man was supposed to look after himself, "elst he might get hisself skinned"—a common term for dying by live steam, fire, collision, or dismemberment by iron wheels and steel rails.

The harshness of life and the unpredictability of the future helped make the people of Jefferson Township stay close to home. The church, the habit of thrift, and some high thinking was enough for Westboro; a semi-pro baseball team, the pool rooms, saloons, the railroad, and horseplay was more the speed for Midland City.

If an older generation stayed on, the newer generations followed the work, and—like the Mound Builders—were no longer brought here even for burial. This township is not yet a country ghetto, but even when the autumn full moon is aloft, Thomas Jefferson would weep, if only a little. To people who reside here (but seldom work here) Jefferson Township is mostly a name, designates a school district, itself open to new consolidations. The small farm is no longer viable; the once arrogant railroad rolling stock now does not often stop in Midland City.

## As I Knew It

When I was a boy in the mid-1920s, Jeff Township had changed not much from the turn of the century.

Veterans of the Civil War were alive; one of my grandmothers remembered the day Lincoln's funeral train passed through.

The last flicker of pioneer and later rural cooperation was evident when my grandfather and others, with a grader and horse-drawn scrapers, "donated" a day's work and a team of horses for maintenance of township roads. Whether this was voluntary, or credit against property taxes, I do not know.

Those were both Jazz Age and Prohibition times. This brought the new small businessperson, the bootlegger. All formal bootleggers were from or around Midland—never Westboro.

There was a surprising tolerance for bootleggers from a township that had righteously voted "dry"; there was a curious tolerance for all crime, sometimes said to beat "work for a living." The rationale was something like this: "Arrest too damned many of them, and you have to build a bigger jail."

There were elaborate, on-going practical jokes, something like folk theater.

With the connivance of the local telegraph operator, there might be an authentic-looking telegram delivered by bicycle perhaps late at night to a skinflint farmer, ordering him to report to the nearest U.S. post office—a matter of taxes on "said Terwilliger tract" (the man's own farm).

The postmaster would be entirely sympathetic, and suggest consultation with a deputy sheriff, and so on. In those days there were still boobs in America, and the man who got such a "telegram" was not suspicious that it was signed, "The Government."

During WPA days, a hundred men, fifty on each side of a ditch they were cleaning, to the man, contrived balletlike, to be leaning on their shovels each time the landowner came past to view their progress. Or, when a garage mechanic was hungry, was working very late at night—on a bread truck—and sent someone for a ham sandwich, the local restaurant cook might first send back a fried mouse sandwich (on a mouldy bun) followed not too quickly by the correct order.

For such things to happen consistently, members of a community must know one another very well—and know just about how much a man will stand for. I do not remember a time when I did not think there was something hilarious about life, just in general.

More seriously, a political, an educational issue of importance was finally settled: to consolidate all Westboro and Midland schools into a modern brick building.

The contention was over the new location, the site. The Westboro and the Midland state of mind squared off.

In the end, there was compromise and the Jefferson Consolidated School was located within a surveyed inch an equal distance from the two towns.

These school board meetings were for keeps: on one vote my father allegedly was locked in the broom closet, then in the minutes of the meeting tallied as "absent."

At any rate, one of my early memories was of the school site: the basement was being blasted by dynamite, and I saw the dirt shoot skyward, heard the noise, felt the earth shake.

The seemingly very large building, the largest building in the township, was finally finished. To me it seemed mighty against the sky—for my parents thought it so. Everything was new.

And when I was six years old, ready for first grade, my mother—once herself a schoolteacher—took me there.

And Miss Osborne, a spinster teacher from an old Quaker family near Hale's Branch and Westboro, showed me my little desk.

I was to sit there and be a very good boy.

And I did.

And I was.

* * * SUSAN HAUSER * * *

# WHEN THE BOUGH BREAKS

The early afternoon sun worked at the drawn shade of the south window. From my bed, where I was supposed to be napping, I watched. Some light sneaked in through the fabric of the shade itself. In its passage through the cream-colored fibers, it lost its edge. More yellow than white, it breathed into the room, betraying the civilization of dust motes that eddied about.

I almost fell asleep staring into that microcosmic dance, but then a breeze found its way around the outside of the house and in through my open window. The shade was no match for it. Easily, as though with a hand, the moving air pushed in and lifted the shade just a little. The weight of the pine slat sewn into the hem slapped it back down as quickly as it had risen. It was time enough. The outside air was in, accompanied by a stab of light. The dust motes scurried about in panic, then quieted. Then the breeze did it again and then again and I wearied and slept.

I was in first grade, old enough to be conniving, but young enough to be inept at it. I had played sick that morning. I had to. I had asked and then begged to be allowed to stay home from school that day. The tree cutters were coming. They were going to saw down the oak tree next to the house. I had tried to talk my parents out of it. They would not relent, even when I explained about the nest, the bird nest, that I could see from my upstairs bedroom window. The tree was old. In the right wind, it would fall on the house. It had to be cut down.

They said the birds would be all right. I did not believe them. I wanted to see for myself. Would find the nest in the fallen tree. Maybe I could hold birds in my hands.

I thought my parents believed me when I said I was sick. They did not argue with me. I went to my room to wait for the men to come. Dad stayed home too and also waited. When the men came,

I watched him in the yard with them. Sometimes they moved around to the other side of the virgin oak and I could not see them through the leaf-ridden branches. I could still hear their voices though, the words scrambled in their passage through space up to my window.

When it fell, the oak tree filled the entire yard. I tried to watch the branch with the nest in it plummet toward earth, but lost it as all the branches shuddered and collapsed into each other. I ran down the steps and out into the yard but stopped short by the back stoop.

The tree had changed. The clusters of leaves that whispered to me in the night were gathered into fists. The branches that had held the nest out to me now kept me away from it. I tried to see it but could not. No birds flew out of the wreckage.

Then my father discovered me. I was home because I was sick. Even though I felt better, I would have to stay in my room. Already shaken by the deception of the tree, I was hit again from the other side: my father knew I had lied, and he let me get away with it.

I was glad to be going back up to my room, but when I got there, it had changed too. With the oak tree down, the sun came straight in the south window. It illumined the grain of the knotty pine wall, and I could see how much more there was to wood than I had understood before.

I wondered what they were doing at school right now. I looked out the window in the direction of Lincoln Elementary. With the oak tree gone, I could see past the roof of Newton's garage, into Cochran's yard kitty-corner to ours, and even over to the houses on the other side of Fremont Avenue, a block away. Somewhere beyond that, another dozen blocks or so, my friends and siblings were bent over their desks.

In the yard, the men were working on the tree. The smell of cut wood found its way up to me. This was familiar. There was always a new house going up in the neighborhood, and in the evening, when the carpenters were gone, we kids retook our territory. Vacant lots belonged to us and, until the grownups moved in, we claimed eminent domain.

We played house in those incipient homes, sawdust gripping our clothes, slivers finding the soft spots on our callused bare feet, and the sweet odor of pine lodging forever in our hearts. Sometimes we found wood knots on the floor and sometimes we could even find the boards they'd fallen out of. Then, sometimes, we would slip them back in, happy to see how neatly they fit and making that house somehow our own.

Sometimes, though, we kept the knots. They were red as though with the blood of the tree, and sap sometimes wept from them and you could carry one in your pocket and reach in there for it when you needed something solid to hold on to.

In the yard, beneath my window, the men pulled the severed branches away from the tree. They dragged them over to Emerson Avenue, east of the house. The long skirts of leaves trailed behind them. I did not want to watch anymore. That was when I pulled the shade, blunting the light.

That was when I slept. When I woke up, the sun had moved on and was working its way around to the west window. Soon it would look straight in, and the other kids would be coming home from school.

I went over to that window. From there I could not see the carnage of the morning. I could see 73rd Street. I watched for the orange splash of the bus. For a long time the street, which did not really go anywhere, was empty. So were the yards on the other side. Like my mom, Mrs. Walters and Mrs. Kimm were in their houses. The dads were at work. Even my dad had gone back to his store.

Then the bus was there, at the corner of Fremont and 73rd. It stopped and the door opened and Lottie Lee and Patty and Kippy and BeeZee and Cary Lou and Nicky and Joey and Bobbie and Diane and Kerry and Gretchen and Julie and Margaret Mary and Paul spilled out onto the road and scattered like leaves let loose in wind. Sunshine fell on them like rain. I wanted to cup my hands and gather them in.

* * * C. J. Hribal * * *

# The Landfill of Memory,

# the Landscape of the

# Imagination

When I was ten my parents quit Elmhurst, a post-Korea suburb of
Chicago where there were drugs and divorces and even suicides,
where the last lot had been purchased and built on two or three
years previous, and we moved to a farm three and a half miles from
the nearest town. My parents went back to the land at a time when
doing so put them unknowingly at the vanguard of a hippie movement they also disdained. Being ten, I thought it was cool, having
all this space suddenly available for traipsing and discovery. My
parents' thinking exactly. With "room to move, room to grow,"
we'd be safe. It was a noble, misguided idea, postponing the inevitable by a decade at most, in some cases not even that, but in looking back I am awed and filled with pride at their undertaking. My
parents left everything and everyone they knew and loved and
hiked their children two hundred miles north to give us a chance to
play in unbounded space, the only boundaries being fences you
crawled under or through, or creeks too wide to leap across.

There were two towns, actually—Stephensville and Hortonville—
nearly equidistant from the ninety-five-acre farm my parents had
purchased. They were, however, in different townships. Ellington
and Hortonia. Coupled in speech, they sound like the names of a
30s bandleader and his exotic, heavyset scat singer. Or maybe a
British vice-consul and the Marx Brothers–like principality to
which he's been posted. But except for a line drawing in the front of
the phone book (Faulkner did better) that I occasionally looked at,
it made no difference to me where one township ended and the
next began. I was much more fascinated by the aerial photographs
of the area my father had ordered. All those farms outlined in black
ık. Rivers, woodlots, lone trees, the curves of hill and swell, the

matted look of marshes: these were the things that determined boundaries. Our farm was a perfect rectangle except for two double L's on the left (west) boundary line that showed where previous owners had sold off acreage. I studied the maps to learn where things were and where things ran: the Wolf and Embarrass and Fox rivers, Pappy's Rock, Mosquito Hill, Highways 76 and 45. People knew where the rivers oxbowed or spread out close to the roadway, where fog was likely, what houses had gone up on which hills, who had a place on the river for sheepshead fishing and who didn't. I wanted to know this, too.

The differences between the townships, as near as I could tell, were based on their relative populations. Hortonia (the town of Hortonville squared off and added to for the sake of neat corners) had more people so it had the grade school. Also the high school and the supermarket. Ellington (Stephensville, really; everything outside the village was farm or forest or swamp) could boast only a couple of corner groceries, the kind of family-run places that doubled as gas stations before the Quick Trips and SuperAmericas rendered them as obsolete as Zep soda. We were taxed, got our fire numbers, voted, and went to church in Ellington. We got food and education in Hortonia.

*

The fire numbers thrilled me. Red upright rectangles with white numerals, each green fence post rising from the ditch out front. Here was a more practical order, a sequential logic in this crazy quilt of curved and diagonal roads and irregularly shaped farms. At one time it was all clean, people bought in sections, but as farms changed hands or were subdivided among inheriting sons or city folk (we were city folk, once upon a time), the order and cleanness vanished. You were as likely to farm three squares and two trapezoids set three miles and a highway apart as you were to have regular, contiguous borders. Only the fire numbers, one per dwelling, made sense. We were number 187. The way I imagined it (what did I know? I was ten), if we ever had a fire, someone at the Ellington Town Hall would answer our phone call, check the map to see where number 187 was (maybe it lit up or something, a tiny white or clear bulb flaring to life to let people know we were in danger), and the volunteer fire department would come over lickety-spiit

Later I learned they'd probably ask instead if we weren't the old Hawley place, or they'd ask "Is that you, Claude?" if it was my father or "Is this one of Claude's boys?" if it was me, but I continued to believe 187 was a magic number, important in itself. Now there are enough ex-urban subdivisions that the numbers do matter, and they're four digits, not three, and they might as well be anonymous house numbers, something you deliver mail to, not count on to direct somebody to the saving of a life. But that's another story.

Another thing that thrilled me about Ellington (Ellington was the wild open spaces compared to Hortonville, which had a nine-hole golf course and a press box shakily erected above the football field) was Larry's Country Club. Larry's was not a real country club. It was a supper club on Double M that specialized, as supper clubs do, in steak and walleye and Friday fish fries. The potatoes came wrapped in foil with a plastic cup of sour cream nestled alongside. If they knew you, the sour cream came dolloped right on the potato, Larry's version of fast food. What made Larry's special was a spring nearby that Larry had damned, squared, and concreted. Instant neighborhood swimming hole. The kids could go off a high board, shriek and go crazy under the bug lights while their parents caught an early dinner, then had a few beers out on the lawn while their kids' lips turned as purple as the bug lights. It was kind of a public service. Then one spring Larry opened the dam and let the swimming hole drain away. His insurance had gotten too high.

I think that was the end of another idyll.

What I remember most clearly about those days is the drinking. Everywhere you looked it seemed somebody was holding a seven-ounce fluted bar glass or a twelve-ounce plastic cup. It was part of the culture. Skinny-chested kids splashed for free while their parents swilled Larry's drinks. For certain homecomings highway and county trunk roads got closed off where they went through town. Intersections became beer gardens. Churches raised money in beer tents, and during parades men with trays of plastic beer cups worked the crowds, dollar bills stuck between their knuckles like diagonal fingers. Drink Beer for Christ! I thought in my more cynical moments, though later I'd down a few for Jesus, too. This was Wisconsin, after all, a state where the legislature can't decide if milk or beer is the state beverage. Local and regional breweries were still making a go of it and not charging microbrewery prices. There was Gettleman in Appleton (later to become Walter's of Eau Claire), Chief Oshkosh, Adler Brau, Rhinelander, Point. I remember my parents being amazed by this, at the unabashed consumption and the pervasiveness of a culture fueled by drink. In winter people sealed themselves in snowmobile suits and ran high-throttle engines across miles of near-arctic waste in driving blizzards just so they could have a beer away from the house. Whole parties would be organized this way. Twenty, thirty snowmobiles whining in unison at eleven o'clock at night, traveling thirty-five miles an hour across farm fields to get to Bean City, which was a dance hall and bar in the middle of another field. Bean City. It might as well have been Oz.

*

We had Germans around us, mostly. Bavarian Germans, which meant equal numbers of Catholics and Lutherans and alcoholics. Hortonville when I was growing up had thirteen bars on Main Street, not including the bar in the Black Otter Hotel or anything on the side streets. Hortonville also had just a tad over thirteen hundred people. Stephensville had another three taverns—Gene and Lou's, Banana's Never Inn, and one whose name I've forgotten. Banana's was right across from St. Patrick's. The Irish had moved out long ago, perhaps because even they couldn't keep up with the hard-drinking continentals, but more likely because once the area was timbered out they moved on and left the Bavarians the farmland.

Our first Sunday in our new parish my father noticed that everyone left the church after the High Mass at ten o'clock and went straight across the street to Banana's. My parents assumed they had a brunch, but asked Monsignor Gehl anyway. Monsignor Gehl was a stiff-backed, grim-toothed priest with absolutely clear gray eyes behind rimless glasses. He wore his hair in a pure white brush cut and lacked, I thought, only the dueling scar on his cheek to be a full-fledged Prussian officer. Monsignor Gehl shrugged, the shrug of a man who's seen everything twice and is not going to get all worked up over changing what he can't.

"Sometimes," he said, "sometimes after my sermons what everyone wants is a good stiff belt."

Wisconsin leads the nation in drunk driving, a distinction borne out Friday and Saturday night after Friday and Saturday night. And every other night of the week as well. Part of that is the expanse— you have to drive to drink unless you're one of those stay-at-home drinkers, and it's only the stay-at-homes who are problem drinkers, right?—part of it is the culture, and part of it is a geography that frustrates and subdivides the neat political squares of a town-shipped Wisconsin. On cold spring or autumn nights, or cool summer evenings, or in the winter when there's a thaw, ground fog rolls up from the rivers and the low-lying fields draining into them, and what you wind up with is a recipe for disaster: drunks in tin cars wobbling and whipping around in a pea soup fog that usually starts collecting over the roadways about midnight and stays through morning.

The first time we saw this first-hand it was funny. After moving from the horrors of Chicago, the first project my parents decided on was repainting the house. It was the color of dried blood and so weatherbeaten that the paint we applied soaked into the boards as though each silvered, blood-colored board was one of those sponges they compare paper towels to in the Bounty commercials. My mother did most of the painting. My father, a traveling salesman by profession, was away most of the time, and when he returned late Friday night after a ten- or twelve-hour drive, taking brush in hand was not an option. A seven-ounce fluted glass from Banana at his Never Inn, however, was a different matter. Anyway, the house was painted an off-white.

About the same time my parents discovered that our two hundred–foot–long driveway was something of a lover's lane. Cars would creep down the drive, gravel crunching, and then the headlights would go out and from the front windows we saw jerky, furtive movements, the kind of wrestling possible only in confined spaces. My mother was terrified until she figured out what it was. We were at the windows with her, our lights doused, our faces pressed against the glass. The storm windows were open. It was summertime and the occupants of the cars had their windows open, too. So over the hum of the crickets and the buzzing of the June bugs we heard heavy sighs and engines ticking heat. And the occasional clink of a bottle being dropped onto our gravel drive.

My parents had a crime light put in. This seemed odd to me. A crime light. I had only the vaguest idea of what the occupants of those Dodge Darts and Camaros were doing, but it wasn't a crime, was it? I mean, no one came up to the house afterward and tried to break in. They just sat there, faces welded tight, bodies writhing like snakes in a blanket, and after an hour or two or three they started the car and backed out our drive and were gone.

"Look," my mother would whisper to my father those nights he was home. "They're at it again." My father would get the same half-grin on his face Monsignor Gehl got on his and then he, too, would shrug. Nevertheless, the crime light went in and the house was painted, and nobody parked in our drive anymore. We felt new and safe, just as though we'd moved from Chicago and nothing could hurt us.

Then one Friday night a few weeks after the house was painted we awoke to a terrific series of crashings and thumps. Something metal was being torn from its moorings and ferociously bumping its way down our side field. A big hulking Buick, one of those 1950s jobs with the clipper ship steering wheel, had leaped the ditch, plowed through our fence line where North Road T'ed onto Grandview, and had just come to a rest two hundred yards down the field on the east side of the house. It was our neighbor, Ernie Ott. (Names have been changed for obvious reasons.) He was driving himself home from the Dugout, a tavern located where Highways 45 and JJ veered together. My father threw on a blue terry cloth robe and boots and struggled across the field to where Ernie Ott's Buick sat, its wheels deep between a couple of furrows. That field wasn't in use and the previous owner had a curious way of rendering it fallow. He set the blades on his plow to turn up, but not over, each furrow, so that the field had the look of a baby's curlicue, row upon row of upright waves, like Mohawk haircuts suffering osteoporosis. No doubt Ernie Ott had a broken axle.

We were all up and watched from the upstairs window as my father helped Ernie stagger across the furrows back to our house. There was a clumping up the stairs of our mudroom and then there he was, in our kitchen. Mother was making coffee. Ernie Ott was huge. Imagine a bowling ball in overalls, with another bowling ball, much smaller, sitting on top of that, and three rubber dough-nuts for the chins that connected them. He was wearing one of those plaid Canadian baseball caps, the brim of which was pointing toward the corner of the ceiling. "What happened?" my father asked. My mother eased a cup of coffee across the kitchen table to Ernie Ott's waiting fists. Ernie looked dazed. Even the coffee didn't seem familiar to him. His eyes were grizzled with tiny broken veins and they rolled slightly in his head the way cartoon animals do when they've been whupped upside the head with a two-by-four or a crowbar. His head tilted slowly to take in my older sister, who'd just turned fourteen. Ernie's eyes got bigger, and I suddenly under-stood what "leering" meant. "I've got a son about her age," he said, his eyes cutting across to my father and then centering back on Carey. "Maybe me and her can work out a deal. My boy and her boy, eh?" My father nodded a stiff-lipped agreement even though Ernie Ott misspoke the deal. This was the stiff-lipped nod my father gave in bars when somebody said something particularly heinous and my father, being a salesman, didn't want to contradict or offend anybody. My mother shooshed Carey a little farther back behind her brothers. There were five of us; we made a pretty un-even picket fence. I was in the front row now, and I could see how heavily Ernie Ott sat. Like a sack of concrete, solid and sagging. "So tell me what happened," my father said affably, as though he would really like to hear the story. "Claude," my mother said. My father held his hand up, meaning it was all right, he could handle this.

Ernie Ott waited a minute. Two minutes. He bit his lip. Clearly he was gathering himself. He couldn't understand it either. Finally, he said, more to himself than to us, "The red house. I always turn at the red house." He shrugged and grinned like the idiot that he was. And this is what has always puzzled me. My father clapped him on the back and then helped him to his feet. "Well," my father said, "that happens." And that's what my ten-year-old brain couldn't understand, this affableness of my father in the face of a man who'd torn out our fence, left his car wheezing in our field, and had just suggested his son mate with my sister. Yet here was my dad suddenly as affable as Monsignor Gehl telling us about his parishioners having a drink right after Mass on a Sunday morning. At age ten it was horrible for me to see these three men yoked like that, and my father and Monsignor Gehl went down a peg in my esteem for philosophically consorting with the likes of drunken Ernie Ott. It was not until I had to deal regularly with drunks myself that I realized what a great salesman my father was, and I think now that part of it was this ability to nod pleasantly at other people's inanities as though he agreed with them. He got Ernie Ott out of our house and back to his own and Ernie now rents forty acres from us. He usually pays the previous year's rent about halfway into the next year's planting season, but that, too, is another story.

✳

Usually it wasn't quite so funny. My adolescence was chock-full of stories of so-and-so being killed when their car spun into a ditch or collided head-on with somebody else. As often as not, the drunks walked away. The people they hit didn't. The fog came up thick and frequent, and people with nothing better to do than drink themselves silly did so at the neon beer sign–infested bars that bloomed at crossroads like unkillable weeds. And then they drove themselves home, killing whatever deer or skunk or raccoon had the misfortune of stopping their drift over the center line.

Sometimes it was people.

Almost every graduating class from Hortonville High School had somebody listed in the back of the yearbook "in memoriam." They were dead because either they had been driving drunk or the people who hit them were. For years after I left, my mother would call me and give me the latest casualty reports. So-and-so was killed by a drunk driver on County M, so-and-so collided with some-and-such where JJ dumps into 45. The catalog went on and on. I could barely stand listening to it. The stories were as shocking in the plainness of their tragedy as watching one cow lumbering atop another was shocking in its possibility. Once my mother called with the news that a girl I had dated in high school had been killed. She'd been returning home after going bowling with some girlfriends (people in Wisconsin do that) and a drunk had drifted into her lane. He walked away untouched, not even aware he'd killed somebody.

✳

They start you out drinking early in Wisconsin. You'll get served in a tavern as long as you're with your parents. Or the bartender knows your parents. Cirrhosis is earned, after all, it's not just given freely to anybody who comes along sniffing. And for those of us who didn't drink much, who didn't get smashed in the back of some stubble field where the land dipped and the river and the woods came up close, sheltering the revelers from the wind and the town cop, well, we were wusses. Pansies who couldn't hold our liquor, much less tie one on with any efficiency. You learned to hold a beer cup belt high at parties even if you weren't drinking; it saved you a lot of grief during the chug-a-lug contests if you seemed to be joining in on the fun.

My father had a wonderful way of combating this peer pressure, and as unorthodox as it sounds, it worked for nearly all of us. When each of us turned about thirteen he took us to the refrigerator, swung the door open, and pointed at the bottles of Old Style, the cans of Strohs. "See these?" he'd say. "Any time you want one, you take one. Just do it in front of me so I know about it. If I hear you're drinking in somebody's field, though, you're grounded for life." In an odd way the magic was out of it for us then. Your dad says it's okay, anytime you want, and what do you have to live for except Thanksgiving and sneaking more than the one-third glass of champagne that was doled out just before the stuffing bowl made the rounds?

✳

There was one time when drink was something you looked forward to. It took on the aspect of ritual, and ritual for a skinny teenager shaky about his status in the male gender was a welcome thing. It would happen in July and August. Baling season. Nobody around us had enough equipment themselves to do all the tasks associated with harvest, so usually we'd make rounds of each other's fields. Somebody'd contribute two wagons, somebody else a rake, some-

C. J. HRIBAL ✳ 103

body else the baler. My father contributed five sons as his communal offering, also a small gray Massey Ferguson tractor that was okay hooked up to a rake but didn't have enough power for much of anything else. Later he bought—and there was quite a laugh about this, since my Dad was a staunch Legionnaire and later served as post commander and later still as Wisconsin State Chaplain—a Russian-made tractor painted bright Soviet red. That was during the early Nixon years when such things were possible. We were selling sturgeon to the Russkies as well, then buying back Missouri-bred sturgeon eggs as Russian caviar. It's a world for head-scratching. But I digress. At dusk, after a hard, sweaty day of baling, the person whose house we were at would bring out a case of beer for the baling crew. That beer went down faster than ice-cold milk. The cold, tongue-grouting scorch and bite of it. With my hands torn up by the cut hay's sharp edges, my palms blistered and rubbed raw from the baling twine (even though I was wearing gloves), my forearms sliced (it was too hot to wear long-sleeved shirts)—it was the greatest taste on earth. Nothing had ever tasted so wonderful. And except for a single incident when I was sixteen and my brother and John Cooper (he was going into the military!) drank most of a case between them playing poker after baling, and I could see that even with a learner's permit I was going to have to drive them home later, and I did, the two of them asking me to slow the car down so they could open the doors and barf across the running boards, rolling down the window being too much trouble after the first volley streaked the sides of the two-tone Chevy—guess who hosed that baby down later?—except for that single time, when even I nervously sipped three beers to completion, the only times I drank before I was legal was at baling time. Even after baling, when they'd set the case down, I'd be thinking, Okay, are they going to offer any soda? No? Well, okay, then, and hold my bottle the way I'd seen the older guys do it, casually around the bottle's neck, the thing hanging off the sides of their belts like they were lounge singers taking a break between numbers. They'd slouch their backs against tractor fenders, even have their butts leaning against a wheel, or sit on the very edge of the hay wagon with their feet dangling or lined up on the hay wagon's tongue, like the lot of us having a beer in a field after a day's work was no big deal, just the way you capped the day. Tony Lauer or somebody, Cooper maybe, would say something about the weather tomorrow, whose field we'd do then. Five, six, eight guys, also maybe Joan Stadler, Ron's beefy daughter, all standing or sitting or leaning against the equipment as the last light lingered orange and yellow, outlining the far line of trees and the radar hill towers (they were microwave relay towers put in by the government as part of NORAD, but nevermind), the sweat trickling through the dust and chaff on our faces, our fingers, knuckles, forearms caked with fine rivulets of blood, each of us with a long-necked empty with maybe just a swallow or two of starchy, bitter beer still to swallow, a few grins, some low talk . . . I realized I was being admitted into the company of manhood in as formal a ceremony as I was likely to see. It was not some phony pageant worked out for parents and relatives and the larger community. It was what they called the real thing. The idea, see, is that it was no big deal. No Kool-Aid mixed up in a gallon milk bottle or tin pail for you. No extra soda pop. It's late, you worked hard—here, kid, have a beer.

*

There's another side to this, of course. I said my father's plan worked for nearly all of us. It didn't work for one of my brothers, and it didn't really work for my dad, either. Something about being on the road all those years, the separation from wife and family, your strongest connection being between you and the steering wheel: when my father came home he'd as often as not take one of us to the Dugout, or Banana's, or even Larry's Country Club for a Saturday or Sunday afternoon of beers (him) and soda (us). When my mother put her foot down and demanded he not throw away good money at some tavern, he'd come home, open the refrigerator, and there'd be the very thing causing him grief elsewhere. All those tin and glass soldiers waiting to be killed.

My father was an armchair alcoholic. He'd drink his two-three-four beers a night, chase it with a Rob Roy, and settle in to do his expense reports and other paperwork, occasionally lashing out at the TV that Walter Cronkite was a pinko, a friend and supporter of that communist Hubert Humphrey. Broken green and bloody glass replaced my father's normal eye color. Little red dots leaped to his cheeks. He did not look good. Years later he was pulled over for DWI and my mother finally got him to see a doctor. It turned out he had diabetes. The doctor told him he needed to quit drinking or risk a coma while he was driving. A diabetic coma while he was on the road: that scared him. He quit drinking, he takes his medicine, he watches his diet. Or rather my mother watches his diet for him. In odd ways my father is a disciplined man. He quit smoking thirty years ago when he developed an ulcer. He imposed limits even on his drinking when he was drinking too much. He'd drink until the broken glass appeared in his eyes. Then he'd stop. Now, at Thanksgiving, he's the one who receives the one-third glass of champagne, and sneaks the second third. And when it's time for the toast he holds up his puddle of bubbly and gets this elfin grin on his face like he knows he's getting away with something.

We smile, too, relieved he's alive and relatively healthy.

*

We—my friends from high school and I—couldn't wait to get out of there. Hortonia, Ellington: small time, strictly, stupidly small time. What was a township anyway? We wanted to be where nobody knew us. Appleton was where all the real action was anyway. Fifty thousand people! Imagine that! A city! Even geography was on our side. With three rivers to the north and Lakes Poygan and Butte des Morts to the south, Hortonville was, quite literally, in the pits.

The funny thing is, we're now all trying to get back to it. One of my friends, after five years in California as a Silicon Valley techie, has bought the town feedmill from his father; another, a research biologist for a Philadelphia chemical conglomerate, is buying vacation land with his parents just north of us. And me? After ten years of being away in New York and Minnesota and Tennessee, I now live in Milwaukee, land of ten thousand bars.

My imagination returned long before my body. In two books I peopled a whole town of people I'd never met but knew existed. The landfill of my memory; the landscape of my imagination. I don't worry too much anymore about which is which.

*

Milwaukee is remarkably like Hortonville except for the lack of open space. My neighborhood is a township in itself. It has a bar on every corner and sometimes one or two midblock. No one seeking beer or the cool darkness of a place where people don't want to open their eyes too much will go wanting. And when I think back now on growing up amidst this plenty, two things occur to me: I was fueled by my desire to be away from it, and I'm glad to be back. My friend Ron Block says of three bulls in his poem "Dismal River," "The land was theirs, entirely; / their sleep entire; they were entirely / themselves . . . ." People sitting in the cool half-dark of a bar are entirely themselves.

I don't know what it is about Wisconsin, or particularly about Ellington and Hortonia (though I suspect this is state-wide), that causes people to drink too much, or to risk doing so on a regular basis. Suicide, dismemberment, bankruptcy, the three occupational hazards of farming: these could have something to do with it. So, too, could the gnawing knowledge that you're in the middle of the middle of nowhere, at least as far as the rest of the country's concerned. Flyover country, as we're known to the coasts. You say to someone you're from Wisconsin and their eyes glaze over. Oh, yes, they say. Winter. Cheese. MOOOOOO! Repeated a few million times, that sort of gets to your self-esteem. You want to shout at people, we are not "Laverne and Shirley" reruns. "Happy Days" was a long time ago, and it wasn't true when it was true! But it's too late; the national consciousness is set. And even if you never leave the state, you know what they're saying about you. But it's not that so much as the feeling of insignificance that gnaws at you. In another poem, a friend from a state with mountains asks me what it's like, living where "what's vertical's made"? A decade after he wrote that, this is my answer: my wife and child and I took a drive recently through the Kettle Moraine (where the glaciers got tired and dumped dirt and rock all helter-skelter). It's pretty, rolling hills and ridges, cornfields and woodlots. The wind blusters with the nip of winter and the trees are going buttery yellow-green and orange and red. It's not dramatic (nothing in Wisconsin is dramatic, except the passion plays that wind up in the tabloids), but pretty. Wisconsin is one of those girl- or guy-next-door states. Not your first choice to ask out, but if New York is busy, you might think about giving Wisconsin a call. Wisconsin knows it's being called on the rebound, and is good-natured about it.

Reason enough to drink? I don't know. But I think about my father a lot, and about Monsignor Gehl, and even about Ernie Ott. I think about all those women who had to put up with alcoholic husbands. I wonder if there was a point when these people knew their lives were controlled more by whimsy than reason, and they could either get bitter, go crazy, or accept the things life gave them. The crazy and bitter ones drink like crazy. The rest shrug, then have a beer.

I'm learning to shrug.

# ACTIVE VOICE

*Wayne Township, Jay County, Indiana 1931–1948*

We had no pails. Carrying water to the backyard garden, giving the kitchen floor its Saturday scrubbing, we managed with what we had, buckets. Also missing were shops. Portland's Meridian Street, known for its extraordinary width, the first step in some grand plan begun and then abandoned before the turn of the century, was lined with stores. The Hines Theater did no traffic in movies. Beyond the ticket booth where an always suspicious woman sized us up and decided if we should pay adult price, beyond the art deco lobby that we took to be a piece of Hollywood itself, lay shows. To shop we went uptown—never down—and carried our purchases off in sacks, not bags. Until I went to college, I thought tedious and "tee-jus" were two discrete words. As we used them, they were.

What persists, finally, is language, surpassing in importance even that which we call memory, because it is the carrier and arbiter of memory. Its symbols and systems define our reality. Asked how a story starts, many writers reply, "With a picture." Perhaps. But I wonder. For me, the picture must have a caption to quicken it. Wittgenstein said it best: that which we cannot speak of, we must pass over in silence.

We lived in several worlds simultaneously and understood each spoke a slightly different language. I manipulated diction with consummate skill, never slipping, speaking always a little differently to: parents, friends, teachers, grandparents. My first paying job as an author was writing letters for the old woman next door who was illiterate, a phenomenon that was still fairly common. Five cents per letter. I was ten years old. The letters went to a daughter in another town, and always went out in the old woman's voice. I was a trustworthy amanuensis.

Differences in diction among generations could be striking. I understood my grandmother's "man" ("Her man never comes to church with her") was a solid, sober word meaning "husband." It was actually a homonym for the word used in popular songs ("I lost my man"). That one meant "boyfriend," and not the best sort. To my grandparents' generation a bicycle was a "wheel," an automobile a "machine," corn on the cob "roasting ears," although they were never roasted. We compared ourselves with our grandparents and discovered that *we* were the future. Was it possible? Hopeless children so imperfectly made? So full of grief for our awful incompetencies? Yes. Evidence was conclusive. By our masterly command of current idiom, we were empowered.

I am speaking here of diction, not accent.

When I give a reading in the East, I sometimes begin by saying, "I grew up in Indiana and I have an accent. There's nothing I can do about it." I know that before the reading is done my tongue will have glided into "warsh," or "feesh," or "aigh." My statement is not an apology; none is needed. It is a simple acknowledgment that I hope will calm my listeners' anxiety. Often they seem to think I do not know what I sound like. Their eagerness to be the first to tell me sometimes becomes a troubling presence in the room. I'm exaggerating, of course. At least a little. In any case, an acknowledgment takes less time than a recital of the history of these pronunciations. "Warsh" is more than it first appears to be, "wash" with an *r* included. The circumlocutions required of mouth and tongue to insert the *r* produce a bountiful splendor of vowel sounds. These sounds are English, from a long-ago England whose vowel-rich voice has vanished, except as it survives in vestiges, in pockets such as those in Indiana. As if to enhance this melodic quality of the language, it is spoken rather slowly. (Keep the tempo down, say musicians, if you want the notes to "sound" and "sing.")

My ancestors carried their speech from England to Virginia, through the Cumberland Gap to Kentucky and Tennessee, and finally, when the Indians had been dispossessed of it, into Indiana. There, farmland was good, plentiful, and cheap. There was no point in going farther. In 1836, my great-great-grandfather rode his horse seventy miles from Portland to Indianapolis. There he sold his horse and used the money to buy his Wayne Township farm. He walked back carrying his saddle.

Our three sons, who grew up in the outskirts of ethnic Milwaukee, always felt a little left out when classmates described their multinational backgrounds. Our children could report only "English." English, English, English, four grandparents and eight great-grandparents. It's a testimony to the quality of Indiana farmland. The first white people who took it, held it. When no land is offered for sale, no newcomers are admitted. The birth of factories altered some of this, but that's another story, a later story, and it is the story of Gary and South Bend, of Hammond and East Chicago, Muncie, Indianapolis. It is not the story of Wayne Township and Jay County, even today.

Over time, we expanded our diction: nuclear, frozen food, television, fallout shelter. But hardly anyone arrived to modify our accent: four war brides, three from Asia, one from New Jersey.

How I regard my accent varies with where I am and what my frame of mind is at the moment. I have been made to feel the most uncomfortable in Philadelphia, although I am a birthright Quaker and feel a twinge of proprietary annoyance at this rebuff. Shouldn't I be admitted here? I am least uncomfortable in California. Baltimore makes me nervous, seeing how easily I could slide into a full Southern accent and lose my identity completely.

"Warsh." "Feesh." "Aigh." I am curious about what has survived, but I am even more curious about what was lost. My first career was music. If the whole could be reconstructed from the parts that remain, what might an entire choir sound like singing in that voice? Enriched by all those vowels?

Ethnomusicologists look for people in their music; song lines are especially revealing. Had anyone come to town and looked—they didn't—we'd have been easy to find. My father was a violinist and a music teacher. He picked up extra money playing for church services, for weddings, and for funerals. Often I played his accompaniments on piano. We knew the workings of every church for miles around. Protestant churches, of course. For better or worse, nearly all musicians will spend a portion of their lives in church. In small communities, it is often the only show in town. Many people thought we played free, for the love of it. We did not. The pay was meager, we lived in genteel poverty, but we did not play free. One Easter we managed to get ourselves hired to play in three different churches. To make the schedule, we had to race up and down country roads at great speed in our old Chevrolet. It was a financial bonanza but I was in terror every minute, not of an automobile accident, but that we would get the music mixed up or misplace it. If my father did not have the notes before him, he would simply improvise. I was expected to follow, and my improvisations were not reliable. Sometimes they came off so well I was amazed, but other times they were so dreadful I gave up and sat in humiliated silence. I was an adult before I realized I was not an inferior musician. It is fairly easy to improvise on an instrument like a violin, that plays a single line of notes. Keyboards are a different matter. Imposing order on a multitude of notes, at the instant, is an undertaking of some complexity.

Each church—and there were many—believed it had its own music, but the hymns were all alike. If they were not actually identical, they were in the same rhythm, in harmony, and in the messages they carried; whether the hymnal was red or brown, whether the preacher was robed or in a business suit, whether the altar was simple or glowing with brass and candles.

Salvation was not of this world: "Hail the glorious golden city." "Jesus calls us o'er the tumult of our life's wild, restless sea." "There'll be no dark valley when Jesus comes." "There is a home eternal bright and beautiful."

Life was to be lived with a good deal of thought, a good bit of care: "I would be true for there are those who trust me." "This is my Father's world." "My stubborn will at last has yielded." "Have Thine own way Lord." "I'm pressing on the upward way, new heights I'm gaining every day."

But if the above cautions were observed, happiness was permitted, and even encouraged: "In my heart there rings a melody." "Sunlight, sunlight in my soul today." "God who touchest earth with beauty." "Love divine all loves excelling, joy of heaven to earth come down."

Later, in college, I would write a term paper on light imagery in the hymns of the Great Awakening, drawing comparisons to imagery in *Paradise Lost*. Today, the implications of that paper astonish me. At the time, at nineteen, choosing the topic seemed a completely arbitrary act; I recall there were other possible subjects I crossed off the list. But it seems to me now that everything I would ever be capable of—being, thinking, seeing, feeling—was present in the paper in embryonic form. All that came after would be elaboration, extrapolation, examination, implication; variations on a theme with a handful of ideas: light–what we can know, religion–ethics, imagery–aesthetics. The lost paradise, of course, was childhood, with all its complex vagaries and permutations. Out of these would come, again and again, evocations of the church, music and musicians, school, the small town, the farm, the war, the world as received through films and books, the young girl in all her guises, and speculation on how everything came to be as it was. We write what we are given; in our narratives, we seek to experience our own lives.

We went to school to films and books. We children didn't think anything in our town, including school, amounted to much. How could it? We had seen the real world on film, Paulette Goddard's clothes, Myrna Loy's apartments, the palms of exotic California, the revolving doors and elevators of New York skyscrapers. We took a cold, unflinching view of our woeful inferiority, and plotted our escape.

We would discover later, taking our college entrance examinations, that our schools had actually been quite good.

But a substantial part of the world came to us through our own reading, outside of school. At fifteen I could recite, "When as in silks my Julia goes . . ." but I thought the poet's name was "don." My mother liked Proust, which she pronounced to rhyme with "Faust." Books came from the library. As an adult, I had to teach myself to go into a bookstore and buy a book. The act seemed unspeakably profligate. I mean single books. The purchase of sets of books was approved: the Harvard Classics, the Delphian Society Reading Series, the World Book Encyclopedia. These were to be kept in trust, like fine china, and handed down through the family. One set was sufficient. I recall no one who owned two. But the books we read, and we read a great deal, came from the library. In our family, one exception was made to all of this. My father *bought* autobiographies of musicians. There weren't a great many of them, and their subjects were an eclectic group. On the shelf, they must have sat in uneasy company: Albert Spalding, Rimsky-Korsakov, Oscar Levant. As we read, of course, we translated. Whatever their origins, the words came in to us in the leisurely voice of north-central Indiana, our voice.

The anomaly here is radio. It seems to have been a colorless sustenance that passed through us to little effect. An earlier generation had predicted radio would abolish regional accents; it did not; and while we listened avidly—Lowell Thomas, Fibber McGee, "The Bell Telephone Hour," "Portia Faces Life"—I recall no aspiration, no forming process that found its genesis in radio.

The world of films and books—highly selective; of uneven quality; by turns idealized, stylized, erudite, cosmopolitan, provincial, hyperbolic, bathetic—created a fractured reality. I wondered in a quite serious, quite literal way where the center of the world was, that place where all contraries were laid down. One part of me still harbors the idea that such a place exists, that my confusion stems from an Indiana girlhood rather than the basic conundrum of existence.

And still one more voice competed for our attention. "Politics," writ large, was the hobby of choice among our elders. The characters of this story are a small number of dedicated liberals who exist in a larger population of conservatives. If they can never triumph, neither can they be completely banished.

Indiana's liberals are like the thistles that menace good clover hay. Turn your back for a moment and one has sprouted. While they tend to cluster in cities and around colleges and universities, they do not hesitate to take up residence in small, isolated towns or in rural areas. Often they were born there and have no inclination to leave.

I remember an attorney who represented labor unions, although he had to commute to Gary to find employment. He is still the only person I've ever known who could work a crossword puzzle straight through without error or correction. Any crossword puzzle. He used a fountain pen. A local bank director worked in the campaigns of Democratic candidates who always lost. A farmer labored year after year to get membership on the school board made an elective office rather than a political appointment.

I was taking world history in high school when Mao came to power in China. Our teacher, a sturdy woman who had taught for more than thirty years, who was said to smoke cigarettes in secret, told us Mao was an agrarian reformer and his communism represented no threat to anyone, a view held by many thoughtful newspapers at the time. This was scandalous language in the larger community. She was reprimanded, vilified, even made the subject of a sermon on godlessness, but she was not fired, as she had known from the beginning she would not be.

In a curious way, it was the Latin Mass, a graceful assemblage of language, that spared the tiny colony of Roman Catholics among us from the full brunt of Bible Belt prejudice. The high school Latin teacher carried the banner for toleration. She loved Latin in all of its manifestations, and she must have been an exceptional teacher. A Methodist herself, she convinced us the variations between Classical and Church Latin were as engrossing as the clues in an Agatha Christie mystery, and made us long to hear the Mass. She urged Latin students to attend the Catholic church on Christmas Eve, and she herself attended. Her small, neat, respected person crossing that forbidden threshold threw Catholic baiters into confusion.

Once a new Protestant minister came to town, very young, very fresh from an Eastern university. He invited the Catholic priest to play golf with him. They played one round. When talk started, the minister quickly abandoned his ecumenical mission. He had not grown up among us and he lacked the backbone of a true Indiana liberal.

We did not know our elders were disputatious; we thought all of the world was composed of people poised to fall into heated debate at any moment. If the larger community usually prevailed, the smaller always contended. No issue went unexamined. Whichever side we took, we were schooled daily out of the notion that whatever is is right. Our leisurely, vowel-rich voices were often hard-edged, rigorous, foolish, raw, excessive, ridiculing, exultant in their quest for authenticity. When I moved away I had to learn to moderate my speech to fit into a world I perceived as better mannered. Better balanced might be a more accurate term, less lopsided.

Today the alliances of Wayne Township are little changed. The agricultural base has weakened. The Japanese have just arrived with a small factory—I would like to hear them speaking English with our accent. Many churches are gone. They have taken up the tracks of the railroad that ran through my great-great-grandfather's farm.

I never moved back, but that's not saying I never will. The tomatoes are still the best in the world. There is little crime, a good library, an excellent bookstore, culture enough an easy drive away. There is good conversation. I was comfortable there, as happy as I've been in the other places I've lived. As happy, I think, as it is given to a writer to be.

# TOWNLINE

In Iowa, and throughout the Midwest, small towns are commonly laid out along the intersection of two blacktop highways, one running north and south, the other east and west. In open country they are discernibly highways, but a block into town they lose that character and become streets instead. Wire fences fall away and lawns begin. Near the intersection lie the town's shops and businesses, gathered like low-coordinate plottings in an algebra problem. And if the town happens to be a county seat, as ours was, there is often another street of businesses, forming the third side of the courthouse square.

There is also a railroad. In some towns it cuts a diagonal across the blacktop highways, disrupting the rectangular grid of property lines. But in our small town the railroad ran parallel to the east-west highway, parallel to the third side of the courthouse square, perpendicular to our street. It ran one lot away from our house, where town had shrunk enough so that the railroad was really railroad again, with ditches and cinders and a right-of-way, no longer just a bump in the pavement. If you imagine our small town as a cross with beams of equal length, then we lived on the lower edge of the right-hand, or eastern, beam. Standing on the tracks near our house, I could look across the corner of a farmer's field and see the southern beam of our town, its asphalt roofs, bare yards, and low brick hospital. I could look out into the country and still see the town in which I lived. When we visited friends in that neighborhood, I stood in their backyard and looked out across the country to home, though I had not left the place of my upbringing. I was a homesick child.

A number of things occur to me now concerning the geography of my childhood. The railroad tracks were very near, and beyond them stretched farmland—not the five-acre pastures or hobby farms one sometimes sees at townline, but full-scale, oceanic fields of corn and soybeans and whatever else grew there. In my one epiphanic memory from that place, I recall standing with my back toward the blocks of houses near our house, my face to the fields—I associate the time with Easter—and feeling a profound longing, perhaps what C. S. Lewis means by joy. I have always believed that those fields lay north of town, and that by standing on the railroad tracks and looking out among them to distant farmsteads, which rode like ships at anchor, I was looking toward the Arctic Circle. The truth—which I have just discovered—is that I was looking south, toward the poorer soils along the Missouri border where my mother was born.

One thinks of railroad tracks as a line that eventually pierces the horizon, leading the imagination outward. And perhaps if the tracks near our house had not so neatly bounded the part of town in which we lived, I would have thought of them that way. Instead, I thought of them as a fence. To cross them was to cross into the unfamiliar. I could, and did, walk anywhere through the streets of our town with the peculiar freedom of a small-town child in the late 1950s. But not a hundred feet to the south, across the tracks, my personal acquaintance stopped.

Our street, an uncurbed gravel cul-de-sac, crossed the railroad tracks, but once it did so it ceased to be a street and became the private driveway of a small, dark farmstead. I have not seen that farmstead, as it was then, since I was eleven years old, when we moved away. I remember none of its details except a white house, a line of federal corn cribs—common enough in central Iowa—and, in summer, looming, forbidding shade. The inhabitant of that house was reputed to be the garbageman. That was the phrase, *the* garbageman, as if our town could have only one. But how many garbagemen would be needed in a town of three thousand residents, most of whom enjoyed an outing to the dump?

For a time, the milkman lived across the street from us. Between his house and the stucco cottage of a neighboring widow (a category of people with whom our town seemed well provided) lay a narrow flower-bordered path, not quite public, not quite private. It led one between kitchen gardens, past a neat shed or garage, past rusty incinerator barrels whose rims seemed to withstand the fire better than their sides. The path led to a friend's house, a friend whose father was a railroad engineer. My friend's father was rarely home, and when he was he was either razored clean or looked as if his cheeks and chin had been smeared with soot. I was left to imagine his character from his workshop, which, unlike my father's, had nothing to do with wood. It expressed itself in steel and iron and brass, in threaded rods and nuts and washers, and in a calendar whose scenes chronicled the adventures of a plump, scantily clad woman (and by scantily clad I mean bare midriff and slight décolletage), whose adventures always ended in ungainly postures.

Outside that house, the railroad ran past like a levee, raised above grade, eye-level to a man, but to a boy, exalted. It seemed fitting that in the backyard of an engineer the railroad should crowd out the sight of farm fields in the distance, surely an insult to the engineering eye. It seemed appropriate that down the tracks a ways toward town there should appear great culverts where we often sought the signs of hobo occupation—cardboard mattresses, tin-can teapots—with as much fervor as if hoboes were the ancient race from which we stemmed. From the engineer had stemmed my friend and his two older brothers, tall twins with blond crew cuts and twin lawnmowers with which they earned their college money. They were members of Future Farmers of America, always wearing the blue FFA corduroy jacket with the golden FFA seal depicting an owl roosting on a plow handle at sunset. They were surely a surprise to their father. They were a mystery to me, silent, purposeful alien twins. Summer was filled with the sounds of their mowing, with their steady accumulation of change.

What I know about nature I learned first from the railroad tracks that ran past our house. I learned about the tangle of weeds in the right-of-way, how hard rain smoothes the long grasses down like hair, how it mats the thick recesses as if a deer had lain there at night. In winter I learned almost everything there is to know about the cornices and hollows that wind forms in the drifts of snow, silent depravities of structure. I awoke to astonishing mornings when tracks, fences, fields had disappeared under a vastness of purity, unsullied until there came grinding slowly from the direction of town a locomotive snowplow with the skewed grin of a right whale, spraying snow in high arcs on either side of the tracks, leaving in its wake a double line of polished steel flush with the snow.

There was milkweed. There was what we called snakegrass, which pulled apart in sections. There was a pulpy plant with shallow roots, which when broken off short resembled a potato-masher grenade. There was willow, perhaps, out of which my maternal grandfather, who was handy, could make a whistle. There were broadbladed grasses from which I could make a whistle myself, holding the leaf taut between the meat of my hand and my thumb knuckles. There were plants that, in telling what we could do with them, make me sound much older than I am. But mostly, there was the chaos of undisciplined growth, a narrow uncultivated strip between lawn and seed corn. It was not a grove, it was not a park, it was not a forest. But it was always enough.

Especially when the trains came. I believe that our tracks were only a spur off a main line somewhere, the kind of railroad that used to connect grain elevators in small towns all across the state. Trains lumbered slowly down the tracks, and sometimes they stopped, their length stretching all the way into the heart of town, five, six blocks and more. We could see the stains on the tank cars, the official seals; we could see the road-beaten boards of the boxcars. We could see the men playing cards in the caboose, if we were lucky. Because we were children we believed that if we approached a resting train too closely, it would lurch into life.

But the best railroad traffic of all was this sort: on the kind of afternoon that is the finest approximation of eternity in life, endlessly absorbing, summer-soaked: to hear the silence grow around you because, in the distance, a new sound has broken the silence: to look up and to wait and to see, after a moment or two, a lone man on a railroad handcar—nothing more than a wooden platform on railroad wheels—come rolling up the rails, rolling, rolling, past my friend's house, past the garbageman's farmstead, past our neighbor's yard, out of town, into the country, the small engine that powered this handcar no louder than the ringing of the rails. We called those handcars "putt-putts," for the noise they made. Being a homesick child, I never felt the allure of the railroad, which is a kind of disease in my family, except when a putt-putt passed. Then I wanted to be the man on the handcar, wind blowing all about me, children staring from their yards in admiration, the rude smell of soil everywhere in the air. I wanted to roll right out of town and look back and wonder, what was this place where I had lived?

*Villa Grove, Illinois, 1986*

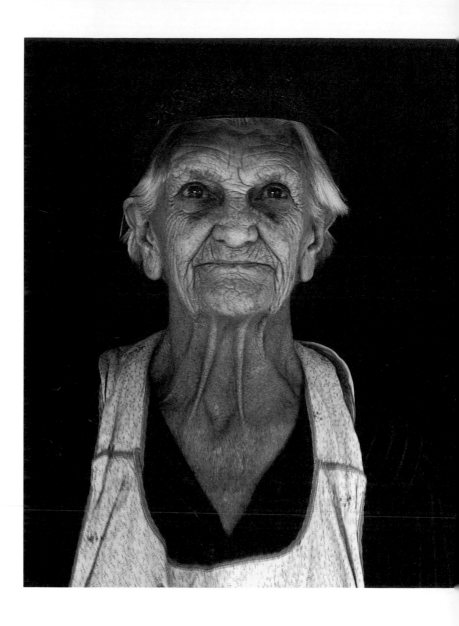

*Fountain, Indiana, 1979*

*Cerro Gordo, Illinois, 1987*

*Brocton, Illinois, 1979*

*Abandoned farmhouse, Indiana, 1989*

*Wallace, Indiana, 1984*

*Bloomingdale, Indiana, 1984*

*Crawfordsville, Indiana, 1976*

*Abandoned farmhouse, Illinois, 1986*

*Marshall, Indiana, 1984*

*Covington, Indiana, 1983*

*Fountain County Home, Indiana, 1976*

*Bement, Illinois, 1982*

*Chillicothe, Illinois, 1986*

*Greenview, Illinois, 1986*

*Mackinaw, Illinois, 1986*

*Woodland, Illinois, 1986*

*Allerton, Illinois, 1987*

*Saybrook, Illinois, 1987*

*Bishop Hill, Illinois, 1985*

*Toulon, Illinois, 1986*

*Kemp, Illinois, 1982*

*Elliott, Illinois, 1986*

*Hugo, Illinois, 1986*

# BEAVER TOWNSHIP,
# BAY COUNTY, MICHIGAN

I was nearly sixteen when, on a stormy evening in the spring of 1963, my father and I saw lightning hit dead on Lyman Schroeder's barn two miles to the west. By the time we got to the scene there was nothing to do but watch the timbers turn red. Lyman had given up on yelling at the bawling, trapped cows. He looked sick, I thought, as the heat drove us back, as the air filled with the smell of burnt hair, but all this time later I wonder: is it possible Lyman's mind was already jumping ahead? Might he have been able to see, even at that terrible moment, how circumstances that seem to be disaster one day can sometimes be opportunity the next? Lyman always had been a guy with a catchy, push-ahead energy. He had a trace of the tycoon. In any event, not more than two months later he was showing me a landscaper's plan drawn in blue. Doglegs and sand traps and water hazards were laid out on acres that for eighty-five years the Schroeders had had in pastures and croplands. A clubhouse was to be where the barn had been. With the insurance money, plus other money virtually free from a program established by Congress to promote recreation in rural America, Lyman planned to create in the midst of yeoman German farms—I could scarcely imagine it—a full eighteen-hole golf course.

A golf course. I remember my father saying, "Well, that's the last we'll see of Lyman," which I thought was a highly dramatic thing for anyone to say, let alone Fredrick Kohn. My father, this big, red-knuckled figure at odds with modern concepts of leadership, in his worn-out coveralls, his face sweat-streaked, might tell you facts no one wished to hear—they knew in Beaver Township he would be the one to speak up—but he never exaggerated, never lied.

I don't know what, if anything, he said to Lyman about the golf course. They did not have many chances to talk because all of a sudden, in fact, Lyman stopped his regular visits to our place and stopped attending also Sunday services at Zion Lutheran. People took note of his absence, which only added to the buildup for what was seen as another inevitable day of reckoning between Fredrick Kohn and the Schroeders. A date was set. Everyone in Beaver Township was invited to a public hearing in front of the zoning board, and you could bet it was going to be the same as the previous year.

The only difference being that the year before it was Lyman's older brother, Elmer, who'd come to the zoning board seeking an exemption to the township code so he could put a trailer park on his farm. My father still had been chairman of the zoning board and presided over the hearing. For as long as I could remember it was the township of Fredrick Kohn everyone was living in. He was the keeper of the body. You went to him first if you had anything in mind that deviated from the township code. Everyone, of course, knew the code involved more than the fine points of the zoning laws. It had to do with the essential nature of a man's worth, and what counted was not how much money he made but how much work he did. The pioneer families of Beaver Township were obsessively hardworking people brought up to abstain from shortcuts and from the vulgarities of easy money. The discipline of working for the sake of work had fallen out of favor elsewhere but not in Beaver Township. Honor and citizenship were about nothing else except work. Working the land, with its insistence on slow returns, never making money near what time went into it, was the given of the place, the purpose for all seasons. It brought you to God. You did not enroll your farm in the federal "soil bank" and collect government checks while you and your land sat idle. Nor, it stood to reason, did you plop down a couple of dozen prefab trailers on skids and start collecting rent.

The pros and cons about sewage and traffic and taxes were not really relevant to Elmer Schroeder's scheme. My father, speaking at the conclusion of the public hearing, his safekeeping words point-blank and almost poetic, told Elmer simply that it wasn't right. It wasn't a right use of the land. It wasn't a right means to earn your way. People in the township had an understanding of life in the quantifiable, in the pitilessly literal—in acres per field, bushels per acre, dollars per bushel—but, for all of that, people had a much larger belief in the higher consciousness of living right. I did not actually see Elmer react to my father, but, according to the version I heard, the changing colors on Elmer's face were like a heart attack. A countervailing philosophy inside him came roaring out. He accused my father of abusing the power of his office, and of a lot more. The short of it is that my father wrote out his resignation from the zoning board on the back of an envelope, after which the remaining zoning commissioners voted as one to reject Elmer's petition for an exemption. One other thing: Elmer was at the time the township supervisor, the highest elected official in Beaver.

The person who, some weeks afterward, described all this to me was Lyman, who said my father had acted in accordance with every important virtue. The curtain would keep rising in Beaver on buildings built for the ages, on farmhouses and barns, on a cheese factory and a pickle factory and a mechanic's shop, even on a beer garden, but not on anything smacking of fast bucks. Uncontaminated, life here would remain: my father stroking milk into a pail, my mother shelling peas under a gigantic maple, my brothers and I bent over hoes in the navy beans, the scrupulous days and tireless people repeating themselves up and down the long gravel roads.

Once again my father crisply and cleanly had defined the township, nevermind that henceforth he was without any official title. "The whole township's behind your dad," Lyman had said. "I told Elmer he better apologize if he expects to win the next election."

But now it was a year later, and the unintentional irony of a lightning bolt, as well as something else, something—let's say it—opportunistic about Lyman, had put him in Elmer's place. If the zoning board could be convinced, Lyman pretty soon would be collecting green fees all summer and taking his winters on a beach, even though at first he tried to tell me otherwise. "The golfing business, you know, is not all that different from farming," he said to me with a kind of perfect phony brightness. We were consulting his landscaping plan and pacing off the fairways. I had biked over to see Lyman. He didn't attempt to explain why he had started to avoid the Kohn farm.

On the evening of Lyman's public hearing my father left early and came home early. Upstairs, I listened through the floor register to him telling my mother that, at the last minute, after he'd stood up, with every eye on him, the words wouldn't come. He found he couldn't force the issue. Have I mentioned that once Fredrick Kohn and Lyman Schroeder were the best of friends?

So Lyman's farm was turned into the Sandy Ridge golf course. Over the next year I felt myself becoming a character in the magnetic pull of the place. Lyman paid me to help lay in the sprinkling system and set the grass plugs in the greens. A couple of times my father dropped me off at the Sandy Ridge driveway, but he stayed in his truck, his face set ahead, muscles like bone. The day Sandy Ridge opened Lyman gave me a lifetime pass. I learned to play a decent game. My memory is of Sundays on the course and an image as luminous as Rousseau's *The Dream*. Dew on a green is a beautiful thing and so is the ball rolling to the cup. I became steeped in the joy of pure leisure under the sky. I felt worldwise, among golfers from the city, their cavalier style, their esprit, flashing a ventilated glove, worn on one hand, and in summer (!). In the clubhouse was a glimpse of another life, free of the familiar drudgeries. It was the life I wanted to chase.

Lyman took a long vacation in California the next winter. I was in my last year of high school, applying to colleges. In the spring, out on the fairways, I heard that Sandy Ridge might be for sale. Lyman said it was true. He planned to live south of San Francisco and play someday at Pebble Beach. I would understand the reason. "There's a whole other world out there," he said.

As far as I know, my father never set foot on Lyman's golf course. Nor, after the sale, did he see Lyman again. The first few Christmases I think my father expected Lyman to show up in the Zion pews next to Elmer and the rest of the relatives left behind, but it wasn't long before Elmer, too, moved away, and then all the Schroeders save for two elderly widows. And to think they used to have the big numbers in Beaver Township, thirty-five or forty of them.

Working the land is the alpha and omega of things eternal, and most of us who quit Beaver went off toward things considerably temporal. All the outside world truly is flesh. Against that temptation, my father held fast. For a long time I thought a strange fear, born out of both a moral superiority and a kind of insecurity, kept him in Beaver. What I failed to understand was his zest for work, the high thrills of his farm. I did not understand that his hard days under the sky and in the barn counted for more than merely a life empty of sin. His days were something virtuous and affirmative, richer and more triumphant than a bank statement, more on the dazzling level of a hole in one, like a love affair you would give up everything for. Even after I understood, I could not bring myself to go see him and talk man to man, although at length, before it was too late, I did.

I was shamed into facing my father by many things, among them a letter he sent. He wrote, "Maybe you could look up Lyman"—I was living in San Francisco—"and say hello for me." I had no success at all with directory assistance and only a little when I phoned around to several of the golf clubhouses south of the city. There were rumors of someone who had cut a swath, of gold chains and parties and real estate deals, but as for the man himself the trail was dead. Around that same time I began to lose interest in the game of golf. My clubs, an expensive set, have been gathering dust under the front stairs quite a while now. I travel the country a lot, and I have noticed there may be fewer old yeoman farms these days than golf courses, but always the sight of mowed fairways and gleaming greens brings back my father's letter and that unexpected, earnest, forgiving sentence.

# ENTERING POETRY

During and after dinner there were always arguments at my house: my older brother Eli and my mother against my twin brother Eddie and me. Eli was sixteen and wore a clean starched shirt and tie to the table; he frequently complained about our manners, our language, and our filthy fingernails. He ate methodically and used his napkin often, making little pats at his lips. He also ate a great deal, so the meals seemed to go on forever. It was no good racing through dinner because we were required to remain until the meal was completed. It was also useless to go to my room after dinner because Eddie's single preoccupation was with getting revenge. His favorite phrase was, "I'll give no quarter and take no quarter." (He'd already discovered Sir Walter Scott.) I'd seen him fight often and knew he was serious. When he got another boy down he would kick him with all his considerable might. Only the tallest and toughest of the Episcopalian boys at our new school still called him a dirty Jew.

The year was 1940. My mother had just purchased a house near the outskirts of Detroit located on an almost empty block. There was a similar square two-storied house on each side of ours and two houses directly across from ours and from the house of Steve Psaris, our neighbor to the north. There was also one house directly behind ours. To the east were two blocks of fields and then Livernois Avenue, famous for its profusion of used-car lots. To the west were two totally undeveloped blocks, still deeply wooded with maple, elm, and beech and thick underbrush. In my imagination this settlement of six families was a tiny America, an outpost of civilization between a vast open prairie and the mysterious darkness of a wilderness.

When I sneaked out of the house after dinner each night I headed directly for the security of the dense thickets and trees.

Once into the woods I would make my way to one of my favorite trees, most often a large copper beech whose low branches spread out almost horizontally, and lean back and survey the night sky. There was no industry in this part of the city, and so the stars were visible and on some nights spectacular. One night I began to speak both to and of them. Immediately I felt something enormously satisfying about this speaking, perhaps because nothing came back in the form of an argument. It was utterly unlike any speaking I'd either heard or made before. I liked the way my voice, which was just changing—for I was twelve—would gather itself around or within certain sounds, the r of "rains," the long open o sound of "moon." I would say "rain" and "moon" in the same sentence, hear them echo each other, and a shiver of delight would pass through me. On cloudy, starless nights when the air seemed dense and close, I'd hurl my new voice out at the sky by saying, "The clouds obscure the stars," one tiny delicious sentence, but for the most part I was not brief. Best were those nights after a hard rain. In the darkness the smell of the wet earth would fill my head almost to the bursting point. "The damp earth is giving birth," I would say, and then in sentence after sentence I'd go on to list all that was being born within and outside me, though in the dense night I could hardly discern where I ended and the rest of the world began.

I was no longer addressing the stars, for often they had deserted me. Was I addressing God? I'm sure I was not, for I had no belief in a God who could hear me even though I was learning Hebrew and reading the Bible and discussing its deeper meanings each week with my instructor, a chubby-handed little man who was preparing himself for the rabbinate. Quite simply, Eddie and I had worked it out together and come to a complete accord: there was no God or any chosen people. "What the fuck were we chosen for?" Eddie would shout out after one of our frequent losing battles with the taller Episcopalians, most of whom were driven to school in long Lincolns or Packards, while we made the mile-and-a-half trek on foot even in the worst weather. No, I believe I was already a blooming Platonist addressing the complement, all that I was not and yearned to become. When I was in the crow's nest of my copper beech the wet earth smells rose around me and the wind quivered the hard leaves and carried my voice out to the edges of the night; I could almost believe someone was listening and that each of my words freighted with feeling truly mattered. I was certain I was becoming a man.

*

One spring day, returning from school through the great prairie east of our house, I came across a wild iris, a tiny purple thing growing on its own, just a single bloom with no sign of a neighbor, doing its solitary best to enlighten the afternoon. I ran home and returned with a bucket and shovel from the garage. I dug up the iris, making sure to take plenty of dirt and being careful not to sever the roots. In our backyard I dug up a few square feet of sod near the back fence and planted the wildflower. I watered it carefully, but even by dinnertime it looked as though it had had it, so pitifully did it sag. By morning it was a goner. On Saturday I combed the open fields and found two more wild irises. I dug a second hole and planted the two side by side, this time preparing the ground with a dark, evil-smelling fertilizer I'd bought at Cunningham's Drug Store. I watered one flower hardly at all for fear I might have drowned the first iris. By later afternoon it was clear they'd both died. I asked the advice of Sophie Psaris, Steve's wife, who seemed able to make anything grow. She assured me that not even she could transplant a wildflower and make it grow. As a girl in Salonika, she'd fallen in love with the blood red poppies that stained the meadows each April, but though she'd tried to get them to take hold in her mother's garden, she'd always failed. "Try rose bushes," she said. "The flowers are beautiful and they grow easily." I decided there was something proper about the irises' stubborn refusal to grow inside our fenced yard, something dignified in their preferring death to captivity. Never again would I interfere.

A week later with money earned from washing windows, I bought my first rose bush, a little thorny stick of a thing with its dirt-encrusted roots wrapped in burlap. "You want something that will grow like mad?" said Bert, the little wizened Englishman who worked in the garden section of Cunningham's. For sixty-nine cents he let me have a mock orange. In no time at all, he assured me, it would be taller than I, but then I was still less than five feet tall. "Why do you call it a mock orange?" I asked. "Because that's its name. You see it doesn't give any oranges, you can't grow oranges this far north. It's not even a tree; it's a shrub, but the blossoms look and smell like real orange blossoms."

The instructions for planting the rose spoke of "sandy loam," and the need to place the roots six to nine inches deep into this "sandy loam." After my disasters with the irises, I was hesitant and so took a handful of our backyard dirt to show Sophie. "Is this sandy loam?" I asked. She took a pinch from my open palm between her thumb and forefinger and smelled it and then put a few grains on her tongue and spit them out. "Pheelip," she said in her heavily accented English, "this is just dirt, you know, dirt that comes from the ground." This didn't really answer my question, so with no little trepidation I took a second handful to Cunningham's to show Bert. Was this in fact sandy loam? He stared at me in silence for half a minute and then cocked his head to one side. Why was I asking? I explained how the instructions had spoken of a six- to nine-inch hole in "sandy loam." "Where'd you get this?" he said. I told him I'd dug it out of a hole in my back yard. "Yes, of course you did," he said, "it's dirt, it'll do just fine. Call it 'sandy loam' if you'd like." He assured me that if I just planted the thing in a hole and gave it some water it would grow. "It's a lot less fussy than we are," he added.

Somewhat heartened, I returned home and planted the mock orange in the already fertilized hole that had failed the iris and planted the rose beside the fence separating our lot from Steve Psaris' driveway. I liked the way my hands smelled afterward. I washed away the grosser signs of their filthiness, but I was cautious to leave just enough dirt under my fingernails so that whenever I wanted to I could catch a whiff of the earth's curious pungency that suggested both tobacco and rust. Though the soil of our backyard was a dull gray brown, the perfume was a foxy red. For once, I looked forward to Eli's complaints.

The rose especially was such a sad little thing that in spite of Bert's encouragement I was certain it would not survive, but within a week tiny reddish twigs began to jut out from the woody gray stick. I would press my thumb against the new thorns just to feel their sharpness against my skin. Eddie liked to speak of something he called a "blood oath," a vow taken by two strong men and sealed by the mixing of their blood. At the time he was reading Dumas and Sabatini and often spoke also of taking fencing lessons, though we knew no one in Detroit who gave them. One day I considered puncturing my skin against the largest of the thorns, but I stopped short of this gesture. Sophie had assured me the buds would come as they had on her bushes. I knew from watching them they would transform themselves from hard green almond-shaped stones to the swelling red-tipped about-to-be-flowers.

✻

One late May morning I glanced out of the back window of the breakfast nook to discover the mock orange in bloom. Caught up in the excitement of the beginning of the baseball season, I'd not been paying attention and was taken by surprise. There were suddenly more than a dozen tiny blossoms and a rich, deep perfume that reminded me of the perfume of my Aunt Belle, my mother's younger sister. After school I cut a small branch of three blossoms and placed it in a glass of water and set it in the middle of the dining room table. To my surprise, that evening no one noticed it, and dinner passed with Eli discussing his plans for a camping trip in northern Canada. I listened in silence, and when the others had left the table I dropped the little branch down the front of my shirt.

The days were lengthening, and it was still light out when I sneaked out of the house after helping with the dishes. I made my way to the deepest center of the woods and climbed a young maple tree and gazed up into the deepening sky above. I must have dozed off for a few minutes because quite suddenly the stars had emerged in a blacker sky. Although I did not know their names—in fact, I did not even know they had names—I began to address them quietly, for I never spoke with "full-throated ease" until hidden by the cover of total darkness. A soft wind shook the leaves around me. From my own hands I caught the smell of earth and iron, which now I carried with me at all times. I reached down my shirt and extracted the mock orange branch and breathed in the deep feminine odors while between thumb and forefinger I fretted the blossoms until they fell apart. I began then to address my own hands, which seemed somehow to have been magically transformed into earth. For the first time a part of me became my night words, for now the darkness was complete. "These hands have entered the ground from which they sprung," I said, and tasting the words I immediately liked them and repeated them, and then more words came that also seemed familiar and right. Then I looked on the work my hands had wrought, then I said in my heart, as it happened to the gardener, so it happened to me, for we all go into one place; we are all earth and return to earth. The dark was everywhere, and as my voice went out I was sure it reached the edges of creation. I was sure too my words must have smelled of sandy loam and orange blossoms. That was the first night of my life I entered poetry.

# QUAKE

*December 3, 1990*

I'm sitting on a balcony in New Harmony, Indiana, waiting for the end of the world.

I don't mind the wait. Every sixty years the sun and the moon battle for the earth's affections, and the body of the earth turns liquid and rolls. Earth tides, they're called, and everyone in the Midwest knows about them now. Something strange and unsettling in the solid earth we've counted on. We live on one of the world's largest fault lines, and most of our lives we weren't even aware of it. Some prophet had predicted that the tide will cause the fault to shift on this very day, and because we're only ten years away from the new millennium, something in us longs for the explosion.

Blow it all up, get rid of it: all the plastic pens and razors, and the World of Dinettes that sold us the one-hundred-dollar chairs that fell apart in one year. Blow up the immense shopping desert with the acres of stone lots and tall mercury lights like drooping flowers and all the brand new vapory objects that pack the stores so tightly it makes us dizzy to walk through them. Blow up the church where we sit without fervor on Sunday, listening to announcements about the sidewalk fund, and the chaos of strip malls where it's impossible to walk from Toys R Us to Children's Palace one hundred yards away, and it takes an hour to drive through a confused tangle of unplanned traffic lights and roadways to the K Mart where last year a five-year-old girl from my neighborhood reached for a silver tube of toothpaste on a shelf and it blew off her hand. I put my own children in a metal shopping cart now like a cage, and I pray they won't reach their hands outside of it.

Because I've lived in the suburbs of Indianapolis all my life and I remember the forest of one-hundred-year-old beech trees that was cut to make that chaos, and because when I wake up in the middle of the night in the same neighborhood I lived in as a child, the sky isn't dark and crisp and starry, but this weird half-mystical shade of orange-gray-violet, when I heard about the earthquake, I ran hell-bent out of my township, down through the detritus of the city's spinning—past Auto Parts and Used Auto Parts and then old tires submerged in winter field, past rows of hay huddled under black trash bags. I ran from my own anger, down to where the earthquake map in the paper was shaded, to where I could feel it if it goes. In 1823 a prophet brought a group of people here from Germany to wait for the end of the world. The earthquake, if it comes, won't be just some minor trembling that shakes the curio cabinet here, and the Harmonists who've been waiting first in line, folded into the ground like egg whites for one hundred years, will shiver: hush, maybe this is it, what we've been waiting for, new life, our chance to rise. So I sit on a balcony overlooking Paul Tillich's grave, waiting with them for the end of everything.

It doesn't come. I try to meditate on important things. Instead, I think about local gossip, some scandalous reason that Tillich is buried here and the Harmonist granary across the street has never been restored. I think it has something to do with the IU calliope. I can't remember the story, and anyway it's probably not true. I stretch and drink coffee and wonder why I am so shallow even on earthquake day. I put my feet up on the balcony. The day is unseasonably warm, the climate turned strange, the globe a candled egg.

Wild geese rise up from the woods behind the Benedictine chapel. They have difficulty forming a V; one goose moves out in front and then another. The others have no idea which one to follow. Is that a sign? Do geese get confused before earthquakes? Supposedly, cats run away; that's part of the mythology. Keep your eyes on the want ads in the paper. I decided that I need a paper.

I walk downstairs and head toward town, past the log houses, the roofless church. I see the granary behind a gate. Private residence, the sign says. Things like that can't matter when you're waiting for the end of the world, so I walk in.

It's one of the largest barns I've ever seen—stone and log windows, the whole thing shaped like a loaf of bread. It's where the Harmonists stored their hay for the millennium. The barn is covered with dead foliage like tangled hair, two cats sitting in the chink of light that's opened by a boarded-up window; maybe they've run away. I try to look inside. Rotted wood and fallen rafters, an expanse of dark like a cathedral, dusky light from windows high up. I walk around the corner of the barn, over to Robert Dale Owen's mad scientist laboratory, a weird Victorian structure with turrets like witches' caps, a metal fish twisting overhead. There were two different utopias here. It was only the first group who waited for the end of the world. The Owenites bought the whole town when it didn't happen and the Harmonists began revising their predictions. If the Harmonists thought that human beings were angels—Gabriel, it's said, even left his footprint in a stone above the Wabash—the Owenites thought they were machines. They were the ones who mapped and classified every inch of this wilderness, the ones who brought in the abstract and the rational. Make the perfect world, they thought, and you create a perfect human being. Strangely, though, it was the spiritual Harmonists who created the buildings that still stand, a simple beauty and order in the life they made, much like the Shakers. It was the rational Owenites who built very little, and when they did, created this wacky laboratory. Toward the end of his life, Robert Dale decided the spirit was so completely disconnected from the body that he turned to séances, the air so thick with spooky spirits that he could hardly walk outside.

The wall of the granary on the laboratory side is covered with trumpet vine, hard, dried bean pods like the beaks of brown yammering toucans. I break a pod from the vine and put it in my pocket. The pods shake in the wind and it sounds like applause; the fish on the laboratory spins and spins.

I leave through the gate and head into town. I realize that I'll spend the very last day in the world shopping, the way we celebrate holidays in the suburbs. Labor Day Sale. Memorial Day Sale. After Thanksgiving, Pre-Christmas Sale. Armageddon Day Clearance, everything half-off, take it with you. I try to talk to people about the earthquake, looking for a true believer, but only the agnostics are out.

A woman sits in a bookstore putting all the change from the church Sunday school into paper rolls, her finger stuck down inside a roll like one of those Chinese puzzles. "It's old people and children that are worried," she says to me, "people who don't have a thing to do. My mother's boxed up all her stuff and tied the water heater to the wall with cup hooks. My little boy's gone to stay with her; they can be scared together all day long."

A clerk with dangling paper-clippey-looking earrings overhears us. "It's not just old people," she says. "My insurance agent boxed all his stuff up and spent the night in his motor home. I'd be afraid the thing would topple over."

I tell her I talked to an insurance agent before I came down here, one from Anderson who had to hire three extra people to write up earthquake riders on policies even though Anderson's supposedly on a different plate. "You're as safe from this fault in Anderson," I say, "as you would be in Paris."

I buy books for my kids and a newspaper, head out the door. I check the sky, feel my feet on the sidewalk. Is that a rumble? Is everything solid? I put my hand on the cold stone building.

Around the corner to a white house where they sell woven goods. I walk in. Cross-stitch pictures of lambs and bins of colored yarn; maybe I can find a scarf for my brother. He can wear it in January if the weather turns cold enough. January? Yes, I think. January. If I really believed in this prediction, I wouldn't be here. I would have gathered up everyone I love and headed for an open field.

An old woman with short bowl-cut gray hair sits behind a floor loom. National Public Radio is on louder than any rock station. Something crashing and dissonant, the wood loom clacks like the dried trumpet vine on the granary.

"I'm not afraid of no earthquake," she says. "You talk about Kentuckians," she says, "but we're ignorant here, that's all. Hoosiers— damn ignorant"—clack crash, the loom, the radio's percussion.

I try a purple shaw on over my coat, and it turns me into an old woman immediately. Last night in the restaurant, two old women with rounded backs, their eyes inches away from the tablecloth when they sat down; they looked like the handles of two umbrellas hooked over the table's edge. I pull the shawl around me, turn away from the mirror. I'm trying on old age to see how it feels.

"Ignorant," the woman says, "because they've never been out of the state in their lives"—clack crash—"never farther than Evansville, some of them, like my son's wife, they're divorced now, I wouldn't have said ignorant while she was married to him, but the week my son wanted to take her on a vacation to Dallas, my ignorant daughter-in-law said it was too far away, and that was the week she moved out with the baby and the furniture."

"Ignorant"—clack crash—"just damn ignorant."

Another old woman in jeans and a red stocking cap comes in the back door, puts down a sack. There are three of us now. I hunch over, move toward the loom.

"We get the baby every eight days," the weaver says, "and they're beating her."

"Who's they?" the woman in the red cap says.

"How awful," I say.

"They're beating her"—clack crash—"and we can't prove it."

"Scars are being formed there," the other woman says.

"Every eight days then Wednesday Thursday Friday Saturday Sunday, and the baby cries when we try to take her back to her mother."

"Pillar to post," the other woman says, "lifetime scars are being formed there."

The weaver slams the shuttle through the loom. "We don't know who's beating her," she says, "maybe the day care, we can't prove it."

"Are there bruises?" the other woman says.

"No," the weaver says, "but she cries too hard for no reason."

"Scars you can't see," the other woman says, "scars being formed there."

I put the shawl back on the wire and straighten my back.

"I've been to Hawaii," the weaver says, "to my sister's house in California. An earthquake in California, they just look up and go on, not like here."

"Something needs to shake us up," she says.

"Shake rattle and roll," her friend says.

"You like the shawl?" the weaver says to me. "I didn't mean," she says, with a crash, the beater bar shoving the threads so tight they will never unravel, "to tell you a horror story on earthquake day."

I walk outside. Everything is still the way it was, but different. There are earthquake stories everywhere. I walk down the street to the Main Street Cafe, walk in, sit down. Three more old women in a booth next to mine. A man in a John Deere hat walks by. There are all these tired graying faces, but this man's face is a candle. "There were tremors," he says to the table of women, "tremors at 10:30."

Of course! Everyone nods, revisionist history. So that's what it was, we think, the sound I heard—not a truck going by on the highway, not a man moving furniture in the apartment upstairs, not a woman taking out her troubles on a loom. It wasn't one of my spells, I hear a woman saying to a friend, right about then it was I leaned into the truck and started hoping that someone would come along and save me. Tremors! Our new lives can begin now, all fresh, everything bad sloughed off like water through a colander.

"You from around here?" one of the women at the booth says to me, just like you would expect her to. "No," I say, "I'm staying at the Inn." She tells me she lives in the green stucco house across the street, the one with the ceramic elves in the window, sure that I noticed it. I assure her that I did notice it, and I tell myself I'll look for it when I leave. The last day in the world, and I've become a liar and a trespasser and a thief. There's no hope for me, none whatsoever. The woman is getting ready to go home and watch "Days of Our Lives." I tell her I haven't liked it much since Doug and Julie left, and Bo and Hope, and she says yeah, that Patch just got killed too, and I tell her I'm sorry, I didn't know.

"Remember when Patch was a bad guy?" I ask. And she says yes, that he was one of those good-looking bad guys that all the viewers fall in love with, so they turned him into a good guy, little by little. But not too good; he still had a wicked edge to him. It would come out when you least expected it. He died a good-guy death though, a hero.

I ask what's happening now—gossip, shopping, and soap operas are how we spend the last days of our own real lives—and she says they're all on an island and there's been an earthquake. They're holed up together in a building.

Not on earthquake day, I say to her, and she laughs and says, "You're not one of those who believes in earthquakes" as though it's something you need to have faith in, like God or love. And I laugh, say no, I'm not one of those. All of us out to lunch on this day are the ones who don't believe the earth is waiting to swallow us whole for our sins.

One of the woman's friends who lives up near Gary got in with a cult who moved into a church basement a few years ago, believing someone who said there was going to be a killer tornado. She thinks that all these earthquake believers are just as crazy. She tells me about another friend who's rigged up an outdoor generator and put a change of clothes and bottled water in both of her cars, with plans to live in whichever one survives the quake. The woman and her husband are both excited about it; it's given them something to talk about for months.

"I haven't done a thing to get ready for this earthquake," another woman says, as though it's something you have to prepare for, like Christmas.

"If I put all my food in one place," she says to me, "that's exactly the place the wall would cave in."

"You watch soap operas," I say to the women. "When a woman boxes up the baby and the furniture and moves away, what happens?"

"It depends," the ceramic elf woman says. "Sometimes the woman is happier, sometimes not. Sometimes the man is happier than the woman."

"And the baby?" I ask.

"Sometimes an accident," she says.

"Fire, drowning, hurricane, explosion," another woman says. "If the baby survives, she's moved all over the place. Everyone fights over her."

"Babies in soap operas never stay in one place long."

"Sometimes there's a kidnapping."

"Yes!" A woman in her husband's green thermal coat. "Some guy you've never even seen before comes in, claims he's the father and grabs her. Some old lover of the wife—a Mafia guy sometimes, leader of a Virgin Islands cult."

"Everyone comes back together to save the baby," the elf woman says. "The baby's parents fall in love again.

"Months later there's a big wedding, a dress like Lady Di's. We all stay home to watch it, and we cry and cry."

The thermal-coated woman says, "And at the last minute, the bride's brother runs in, his clothes all torn and dirty, holding the baby."

"The bride's brother or the groom's best friend."

"No, the guy the bride left her husband for."

Yes, they agree, that's best. And then?

"Bliss," one woman says. She wraps both hands around her bubbling Coke. "Bliss and bliss and bliss."

"For about a half a year," the elf woman says. "A half a year, then boom, crash, something happens to them. Or they go away for a while and the baby comes back replaced by a teenage actress and the whole thing starts all over."

"And in real life?" I ask.

"Who knows?" they say. Things happen, they agree, you can't predict. Things just go on and on and every once in a while there's an earthquake. The next day the sun comes up, you look around, and you see whether you're living your old life or a new one. It's exactly what I was afraid they'd say.

The problem with this world is that things are so enmeshed. You can't predict a thing, good and evil so bound together that it's impossible, sometimes, to separate them. You try so hard for control and order, and you get disorder. You put your faith in science, and you see ghosts. How do you know how to live your life? The ground is always shifting underneath your feet.

Out here in the heart of the country we've rationalized every inch of earth—all the straight lines of highway and farm and township—but mystery and wildness still lie waiting deep inside every particle of the world, waiting to whirl or crack or ooze into our ordered lives, whether or not we've prepared for it. And the more we deny it, cover it with concrete and lights, the tighter it crouches until it's as small and ordinary as a tube of toothpaste or as large as a crack in the foundations of the world, and we have to pay attention.

I leave New Harmony late in the afternoon, heading for the half-moon of my own confused township. The Harmonists still sleep. Another day almost gone, and still, they're waiting.

Halfway between New Harmony and Indianapolis, I pass two men butchering a deer. The deer hangs by its legs from a tree, its front hooves touching the earth. The men have hollowed the deer body, the ribs turned inward, something so graceful and terrifying in the curve of the animal and the curve of the branch it's hanging from, the men with their silver knives and orange caps, their jump suits the bronzy cinnamon of the oak leaves, the dark flesh of the skinned deer mottled with fat, white like the bark of the sycamores in the woods behind them.

# NONE OF US WENT BACK

We left my hometown when I was eight years old, and we never went back, any of us, ever. My parents loved it too much, and to my sisters and me it soon meant nothing but the past, that under-developed country of stories and dreams. The town was Concordia, Missouri, between the Blackwater and the Missouri River, fifty miles from Kansas City on I-70, which didn't exist then.

I remember no pain when we moved. In fact, I don't remember the move at all, though I'd expect my own daughter, now eight, to remember an event of such significance. I wonder sometimes if that uprooting doesn't account for a certain bluntness in the branching deltas of my nerves, if a certain intuitive understanding wasn't lost with the invisibly fine root hairs left wrapped around sandgrain and pebble. "What if we had stayed there?" I remember my father asking my mother over the years, expecting and receiving no answer. "We moved for your sake," he often told me, for the better schools a city could offer. That was all right with me, but I didn't want to feel responsible for the pain he clearly felt at times. The move was to Ft. Wayne, Indiana, after all, not Heidelberg or Paris.

I feel there's something wrong with the name—Concordia—self-consciously Latin, its very placeness compromised for me by the name's being attached to most of the colleges and seminaries in the German Lutheran universe I inhabited for twenty years. In St. Paul, Minnesota, where I live now, there's a Concordia College. Another is across the state. I attended Concordia High School in Ft. Wayne, went for two years to Concordia College in Bronxville, New York. Concordia feels strange in my mouth, the way your own name does when you say it about a hundred times in a row. The names of the towns surrounding Concordia are more real to me. Higginsville, Odessa, Sweet Springs, Emma. Aullville, Alma. Warrensburg, Corder, Sedalia, Knob Noster. I wasn't actually even born in Concordia, but in Marshall, thirty miles away, where there was a hospital. So Marshall, Missouri, is the name I write down in the space marked "place of birth." It has no other reality; I'm surprised to find it on the map. I'd pay two hundred dollars to have been born in Knob Noster.

It's probably a delusion that the instinctive sense of belonging, fitting in, being part of the tribe, is dulled when a child is removed from the place of his first memories before the hardening of puberty can happen, that it somehow condemns him to being a part of someone else's reality. (I remember standing at the window of my first apartment in St. Paul, bone lonely after the long snuggle of education. In the courtyard below, my landlord's children were playing with some neighbor kids, mostly fighting and screaming, a dog tearing around. The youngest, about four, the age of my son now, looked up and saw me. He poked one of his brothers, who looked up, too. They all looked up. I held my ground at the window, expressionless. "What do you think you're looking at, Mister?" one of them shouted at me. I didn't respond, didn't move, allowed the weirdly fitting mantle of alien adulthood to settle psychotically around me, float me into their dreams.) It's probably a delusion, but who knows?

Too small for me to be born in, Concordia was the right size for a four-year-old to ride a tricycle anywhere he wanted to go, as long as he avoided Main Street, where somebody would recognize him and send him home. Intoxicated with independence and the fragrance of freshly oiled streets, I would have gone on forever, pedaling through stranger and stranger neighborhoods to the end of civilization, if I hadn't been dragged to a stop, arrested by a blueness so absolute I couldn't take my eyes off it—morning glories, drenching a weathered gray house from foundation bricks to rotten gutters, overwhelming the trellis that must have supported them. I stared and stared, and then a door at the side of the house flew open and a witch-haired woman sprang out and I screamed and flew home.

My father and mother loved the town. They were newlyweds there, lived in five different houses, none theirs, knew everybody. When he was fourteen years old my father had been sent away from home to go to school there—high school and then college, preparing for the ministry. He broke his nose there playing football. Not daring to notify his folks back in Omaha, he had his roommate set it, changing his face forever. After seminary and parishes in Idaho and Oregon, the Synod told him they needed a teacher at the college in Concordia and sent him to graduate school, and he came back to the town as a professor. When they needed a librarian, they sent him to library school, and from then on he was a librarian. Shortly after he married my mother, he got in a race with some kids on Main Street and crashed his bicycle, screwing up his back. My parents always referred to their first house as "the crackerbox." They raised chickens there. Nupps Schackenberg sold my father an old shotgun: "seeing as it's you, Prof," asking twice what it was worth. The town was dense with stories, and my parents loved it. Two times my father turned down the call to a new college in Indiana that wasn't even built yet. The third time the call came, he accepted it. We'd be in a city, there'd be better schools for me and my sisters. We left, and none of us ever went back.

Concordia was a market town, and on Saturdays it filled up with farmers. I remember a hatchery and a feedstore downtown, and a produce market beside the railroad tracks. There were two groceries, Schumacher's and Alwell's; two restaurants open on alternate Sundays, Topsey's and the Favorite; a firetrap movie theater above some business, maybe the variety store where we shopped for presents, Wookash's. I'm guessing at the spellings. My father bought me my first baseball bat, a half-size Louisville Slugger, at a shoe store that sold harness and saddles, and I remember a furniture store oppressive with towering purple columns of rolled carpet and a room in back where they kept the coffins. A tavern, the Palace, I think. A blacksmith shop. A rusty, putrid jail.

Once a year there was the Street Fair, town clogged with rides and carnival booths and all the gaud and possibility of the world. Playing hoop toss, trying for a sheath knife, I won a ceramic creamer shaped like a Holstein cow. My older sister somehow won a conch shell that I later appropriated, pink and smoothly disappearing inside itself. From the height of the ferris wheel you could see the hole Jesse James shot in the eagle on top of the bank flagpole. Beneath the ferris wheel one year, either my sister or I found a huge old Liberty Head penny, which I still have, thick and brown as a Hershey Bar. We always figured it had to be worth a lot. I looked it up in a book yesterday, which said $4.51.

As my father gained seniority and the family grew, my parents moved from house to house owned by the college. The three houses we lived in after I was born were on the north end of town, the college end, and at least one of them was close enough to the old highway that I could lie in bed summer nights and listen to a sound so beautiful I have difficulty now accepting it for what it must have been, the hum of truck tires on blacktop, audible a long time coming and a long time going in that flat country. One of the houses had a big side yard, fronted with catalpas, and with two ancient peach trees. The summer of the sad, endless year my father was in Austria on a Fulbright grant, both trees bore prodigiously. I remember helping my mother wedge long forked poles underneath the branches to keep the burden of fruit from tearing the trees apart. One tree was loaded with peaches that were all as small as apricots, even when fully ripe and sweet. The other bore fewer fruit, but they were enormous, grapefruit size, full of worms.

A neighbor boy older than me helped with that harvest. My mother thinks there was something wrong with him, he wasn't all there, she says. I never noticed anything. She seems to feel that about a number of my childhood friends—"He was never quite right," she says. "There was always something funny about him." Some of them are dead, now, at least one from suicide. Maybe she's right. I'd go over on Saturday mornings and help him with chores—shelling peas, pulling succulent weeds for their chickens. He always had a lot of chores, like a farm boy, though this was town. In the fall, his mother would set a cannibal cauldron over a wood fire in the lot between our houses and make apple butter. His dad had the thickest, yellowest toenails I'd ever seen. He'd pare them in the evenings with a fishing knife, the gnarled pale foot he wasn't working on stretched toward us where we played some game on the living room floor.

My memories of the edge of town are scattered but intense. There was a creamery out there somewhere, butter yellow and rancid smelling, the only place in town, besides the jail, that I truly feared. Closer to us on the highway was the Shady Rest, where we bought firecrackers on the Fourth of July. It had a lunch counter (my mother says she thinks it was a "dive," though she won't elaborate) and served as the bus depot. The year my father was away, we'd wait there for the bus into Kansas City, where we had to go to get special shoes for my bad feet. My little sister, who must have been two the year my father was gone, learned to love the escalators in Kansas City. I liked the fluoroscope, the green light that melted away the flesh of my feet, showing exactly how my bones stood in the hard new shoes. I don't know what my older sister got out of it. Responsibility, maybe.

I remember putting on my coonskin cap at the end of that year and walking out to the Shady Rest with my mother and sisters to meet the evening bus bringing my father back from Vienna. Hours later, fondling a German pocketknife with a corkscrew that he'd brought me, I lay awake as long as I could, listening to an almost forgotten music from downstairs, my father's voice mingling with my mother's. Kathleen, my wife, asked me once what was the happiest moment of my life. I told her, the night my father came back from Austria.

We're shaped by our severings as well as our attachments, that much is clear. Last year, trying to calm my daughter's anxieties about our impending move to Costa Rica, I pointed out to her that when my father had gone abroad for a year, the rest of us couldn't go along with him, I'd missed him terribly. I was her age, then. He was my age. We at least were all going to be together, I said. How could he do that, she wanted to know, leave his family for a year? I didn't know how, I told her. But he was a good father, he had good reasons.

It's not completely true to say that none of us went back. Eleven years ago I found myself in Kansas City, spending part of the holidays with my wife-to-be and most of her family. A few days earlier we'd been with my parents, in Milwaukee, where my father was in semi-retirement, starting to die from cancer. By New Year's afternoon I felt as if no blood at all was making it to my brain anymore, and I had the idea of borrowing a car and showing Kathleen my old hometown, whatever might be left of it. Not much, I thought, as we approached the Concordia exit. I-70 there was bright with truck stops, motels, fast-food places, I don't remember what all. But a half mile or so off the freeway, time peeled away again, I was back where I'd started.

It was getting late. We wouldn't have much time. I drove around where I thought we must have lived but couldn't find any of the houses we'd lived in. The college was deserted, the buildings undistinctive. It was getting dark already when we drove down Main

Street, cold, a little snow on the ground. No one was on the streets, no stores were open. My heart jumped a little when I saw the sign for Topsey's, Alwell's, other places I recognized but have forgotten again. The park where there were band concerts in the summer was either too close to the center of town or too far out, I can't remember which. I found a plaque that explained how the town had come to be named Concordia. It said it was something else before, I forget what. I think the plaque said the town was renamed at the end of the Civil War, maybe at the suggestion of a minister. The plaque might have been a part of a Civil War memorial, or maybe not, I just can't remember.

The church where I'd been baptized was open. We went in, I looked at the glossy, brown-robed statue of Jesus that I'd studied critically during so many sermons. I climbed up to the balcony, where my mother could never sit, dizzied by height. No one was around.

When we went outside, it was definitely getting dark. I'd decided on the visit too late to make it properly, to learn anything from it. If I'd thought, I could have pumped my parents for information when I was with them. They could have drawn maps, named streets, given me addresses.

We'd promised to be back in time for supper. We'd have to hurry. We got back in the car. I drove to the far end of town and made an easy U-turn on the wide street and drove slowly back through town. I saw things that meant something, but I can't remember them now, the trip was too rushed and I was careening too busily into my future. We saw nothing moving until we got back to the freeway. I might as well have dreamed it all.

# THE TOWNSHIP ARGO

This box contains uncanceled postage stamps from my term in Grenada, West Indies; a homemade microscope slide of one of my eyelashes; WCOL's Top Forty Hits for most weeks of 1969; a real stethoscope my pediatrician cousin gave me, a self-proclaimed pre-med student at nine. . . . Under the impetuous need to find some long-lost essential that, rightfully, should be junked in my own basement barricade of boxes, I spend an hour in my parents' basement among the cast-off possessions of not only my childhood, adolescence, teens, and twenties, but also those of my sister and my brother. Something in my parents' good nature has given space, if not credence, to the accumulated, unaccountable possessions that never left their home when I went to college or that returned from the various rented rooms which, more than years, divide my life into apprehensible units.

College notebooks are crammed inside many boxes, their spiral bindings combined into double helices, creating mutant subjects such as musical survey of vertebrate anatomy or clinical psychology of glaze chemistry. Indeed, it is hard to remember—to imagine—what future I had intended for myself that would have made each of these volumes indispensable. For basic education requirements—Intro to Soc. or Biology—my parents' basement offers three sets of course materials that differ only in handwriting and the years that separate my brother, sister, and me from undergraduate careers at the same university.

Wayward, haywired electronics occupies another corner. Placed end to end, it creates an evolutionary timeline, mid-to-late twentieth century, of music-playing devices. Extinct creatures include a litter of plastic microphones, a reel-to-reel tape recorder, car stereo speakers, headphones the size of Hostess Snowballs, transistor radios stuffing various stuffed animals, and strata of successively more compact cassette players.

A transparent model of the circulatory system that pumped food coloring through a torso of tangled tubes; shoeboxes labeled *Notes* (folded paper scraps of coy and candid junior high intrigue); huge acrylic canvases (in my teens I had discovered both the overhead projector and how masking tape can make crisp borders between adjacent colors)—perhaps there is no reason to keep the cuttings, residues, stepping stones, souvenirs, and dunnage (all the baggage that doesn't travel) that pad the corners of our houses. Is this stockpile the foundation of a home, as concrete blocks are the foundation of a house? Is it insulation against the cold hard facts—losses—of our occupancy? In any case, each piece is an artifact of a personal habitat, an individual civilization.

Expensive toys like Vacuform and Creepy Crawlers; vaguely indigenous crafts brought from my parents' tropical vacations; the amazing finger-guillotine, a trick from my stint as birthday party magician for my siblings' friends; a statuary of sports trophies; a lanyard long enough to measure a summer's worth of knotting, with a key to who-knows-what safe place: it's easy to believe each object is interchangeable with any other *impersonal* thing, any other inanimate object. But, for better or worse, weren't these very relics my animators? The "Wild, Wild West" belt buckle whose cap gun would explode when I thrust out my stomach: didn't it suggest the hours of playing spy among the half-built houses of our new development? Didn't my parents' old breakfront, emptied now of its nature displays, provide the vacuum we had to fill with specimens collected from nearby vacant lots? And so on, until I've composed my own relatively longer history from the brief life histories of these salvaged yet outlived things.

Sparked by my father's justifiable need for storage, we children have performed a few rounds of triage over the years. Pitching load after load of basement trash that no one could see why anyone would detain, we simultaneously renewed equally tenuous reasons for maintaining other things in indefinite storage.

The appeal of such objects is their silence. They need us to animate them, and thus we catch ourselves, most often unaware, animating ourselves. Things do not embarrass us with our feelings, but we recognize that feelings are confined like a genie in each tarnished vessel. And the memory of each can be released like a genie: as suddenly and unmistakably as a forgotten sensation (say, the unscrewing *pop* of a Tinker Toys' lid, or the pulpy scent of its deep canister), the memory can appear . . . although the thrill and fascination and wonder have been spent; the genie's three allotted wishes have been granted.

Left with the pleasure of memory—not the immediate pleasure of innocent abandon—there's nothing to do but replace the lid, having updated the recollection. Now the original memory and its recollection are both logged in the brain; perhaps such an early memory would have been lost if not for this recent reminder. And so I wonder: can I always recall an original experience, or, as I grow older, can I obtain only experiences that previous recollection has forwarded into retrievable compartments? And, as a consequence of this repeated process of selection, have these updated memories already been foreshortened, misconstrued, and elevated to an undeserved status that I mistake as an exemplar of early experience? Another way to pose this: can I find some precious object from my childhood (a first-time memory) if I haven't already stored it (a subsequent *re*-collection) in my parents' basement? Already saved it from the refurbishing of my childhood bedroom as a guest room?

I riffle through another carton. It's all safe, extant, and in the jumbled but loosely associated company of such familiars as a personality analysis on punched computer cards from the state fair; a chart of the Milky Way that had been taped to my bedroom ceiling for years, save those mornings I'd awaken beneath a crackling but heavenly bedspread; and finally, a gift subscription to *National Geographic*, 1967, that might be worth something one day, or so I tell my parents, stooped at the top of the basement stairs to see what's keeping me.

In my personal geography, this township is zoned in memory not square miles—ephemeral and variable associations of my own travel, frequentations, and, as William Meredith suggests in his poem "Examples of Created Systems," loved ones:

> Incorrigibly (it is our nature)
> when we look at a map we look for

the towns and valleys and waterways
where loved people constellate, some of
them from our blood, some from our own loins.
This fair scattering of matter is all we will know of creation, at
first hand.

The six-by-six-square-mile area where I lived all but three years of
my life does not correspond precisely with one official township on
the county map. The area is pliable as memory—a perpetual exchange of losses and gains, discoveries and misplacings. Overdeter-
mined as a dream, this reconstructed map is charming and respon-
sive as the patchwork crazy quilts I've slept under where my resting,
dreaming body is, itself, a heaving topography beneath a blanketing
vista of fields and forests, dotted livestock and homesteads. The
seismic revisions of a fitful sleep! The adventure of the hands' five-
membered families resettling the territory!

In this part of the Midwest, the quilt's divisions are already plotted on the landscape, miniaturized and made manageable by each
farming family: a grid of occupancy: property lines and county
roads dividing the fields and pastures sown and harvested each
year. Each of these agricultural blocks—acres of soybeans or grazing sheep or fallow grasses—resembles a township or, from a higher
vantage, a county, or even a state or a country, depending on the
imagined altitude. Ingrained into this landscape (and in-livestocked,
in-housed, in- all the other created patterns of our temporary civilization) is a singular version of geography: the way someone has created dominion—whether with stitches of thread, seed, or verse—
within the invisible rules of the undeeded universe.

Issues of ownership aside, this township is another repository of
individual experience. So far, I have accumulated material as a
child, a youth, a student, an adult, and, I admit, as a writer willing
to gerrymander boundaries and environments to support some present purpose. Despite the absence of inscribed plaques, the streets,
buildings, landscapes, *developments* of any kind, all serve as private
monuments. Occupants replace one another, facades and landscapes convert or revert, parades of dumpsters disperse the rubble
of razed landmarks and eyesores, and, even as an ambitious salvage
operation, a block of ten houses moves from one declining neighborhood to one in an aspiring target district—the elements of this

township are continually redefined, like a civic parlance, with the shadings, ambiguities, and paradoxes of current usage. As each denoted place evolves, intensifies—can I suggest *densifies?*—this township produces a text of connotations that I continue to read and interpret and write.

In *Roland Barthes on Roland Barthes*, the sage demystifier of society offers the ship *Argo* as an allegory for a structure "created not by genius, inspiration, determination, evolution, but by two modest actions . . . ," that of gradually replacing each part of the ship as it weathers the calamitous travails of its journey, and that of retaining its original name. The Argonauts' ship completes its journey with nothing but its name and its shape intact.

For my purpose, the ship is a township. The borders and the name of this township have not changed, although how many times has it been reinvented as I have repaired across it? How many times, reinvested as I have populated the residences of my work?

A translator friend of mine insists that every writer should possess fluency in a second language in order to enrich the possibilities of the first; that, or possess the one language with a lexicographer's vigor so as to conjure a ghost of another language: the etymological resources of roots, entendres, and obsolescent forms.

Alas, foreign language, like anything for which I make no current use, is not readily accessed in my brain. Directions in a foreign city, names and events in a recently read novel, pre-med years of organic chemistry, poems memorized for the very purpose of being able to recite them from memory, and most gorgeous but sinecured knowledge has a brief half-life in my mind (unlike the profane objects in my parents' accommodating basement).

It has dawned on me that forgetting must be an active part of my creative process, a vital winnowing and shuffling and depositing that permits certain items to resurface, less rhetorically and self-consciously, in half-recollected guises, unattributed fragments, juxtaposed associations—independent mysteries that offer themselves as aimless directions on a map or nonsense clues to a treasure hunt. The final destination (coherence or revelation) would then be the tracing, composing, and scrutinizing of all these *browsings*, these unobvious points selected by the process we're wont to call inspiration, so as not to expose the circuitry for our own cheaper imitations.

Living in this recurring place of my township stores and, more crucially, restores me to my own knowledge. It provides a second language of dense familiarity that invigorates the perceptions made in this, my single language. A day of slate crashing from a neighbor's roof as workers prepare it for shingle; a new, or possibly the same, litter of feral kittens in the alley—such minor instances startle me into paying heed, an homage to what survives the routings of routine.

While other writers' recollections of their townships may be sparked by a return after so many years away—gross unfamiliarity, grand substitution, broad eradications—that precipitous experience is not mine. Nor is the temptation to bask in or bolt from nostalgia. Where others' experiences of return would necessarily be overwhelmed by the indiscriminate onslaught of remembrances, the routes of my quotidian encounters afford me, amid discrete recollections, a similarly extensive process of endless forgetting.

Over the last six years I have written nearly a novel's worth of poems about a fictional character thirty years my senior. Without designating his particular city, I realized, late into the characterization, that his unspecified home was this township. Whether or not Gordon Penn, a soon-to-retire notions salesman, is someone I expect to "inhabit" in thirty years suggests too simple a model. But his longer occupation in this township has convinced me of the details that recognition, rather than surprise, reveals.

In the following poem, I have projected not simply a situation from my own circumstances, but the very oxymoronic idea of sustained change, a concept that Randall Jarrell may have welcomed in his poem "Hope": "You wake up, some fine morning, old. / And old means changed; changed means you wake up new."

VOTING AT HIS OLD ELEMENTARY

Under the fifth-grade autumn mobiles
(stringers of leaves that spiral in the heat)
parents are crouched behind knee-high tables
of cupcakes, cakes, and cookies—a class learning
free enterprise and how to make change.

MICHAEL J. ROSEN ✳ 151

Whether or not he likes oatmeal or icing,
Penn leaves a dollar trying to say *NO*,
to say what more can he do than pull the lever
*YES* for children and *YES* for schools, quelling
the question, *Why isn't it simple like that?*

Behind the queue of voters, an elephant-
sized turkey papers the wall, feathered
with everything we should be thankful for:
*ENOUGH TO EAT, OUR COUSINS, RECESS*, the names
of family, superheroes, friends.

The woman ahead of Penn owns the five-and-dime
where the children buy supplies. By the register,
she has posted a tablet for Prayer Requests—
its pencil dangling by a thread of hope.
She intercedes on her customers' behalf:

*MY RABBIT IS SICK. BRING FATHER HOME. MORE HEAT.*
A bolder ink is afflicted with a word
it cannot spell: *LUCKEMEA. HEAL*
*BLACK LUNG. NO MISSILES. FIND A JOB AND JESUS.*
The fifty years since Penn stood within

the stenciled circles, behind a free-throw line,
convince him that much of what he understands
is nothing like the *Preamble* (still memorized),
nothing like the way a noun and verb agree.
There are equivalents of disbelief

to challenge even incontrovertible
beliefs: *How can anyone vote other than . . . ?*
The woman leaves the booth, her prayers
turned, perhaps, to votes. The curtains close,
cupping Penn's hands over his eyes.

What can he wish or wish away? Regardless
of who wins or what passes, the season

in the hall will change: A flurry of doilies,
glittered and just as tangled. The kindergarten
scurries past Penn's voting booth, pretending

to be (and quiet as) a caterpillar.

In 1989, thirty years after I was enrolled in kindergarten at the elementary school of this poem, I returned to visit as an artist-in-the-school, a new children's book author. My kindergarten teacher, a woman I adored all through elementary school, formally introduced me to the assembly. She had taught my brother, and then my sister. My mother, running into her at the store, had kept her apprised of my whereabouts. I had been a student in her first class—she had been, presumably, twenty-two at the time. Now, for present purposes, we were peers, addressing her thirtieth class along with the rest of the school seated Indian-style on the multipurpose room floor. I stood there, thirteen years older than she was when she first began teaching; she stood beside me, probably sixteen years older than me. The children from this neighborhood where I had been a child could have included my children; they could have included my kindergarten teacher's grandchildren.

All through my presentation, I could recall how fidgety I would feel on the cold, crummy, tile floor. I could hear the principal's pre-assembly speech over the intercom reviewing the appropriate behavior we were to show our guest. I could remember the assembly day's wrenching expectation, the giddiness of spotting the presenter in the parking lot or hallway before or after the assembly, the klutzy single-file marching past the drinking fountain, and, after it was over, resettling into our regular chairs in our darkened room—*click*, the teacher, last in line, switching on the fluorescent lights—to resume the day's compromised schedule.

This school in my township is certainly another *Argo*, a vessel of sustained change: the hold of five-year-olds replacing itself each autumn in my kindergarten teacher's room; and, for one day, anyway, a new children's book author taking a provisional place as special guest in the timeless history of replaceable parts.

I buy presents for my new nephew at the same Kiddie Korner where I helped select my own childhood presents with my parents.

Now the children who attended the day camp I directed on the grounds of the community center join me at the health club, discussing stock options in a language as farfetched to me as campfire ballads. My parents' peers, who were my dentist, insurance agent, and lawyer, have retired, and my school chums usurp their places in the township *Argo*.

A few years ago, I wrote a novel about a boy at twelve, setting the story in a reappropriation of this township. That time, I misnamed it Centerburg. I drew on anything that would invigorate the circumstances of the story. I incorporated actual details when they seemed too good to be true, and fictionalized details when it seemed additional facts from the elsewheres of another time or compatible place would serve better. Admittedly, the distinctions between actual and fictional weren't always clear. In the reverie of writing, I hardly knew which of the maps my memory had cribbed from experience I was consulting.

The child in that book is, likewise, more my collective childhood than myself, drawn not simply from one individual's story but from selecting among all the stories that one individual encountered, overheard, remembered. It was only after I had completed the novel that I realized instead of rearing a child of twelve, as my parents had done in their early thirties, I was writing the story of rearing one. Composing dialogue, I would alternately imagine what a version of myself at twelve would be saying, and then what I, as a parent at thirty-two, would reply. Child and adult, myself and my parents, I created one behavior from the untrustworthy perspective of memory, and the other from the equally fraught perspective of imagination.

*

Each element of this township acquires a new identity as I discover a current use for it, just as, at sixteen, learning to drive, familiar routes acquired street names and north-south orientation—a curious self-sufficiency distinct from the disinterested oblivion of the passenger. When I purchased a house, the township rezoned itself into property values and investments; the very word "location" underwent apotheosis. When I acquired my dogs and began covering the neighborhood on foot, the houses revealed their canine characters. When I started gardening, the township metamorphosed into flourishing or neglected specimens of local flora. In this same fashion, perhaps before I began writing, my untrained, unretentive mind didn't select material from the local white noise.

When I reviewed the work completed in the last fifteen years, I was surprised to find that, save a few pieces of reviewing or criticism, place and replacement are penned (the second text, the second language) in a disappearing ink between the other disquisitions. To read this, I simply hold the pages up to the candlelight of self-consciousness.

Most of the time, the message is illegible. However, sometimes it can be decoded. There is a granary not far from my house, erected on the site of Norwoods Amusement Park, a small assembly of rides and booths where my family spent many Sundays in the early sixties. Once again, I delegated the harder thinking to Gordon Penn.

*from* CATCHING HIMSELF AWARE

It is difficult for Penn to imagine
enough seed to fill the granary's hold;
impossible to fit within that city block
the whole amusement park which it succeeded.
When he looks at the flat-white hull, he thinks
less of how each Sunday looped into the next,
a figure-eight turning into infinity,
than of the years he drove past, repeating

to whomever—himself—the fragment he has remembered:
wooden speedboats that clopped inside a sky-
blue moat with chips of another summer's
deeper blue, his cargo of children bobbing
past. Penn could no more foresee than they
what might stand in the places of childhood,
miniaturized or outsized like the granary,
emptied of even what he knows they hold.

Perhaps every element in this place is as empty and full, visible and invisible, as the hold of this granary. Perhaps this township

*Argo* is a phantom ship, like the *Flying Dutchman*, known only by unreliable citings and unverified reports. Floating in a limbo of recollection less corporeal than the treasures of my parents' basement, the township is being still replaced, memory by memory, while it remains, as a whole, irreplaceable.

# AFTER THE FLOOD

A river poured through the landscape I knew as a child. It was the power of the place, gathering rain and snowmelt, surging through the valley under sun, under ice, under the bellies of fish and the curled brown boats of sycamore leaves. You will need a good map of Ohio to find the river I am talking about, the West Branch of the Mahoning. The stretch of it that I knew like my own body no longer shows on maps, a stretch that ran between wooded slopes and along the flanks of cornfields and pastures in the township of Charlestown, in Portage County, a rural enclave surrounded by the smokestacks and concrete of Akron, Youngstown, and Cleveland in the northeastern corner of the state.

Along that river bottom I gathered blackberries and hickory nuts, trapped muskrats, rode horses, followed baying hounds on the scent of raccoons. Spring and fall, I walked barefoot over the tilled fields, alert for arrowheads. Along those slopes I helped a family of Swedish farmers collect sap buckets for maple syrup. On the river itself I skated in winter and paddled in summer, I pawed through gravel bars in search of fossils, I watched birds preen and pounce, I courted and canoed and idled. This remains for me a primal landscape, imprinted on my senses, a place by which I measure every other place.

It is also, now, a drowned landscape. In the early 1960s, when I was in high school, politicians and bankers and realtors ordained that the Mahoning should be snared. A dam was built, the river died, and water backed up over most of the land I knew. No city needed the water for drinking. The reservoir, named after a man who had never lived in that valley, provided owners of loud boats with another playground for racing and waterskiing, and provided me with a lesson in loss. If the loss were mine alone, the story would not be worth telling. My grieving for a drowned landscape is private, a small ache in a bruised world. But the building of the dam, the obliteration of that valley, the displacement of people and beasts, these were public acts, the sort of acts we have been repeating from coast to coast as we devour the continent.

Like many townships in farm country, remote from the offices where the fate of land is decided, Charlestown has suffered more than one erasure. Long before the building of the reservoir, the government had already sliced away the northern third of the township for a munitions plant. On current maps of the township, that upper third is blank white, and most of the remaining two-thirds, flooded by the reservoir, is empty blue. Merely by looking at the map, one can tell that here is a sacrificial zone.

*

Returning to one's home ground, always tricky, becomes downright treacherous when the ground is at the bottom of a lake. Unwilling to dive through so much water, I can return to that drowned landscape, as I can return to childhood, only by diving through memory.

I had just become a teenager when the government began purchasing the farms and trailers and shacks that would be in the path of the reservoir. (If there had been mansions and factories in the way, the politicians would have doomed a different valley.) Among the first to be unhoused was the Swedish family, old Mr. Sivvy and his three unmarried children, who had farmed that bottomland with big-shouldered horses, whose silage I had pitchforked in the steaming silo, whose cows I had fed, whose maple syrup I had drunk hot from the vat. Uprooted, the old man soon died. The children bought a new farm on high ground, trying to start over, but it was no good, the soil too thin, worn out, no black bottomland, no fat maples, no river pouring through it. Oh, they had been paid a market price for the old farm. But what good was money? A stack of dollars reaching halfway to the moon would not make up for the land they had lost. All down the valley it was the same, people forced to move by a blizzard of government paper, occasionally by the sheriff, in a few instances by the arrival of bulldozers at their front door.

While gangs of men with dynamite and dump trucks tore down the condemned buildings, other gangs with earthmovers and cement mixers slowly raised a wall across the river. For a year I watched it rise, while I wooed a girl who lived on a ridge overlooking the dam site. The crooner of the moment purred love songs from the stereo in her parlor, against an accompaniment of chuffs and shouts and whistles from the valley below. I studied the contours of that girl's face while the river's contours were bullied into the shape of blueprints. The huge concrete forms, the tinkertoy scaffolds, the blasting, the snort of compressors, the lurch of heavy machines are confused in me now with the memory of damp hands and quick kisses. The girl and I broke up, but the concrete held. Thereafter, I avoided that ridge, and did not see the laying of the dam's final tier, did not see the steel gates close. By the time I graduated from high school, water was beginning to lap over the banks of the Mahoning, but I could not bear to go down to the river and look.

When I left Ohio for college, my family left as well, trailing my father's work to Louisiana. My childhood friends scattered—to war, to jail, to distant marriages and jobs, to cities where lights glittered and dollars sang. I had scant reason to visit that flooded township, and good reason to keep my distance. Why rush to see a muddy expanse of annihilating water?

✳

A few years later, however, duties carried me through the northeastern corner of Ohio, within an hour's drive of my home ground. I had not planned to make a detour. Yet the names of towns emblazoned on huge green signs along the highway tugged at me. The shapes of chimneys and roofs, the colors of barns, the accents in fast-food booths and gas stations, all drew me off the interstate onto the roads of Portage County, up the stream of recollection toward that childhood place.

The season of my return was late winter, after the last snow but before wheat and corn began to sprout, before grass resumed its green sizzle, before trees blurred with leaves. The shape of the land lay exposed. It was a gray day, a day to immunize one against nostalgia, a day safe, I supposed, for facing up to what I had lost. Surely I was prepared by now to see the great erasure. I was a man, and had put behind me a boy's affection for a stretch of river and a patch of dirt. New places had claimed me, thereby loosening the grip of that old landscape. Still, to ease my way back, before going to the reservoir I drove through the county seat, Ravenna, which had scarcely changed, and then through Edinburgh, Atwater, Deerfield, Palmyra, Paris, Wayland, tiny crossroad settlements where I had played baseball and eaten pie and danced, and these, too, had scarcely changed. Circling, I drew closer and closer to the blue splotch on the map.

The best way to approach the water, I decided, was along the road where, for half our years in Charlestown, my family had lived on five acres with horses and rabbits and dogs. Our gray-shingled house, at least, would still be there, safe on its ridge above the lake, even if most of the land I had known was drowned. So I turned from the highway onto that curving, cracked, tar-slick road, looking for the familiar. But at the corner, where there should have been a farmhouse, a silo, a barn, there was only a billboard marking the entrance to the West Branch Reservation. The fields where I had baled hay now bristled with a young woods. There was no house in the hollow where the road dipped down, where the family of Seventh Day Adventists used to live with their stacks of apocalyptic pamphlets and their sad-eyed children. The spinster's white bungalow was gone, along with the battered bus in the side yard that had served her for a chicken coop. Yard after yard had grown up in brush, and the shade trees spread darkness over their own seedlings. No mailboxes leaned on their posts beside the road, no driveways broke the fringe of weeds. The trailer park was gone, the haunted house was gone, the tar-paper shanty where the drunk mechanic beat his wife and the wife beat her kids and the kids wailed, that was gone, and so was every last trailer and cottage and privy and shack, all down the blacktopped mile to our place.

I recognized our place by the two weeping willows out front. My father and I had planted those willows from slips; we had fenced them round to protect the tender bark from deer; we had watered and weeded and nursed them along. By the day of my visit those twigs had burgeoned into yellow fountains some fifty feet high, brimming over the woods that used to be our cleared land, woods that flourished where our house and barn had stood. I did not get out of the car. I could see from the road all that I was ready to see. The dense thicket, bare of leaves, was the color of rusty iron. Aside from the willows, no hint of our work or ownership survived. I

felt a fool. During the years of my absence, while my mind had suffered the waters to rise through the forest, up the ravines, onto the
margins of our land, I had preserved the gray-shingled house, the
low white barn, the lilacs and forsythia, the orchard and pasture,
the garden, the lawn. And yet, all the while, brambles and sumac
and cedar had been pushing up through my past like the earth's
dark fur.

Sight of the reservoir, surely, could not be worse. I continued
down the road through the vigorous woods. Not a house, not a
barn, not a plowed field. The first clearing I came to was half a mile
farther on, at the spot where a man named Ferry had lived. He used
to let the neighborhood kids swim in his pond, even after a boastful
boy dived into a rock and drowned. We knew that when we knocked
at Mr. Ferry's door, raising money for school or scouts, he would
buy whatever we had to sell. He was a tender man. He loved his
wife so much that when she died he planted a thousand white pines
in her memory. The pines, spindly in my recollection, had grown
into a forest by the day of my return. In place of Mr. Ferry's house
and yard there was a state campground now, encircled by the spiky
green palisade of pines. The entrance booth was boarded up. A
placard outside instructed campers to deposit their fees—so much
for trailers, so much for tents—in the box below. There was no box
below, only a slab of plywood with holes where the screws had
been torn loose. Nor were there any campers on this wintry afternoon. As I drove through the vacant lot, the only sounds were the
crunch of gravel beneath my tires and the yawp of bluejays overhead and the shoosh of wind through the pines.

I pulled away from the campground and drove on. My mind
raced ahead along the road as I remembered it, steeply downhill
between fat maples and patchy sycamores to the river and the steel-
girdered bridge. I had rolled down that hill in a school bus, jogged
down on horseback, hurtled down on bicycle and sled, run down
on foot. The slope and feel of it were fixed inside me, the standard
for all hills. From the bridge I had watched the river's current rav-
eling over sandbars, minnows flickering in the shallows, water
striders dimpling the surface. Now and again, when the sun was
right, I had spied my own face peering up from the stream. In
memory, the road stretched on beyond the bridge, passing the tin-
roofed shed where the maple syrup boiled, passing the Sivvy farm,

rising up the far slope to a T-junction with a ridgeline road. Turn left from there, and I would go to the high school. Turn right, and I would go to the barbershop and feedstore. As my thoughts raced ahead of the car, inside me the valley opened and the river flexed its long sleek muscle.

Rounding the curve, however, I had to slam on the brakes to avoid running into a guardrail that blocked the road. Beyond the railing, where valley and bridge and river should have been, flat gray water spread out as far as eye could see. You know this moment from dreams: you are in a familiar room, but when you turn to leave, where a door should be there is a wall; or you come up behind someone you love, speak her name, yet when she turns around her face is blank; or you behold the story of the universe written on a page, but when you draw close to read it, the letters dissolve. Waters of separation, waters of oblivion, waters of death.

I got out of the car and pressed my thighs against the cold steel barricade and stared. Gray, flat, empty lake. Not even a boat to redeem the emptiness. A lone crow slowly pumped toward the horizon on glossy black wings. Along the shore, a few sycamores still thrust up their pale, sensuous limbs. Except for those trees, the pavement beneath my boots, and hills too high for water to claim, everything I knew had been swept away.

My worst imaginings had failed to prepare me for this. I stood there dazed. I could not take it in, so much had been taken away. For an hour or more I leaned against the guardrail and dredged up everything I could remember of what lay beneath the reservoir. But memory was at last defeated by the blank gray water. No effort of mind could restore the river or drain the valley. Only then was I truly uprooted.

Those who built the dam had their reasons. You have heard the litany: flood control, recreation, development. I very much doubt that more human good has come from that muddy, silting, rarely frequented lake than came from the cultivated valley and wild woods and free-flowing river. I am suspicious of the logic that would forestall occasional floods by creating a permanent one. But I do not wish to debate the merits of dams. I mean only to speak of how casually, how relentlessly we sever the bonds between person and place.

One's home ground is the place where, since before you had words for such knowledge, you have known the smells, the seasons, the birds and beasts, the human voices, the houses, the ways of working, the lay of the land, and the quality of light. It is the landscape you learn before you retreat inside the illusion of your skin. You may love the place if you flourished there, or hate the place if you suffered there. But love it or hate it, you cannot shake free. Even if you move to the antipodes, even if you become intimate with new landscapes, you still bear the impression of that first ground.

Of course, in mourning the drowned Mahoning valley I also mourn my drowned childhood. The dry land preserved the traces of my comings and goings, the river carried the reflection of my beardless face. Yet even as a boy I knew that landscape was incomparably older than I, and richer, and finer. Some of the trees along the Mahoning had been rooted there when the first white settlers arrived from New England. Hawks had been hunting and deer had been drinking there since before our kind harnessed oxen. The gravels, laden with fossils, had been shoved there ten thousand years ago by glaciers. The river itself was the offspring of glaciers, a channel for meltwater to follow toward the Ohio, and thence to the Mississippi and the Gulf of Mexico. What I knew of the land's own history made me see that expanse of water as a wound.

Loyalty to place arises from sources deeper than narcissism. It arises from our need to be at home on the earth. We marry ourselves to the creation by knowing and cherishing a particular place, just as we join ourselves to the human family by marrying a particular man or woman. If the marriage is deep, divorce is painful. My drive down that unpeopled road and my desolate watch beside the reservoir gave me a hint of what others must feel when they are wrenched from their place. I say a *hint*, because my loss is mild compared to what others have lost.

I think of the farmers who saw their wood lots and fields go under the gray flood. I think of the Miami and Shawnee who spoke of belonging to that land as a child belongs to a mother, and who were driven out by white soldiers. I think of the hundred other tribes that were herded onto reservations far from the graves of their ancestors. I think of the Africans who were yanked from their homes and bound in chains and shipped to this New World. I think about refugees, set in motion by hunger or tyranny or war. I think about children pushed onto the streets by cruelty or indifference. I think about migrant workers, dust bowl emigrés, all the homeless wanderers. I think about the poor everywhere—and it is overwhelmingly the poor—whose land is gobbled by strip mines, whose neighborhoods are wiped out for highways and shopping malls, whose villages are destroyed by bombs, whose forests are despoiled by chain saws and executive fountain pens.

The word "nostalgia" was coined in 1688 as a medical term, to provide an equivalent for the German word meaning homesickness. We commonly treat homesickness as an ailment of childhood, like mumps or chicken pox, and we treat nostalgia as an affliction of age. On our lips, nostalgia usually means a sentimental regard for the trinkets and fashions of an earlier time, for an idealized past, for a vanished youth. We speak of a nostalgia for the movies of the 1930s, say, or the haircuts of the 1950s. It is a shallow use of the word. The Greek roots of nostalgia literally mean *return home pain*. The pain comes not from returning home but from longing to return. Perhaps it is inevitable that a nation of immigrants—immigrants who violently displaced the native tribes of this continent, who enslaved and transported the people of Africa, who celebrate mobility as if humans were tumbleweed—that such a nation should lose the deeper meaning of this word. A footloose people, we find it difficult to honor the lifelong, bone-deep attachment to place. We are slow to acknowledge the pain in yearning for one's home ground, the deep anguish in not being able, ever, to return.

On a warmer day I might have taken off my clothes and stepped over the guardrail and waded on down that road under the lake. Where the water was too deep, I could have continued in a boat, letting down a line to plumb the bottom. I would not be angling for death, which is far too easy to catch, but for life. To touch the ground even through a length of rope would be some consolation. The day was cold, however, and I was far from anyone who knew my face. So I climbed back into the car and turned away and drove back through the resurgent woods.

# WEST OF EDEN

Nailed shut, covered with dust and dangling cobwebs, the fruit room window was near the ceiling and difficult to open. Yet my brother, Jim, and I balanced ourselves on the middle shelf and pried open the glass, our Keds toeing between Mason jars filled with sugared peach halves and the floating innards of stewed tomatoes. Hammer and screwdriver in hand, a flashlight clipped to Jim's belt, we worked in sync, anticipating each other's movements, one pulling, the other pounding, until we'd propped the window securely with a stick, hoisted ourselves to the top shelf, and wiggled through the narrow opening between the joists. Jim clicked on the flashlight, and then we were inching along on all fours, our five-and seven-year-old bodies just able to squeeze into this crawl space in the underbelly of our old Manning, Iowa, Victorian childhood home. As we scooted along, we scanned, sweeping our hands in front of us, searching for any treasure we could find, hoping to return to the fruit room with the prize of a tarnished brass doorknob, a mildew-eaten book, or even one of my doctor grandfather's old medical instruments. But that day in the cellar, we found something different. That day our hands wound around a couple of old brown bottles of bootleg whiskey.

By then, Jim and I had probed most of the internal organs of the old "Dutton Place." The two-storied, two-sleeping-porched house equipped with a widow's walk, gingerbread railings, bay windows, stained glass, and an oak hand-carved staircase imported from France was built by Dutton, the town banker, before the turn of the century, only to be abandoned and stand empty through years of vandalism until my grandparents bought it for one thousand dollars in the Depression. By the fifties, my grandfather had died, and the stairway had been carpeted, but the house still held a majesty and the mystery of nooks and crannies that children love to explore.

Jim and I scraped our way back along the dirt floor, the whiskey jiggling and jostling, the corks dried and flaking in our palms as we gripped the bottles around the neck. Upstairs, our faces and clothes smudged with dirt, we held up our bounty to the adults.

"Well, what do you scalawags have now?" my grandmother asked.

"Wait, let me see those bottles." My mother swiped them out of our hands and brought them to the light.

My father was already clicking glasses out of the cabinet.

"It looks like—"

"Is it?"

"Sure, it is. Templeton rye."

The Carroll County towns of Manning and Templeton are only seven miles apart, both German settlements named after British railroad men, both fewer than fifteen hundred people, both listing the same surnames in the phone book: Kasperbauer, Kuhl, Lampe. But Manning, in Ewoldt Township, remains obscure in the world, except perhaps for the fact that it once won the Iowa state boys' basketball championship, while Templeton, in Eden Township, with its famous Templeton Rye brew, knew national fame.

Templeton began bootlegging whiskey in 1920 soon after Prohibition took effect. The activity immediately sparked the economy of a town, which like the rest of the nation, was on the rebound from World War I. At first, the whiskey was made from corn, but soon the "operators" turned to rye and the famous recipe was perfected. Great care was taken with each step of the process to turn out a fine product. Blacksmiths skillfully welded four-by-eight-feet copper sheets into stills, soldering them on the outside to prevent lead poisoning. Only the best ingredients were used, with hundred-pound bags of sugar arriving daily at the train depot. Templetonians are still quick to point out that what made their product legendary was not so much its illegality, but its high quality and good taste.

"If I am allowed an ethnic comment," wrote Lam Schwaller in the 1981 Templeton centennial book, "I would say that it [Templeton rye] reflected the inherent qualities of the German people, that is, clean, neat and efficient, and the industry and inventiveness to accomplish it."

At the peak of production in 1931, a single one of those German brewers sold around one hundred gallons a day, and depending on whether the sale was in or out of town, wholesale or retail, prices ranged from five to ten dollars a jug. Cases of empty bottles, corks, casks, and barrels were deposited on the depot platform each day, and as many as three truckloads of kegs left Templeton each week, heading for speakeasies in Des Moines, Omaha, Denver, St. Louis, Chicago, and New York. Al Capone was known to have been "a paying customer," and during a severe drought when the municipal water supplies were turned off at night, the Templeton mayor opened the faucet at midnight so the distillers could start another batch of mash.

The odor of fermenting rye drifted up and down Main Street, through town and into the countryside. When the federal agents arrived to bust the bootleggers, they had only to follow their noses and look for basement windows covered with burlap to conceal the light at night and what went on within. But instead, an elaborate game began with guards and alarm signals and men fleeing into the cornfields, the agents giving chase and even firing a few shots from time to time. Sales forces involved at least a dozen people, with money exchanged at every turn, no one link of the chain knowing more than his or her own particular customer and supplier. No one ever claimed knowing the names of the operators, but the schoolchildren recognized who brought gum or candy in their lunches, or could afford new shoes over stuffing their old ones with cardboard to keep out the snow. Eventually, the agents and operators got to know each other and despite a few prison terms, no bust lasted long. As soon as possible, the bootleggers went back to business. In December of 1931 Templeton's Christmas decorations stretched over Main Street, and amid the evergreen garlands, a replica of a little brown jug of rye swung back and forth in the winter winds emblazoned with the words "Xmas Spirits." Yes, there was a Santa Claus in Templeton until around 1936 when the repeal of the Eighteenth Amendment and the hold of the Depression pushed the bootlegging business into decline. By 1940, if you asked for whiskey in Templeton, they referred you to the state liquor store in Manning.

Not that Manning was ever a dry town. At the turn of the century Manning sported "the longest bar in the world" that seated nearly a hundred customers. A portion of that same bar now serves as the front counter of the Corner Cafe where seed-capped lunchers slurp homemade turkey soup every noon. My grandmother's ledgers show that in 1933 our own family farm, just outside Manning on the edge of Eden Township, suffered the damage of a major fire. We lost the house and all the outbuildings when a still exploded in the barn. A letter in her files includes a liquor permit issued to my grandfather that same year, allowing him to legally make a batch of beer in the bathtub for "medicinal purposes" for his practice.

Manning didn't lack the thirst for booze, or the spirit of inventiveness. It just lacked that extra twist, that fateful bit of flair that radiated from Eden. We were the fallen ones, always a little behind, a little off-kilter. We had an industry, too. But ours never made the *Des Moines Register* or took orders from Al Capone. Our industry was in the open, right there on Main Street for everyone to see in a white, low-slung building. Ours, too, could easily be located by smell, but it didn't lure in outsiders or anything as extraordinary as a federal agent. The only time the feds came to Manning was when an octogenarian went senile up in an attic garret on Third Street. The old coot sequestered himself away during World War II, attempting to tap Morse code messages to the Nazis. The town, super patriotic and stoical enough to send their sons off to kill and be killed by their cousins, took care of the Third Street spy real fast. No, our industry was the blood-drying factory, our export at the depot, glue.

Oh, the days of the dryings are imprinted on my olfactory.

"'Bout ruins a person's appetite." My grandmother set down her fork at the dinner table, pushed away her chair, and put her teeth back in the cup.

"Darn it," my mother said, hurrying outside to gather in the wash from the line before our bedsheets took on the odor of chicken hemoglobin.

The stench stuck to your clothes, your hair. It pressured your brain like a bad earache. But no one made a public stink about the stink. Instead, we quietly accepted its economic benefits and rushed to close the windows and doors, even in the middle of the ninety-degree airconditionerless days of summer. We tried to find out the schedule from the neighbor kid who plucked feathers for the factory, and avoid downtown on firing days, or better yet, drive the twenty miles to Carroll, the county seat, for a morning of grocery shopping and an afternoon of visiting relatives.

Carroll. You had to drive east, through Eden, to get there. You had to go there to be born in St. Anthony's hospital, and you usually ended up dying there, too. You had to go to Carroll for a marriage or driver's license, to buy new plates, swim in a pool, go out to the movies on a date. When you had a family reunion, you sent your overflow of company there to the motel, and on Sundays, when everyone was dressed up from church anyway, you might end up eating there at the Brown Derby and ordering something like frog legs.

East of Eden meant officialdom, adventure, sophistication. East of Eden meant Des Moines, the biggest city in the state, the State Fair. Even Khrushchev's visit, Iowa's biggest midcentury international story, took place east of Eden in Coon Rapids. East of Eden meant the three state universities, all in the eastern part of Iowa, which received more rainfall and harbored more trees. The three state universities meant libraries, music, theater, athletic teams, good shoe stores. East of Eden meant graduating from school and going farther east for a job in Chicago.

The map of Iowa mimics that of the United States in miniature, even down to the detail of the Florida peninsula that we know as Keokuk. The geography of Iowa, with its two major rivers, the Mississippi and the Missouri, forming the eastern and western boundaries of the state, imitates the layout of the nation with the Atlantic and Pacific oceans. So, the two Iowa "coasts" are hillier, classically "prettier," with the flatter land, the Midwest, in the center section of the state. High limestone cliffs jut out from the banks of the Mississippi on the eastern border, while the sandy loam of the Loess Hills billows up and deposits itself along the Missouri.

Like the U.S., the eastern part of Iowa is thought to be more suave, more oriented toward business with its manufacturing centers in Waterloo, Cedar Rapids, and the Quad Cities, and more full of money. The western part of Iowa, like its counterpoint, is wilder, more independent in nature, more politically conservative. Western Iowa is really the beginning of the western United States. Just over those Loess Hills, out of the Missouri River valley, irrigation begins, corn gives way to wheat and grazing land. In western Iowa, you begin to see cowboy hats and boots, large belt buckles with names like DIRK stamped into the metal.

Linguistics divide the state in half north and south, claiming a Great Divide of Dialect runs on either side of Highway 20. Iowans north of the highway are generally said to have a northern dialect, while southern Iowans speak in one that is known as North Midland. Northern Iowans are supposed to favor the more genteel "chipmunk," the more elegant "faucet," the rounder voweled "toe-may-toe," while southern Iowans settle for the "ground squirrel," "spicket," and "toe-may-tuh." Yet, my own quite unscientific sampling suggests that the real dialectical divide falls into an east-west split. "Have you tried Edith's 'po-tay-toes' au gratin?" you may hear at an eastern Iowa church potluck, while western Iowans help themselves to more "po-tay-tuh" salad, or more often just grab a handful of "'tater sheps."

You say po-tay-toe, and I say po-tah-toe. Toe-may toe, toe-mah-toe. Manning, Templeton. Glue, booze. Eventually, my parents moved us to eastern Iowa where we lived in a new modern house with sleek lines and not one crawl space. In Davenport, I learned to sit down on the playground and throw a little rubber ball into the air while I picked up tiny sharply pointed pieces of steel. In Manning, jacks were almost unknown in a town where on Saturdays girls and boys alike ran errands downtown for their parents while dribbling basketballs. In Davenport, I learned to sit down at the piano bench and plunk out Chopin in the morning, and stand up and curtsey to my French teacher in the afternoon.

"Dumkopf!" we yelled in Manning when on Sundays a car drove the wrong way down the one-way. Manning had only two streets, Second and Third, that were one-ways—and only on Sundays when the Lutheran and Methodist churches let out their congregations.

"Zut, alors!" I exclaimed in Davenport in my teenage years when we rode the one-ways in search of new boyfriends, new parties to attend, and sampled the sinfulness of slow dancing and alcohol.

I grew up to go to college in Washington, D.C., then traveled in Europe where I learned to distinguish dozens of kinds of wines, the delicacy of a good Brie or Camembert. Now, home again, I've lived most of my adult life one place or another in eastern Iowa, but there's something about a wine bottle that isn't a whiskey bottle.

my teens and early twenties, I sought to cultivate the eastern side of myself, valuing all things urban, and exotic. Not until my mid-twenties did I come to appreciate the earthier western side.

Just before I turned twenty-six, my parents divorced, my grandmother and mother dead, my brothers living in California, I returned to Manning for a summer to clean out the old Dutton Place and cull through the family relics. I was about to move to Chicago for that first real job, but before I did, I had to take that gravel road west one more time. In the fruit room, I packed up a box of antique Mason jars with glass seams down their sides that dated them from before the Civil War. In the attic, I found a whole box full of crucifixes that had been on a whole cemetery full of relatives' boxes. In the piano bench, I found not only my Chopin music I'd brought back from Davenport to play one summer visit to my grandmother, but stacks of sheet music from earlier eras with even one title, "Anything You Can Do," autographed by Irving Berlin.

But the special day came one morning when I opened the pantry just off the kitchen and found a lone bottle of whiskey and a shot glass, my grandmother's nightly sedative.

"They tell me they're at it again," a Manning neighbor had reported that summer. "Up in Templeton. Imagine. Now there was a good-tasting whiskey."

"Can I get ahold of a bottle?"

"Well, you have to know the right person to ask, see? Then you pay that guy, and he pays another, and another, right on down the line."

I wiped away the lines of cobwebs from the bottle I had in my hand. Why not? I thought, and squatted down on the staircase landing. The whiskey burned down my throat. Tears eked out of my eyes as I surveyed the empty house, stripped now of furniture and draperies, and toasted myself in the floor-length mirror next to the door. From then on, I knew that wherever I lived, in Iowa, the Midwest, the rest of the United States, or the world, no matter what jobs I had, friends I made, roles I played, I would remain forever just west of Eden.

# DERIVATIVE SPORT

# IN TORNADO ALLEY

When I left my boxed township of Illinois farmland to attend my dad's alma mater in the lurid jutting Berkshires of western Massachusetts, I right away developed a jones for mathematics. I'm starting to see why this was so. College math evokes and catharts a Midwesterner's sickness for home. I'd grown up inside vectors, lines and lines athwart lines, grids—and, on the scale of horizons, broad curving lines of geographic force, the weird topographical drain swirl of a whole lot of ice-ironed flatland that sits and spins atop plates. The area behind and below these broad curves at the seam of land and sky I could plot by eye way before I came to know infinitesimals as easements, an integral as schema. Math at a hilly Eastern school was like waking up; it dismantled memory and put it in light. Calculus was, quite literally, child's play.

In late childhood I learned how to play tennis on the blacktop courts of a small public park carved from farmland that had been nitrogenized too often to farm anymore. This was in my home of Philo, IL, a tiny collection of corn silos and war-era Levittown homes whose native residents did little but sell crop insurance and nitrogen fertilizer and herbicide and collect property taxes from the young academics at nearby Champaign-Urbana's university, whose ranks swelled enough in the flush late 1960s to make outlying non sequiturs like "farm and bedroom community" lucid.

From the ages of twelve to sixteen I was a near-great junior tennis player. I made my competitive bones beating up on lawyers' and dentists' kids at little Champaign and Urbana Country Club ever and was soon killing whole summers being driven through dawns to tournaments all over IL, IN, IA. At fourteen I was ranked seventeenth in the United States Tennis Association's Western Region ("Western" being the creakily ancient USTA's designation for the Midwest; farther west were the Southwest, Mid-Coast, and Pacific Coast regions), fourth in the state of Illinois, and 90th–100th alphabetically in the nation, having flown at regional association expense to Kalamazoo, MI, in 1976 to the U.S. National Junior Hardcourt Championships, where in the second round I got my rural ass handed to me by a California kid named Scott Davis who's now a marginal figure on the ATP pro tour.

My flirtation with tennis excellence had way more to do with the township where I learned and trained and with a weird proclivity for intuitive math than it did with athletic talent. I was, even by the standards of junior competition in which everybody's a tight bud of pure potential, a pretty untalented tennis player. My hand-eye was OK, but I was neither large nor quick, had a near-concave chest and wrists so thin I could bracelet them with a thumb and pinkie, and could hit a tennis ball no harder or truer than most girls in my age bracket. What I could do was, in the words of my township's juniors' coach, a thin guy who chewed Red Man and spat into a Folger's can and used to play indoor exhibitions with Gonzalez, Emerson, and Hoad, what I could do was "Play the Whole Court." This was a piece of tennis truistics that could mean any number of things. In my case, it meant I knew my limitations and the limitations of what I stood inside, and adjusted thusly. I was at my very best in bad conditions.

Now, conditions in central Illinois are from a mathematical perspective interesting and from a tennis point of view bad. The summer heat and wet-mitten humidity, the grotesquely fertile soil that sends grasses and broadleaves up through the courts' surface by main force, the midges that feed on sweat and the mosquitoes that spawn in the fields' furrows and in the conferva-chocked ditches that box each field, night tennis next to impossible because the moths and crapgnats drawn by the sodium lights form a little planet around each tall lamp and the whole lit court surface is aflutter with spastic little shadows.

But mostly wind. The biggest single factor in central Illinois' quality of outdoor life is the wind. There are more jokes than I can summon about bent weather vanes and leaning barns, more down-state sobriquets for kinds of wind than there are in Malamut for snow. The wind had a personality, a (poor) temper, and, apparently, agendas. The wind blew autumn leaves into intercalated lines and arcs of force so regular you could photograph them for a text-book on Cramer's Rule and the cross-products of curves in 3-space. It molded winter snow into blinding truncheons that buried stalled cars and required citizens to shovel out not only driveways but the sides of homes; a central Illinois "blizzard" starts only when the snowfall stops and the wind begins. People I knew in Philo didn't comb their hair because why bother. Ladies wore those plastic flags tied down over their parlorjobs so regularly I thought they were required for a real classy coiffure; girls on the East Coast outside with their hair hanging and tossing around looked so nude to me. Wind wind etc. etc. The people I know from outside it distill the Midwest into blank flatness, black land and fields of green fronds or five-o'clock stubble, gentle swells and declivities that make the to-pology a sadistic exercise in plotting quadrics, highway vistas so same and dead they drive motorists mad. Those from IN/WI/north-ern IL think of their Midwest as agronomics and commodity fu-tures and corn detasseling and bean walking and seed-company caps, apple-cheeked Nordic types, cider and slaughter and football games with white fogbanks of breath exiting helmets. In the odd central pocket that is Champaign-Urbana, Rantoul, Philo, Ma-homet-Seymour, Mattoon, and Tolono, the Midwestern life of all is informed and deformed by wind. Weatherwise, our township is on the eastern upcurrent of what I heard an atmospherist in brown tweed call a Thermal Anomaly. Something about southward rota-tions of crisp air off the Great Lakes and muggy southern stuff from Arkansas and Kentucky miscegenating, plus an odd dose of weird zephyrs from the Mississippi valley three hours west. Chicago calls itself the windy city. Chicago, one big windbreak, does not know from a true religious-type wind. And meteorologists have nothing to tell people in Philo, who know perfectly well that the real story is that to the west, between us and the Rockies, there is basically nothing tall, and that weird zephyrs and stirs joined breezes and gusts and thermals and downdrafts and whatever out over Ne-braska and Kansas and moved east like streams into rivers and jets and military fronts that gathered like avalanches and roared in reverse down pioneer oxtrails, toward our own personal unsheltered asses. The worst was spring, boys' high school tennis season, when the nets would stand out stiff as proud flags and an errant ball would blow clear to the easternmost fence, interrupting play on the next several courts. During a bad blow some of us would get rope out and tell Rob Lord, who was our fifth man in singles and spectrally thin, that we were going to have to tie him down to keep him from becoming a projectile. Falls, about half as bad as springs, were a low constant roar and the massive clicking sound of continents of dry leaves being arranged into force-curves—I'd heard no sound remotely like this megaclicking until I heard, at nineteen, on Fundy Bay, my first high-tide wave break and get sucked back out over a shore of polished pebbles. Summers were manic and gusty, then often around August deadly calm. The wind would just die, some days, in August, and it was no relief at all; the cessation drove us nuts. We realized afresh, each August, how much the sound of wind had become part of the soundtrack to life, in Philo. The sound of wind had become, for me, silence. When it went away, I was left with the squeak of the blood in my head and the aural glitter of all those little eardrum hairs quivering like a drunk in withdrawal. It was months after I moved to western MA before I could really sleep in the pussified whisper of New England's windsound.

To your average outsider, central Illinois looks ideal for sports. The ground, seen from the air, strongly suggests a board game: anally precise squares of dun or khaki cropland all cut and divided by plumb-straight tar roads (in all farmland, roads still seem more like impediments than avenues). In winter, the terrain always looks like Mannington bathroom tile, white quadrangles where bare (snow), black where trees or scrub has shaken free in the wind. From planes, it always looks to me like Monopoly or Life, or a lab maze for rats, running; then, from ground level, the arrayed fields of feed corn or soybeans, fields furrowed into lines as straight as only an Allis Chalmers and sextant can cut them, look laned like sprint tracks or Olympic pools, hashmarked for serious ball, replete with the angles and alleys of serious tennis. My part of the Midwest always looks laid down special, like planned.

The terrain's strengths are its weaknesses. Because the land seems so even, designers of clubs and parks rarely bother to roll it flat before laying the asphalt for tennis courts. The result is usually a slight list that only a player who spends a lot of time on the courts will notice. Because tennis courts are for sun- and eye-reasons always laid lengthwise north-south, and because the land in central Illinois rises very gently as one moves east toward Indiana and some mysterious subtle summit (a moraine? something tectonic?) that sends rivers doubled back against their own feeders somewhere in the east of that state, the court's forehand half, for a rightie facing north, always seems physically uphill from the backhand—at a tournament in Richmond, IN, just over the Ohio line, I noticed the tilt was reversed. The same soil that's so full of humus farmers have to be bought off to keep markets unflooded keeps clay courts chocked with jimson and thistle and volunteer corn, and it splits asphalt courts open with the upward pressure of broadleaves whose pioneer-stock seeds are unthwarted by a half-inch cover of sealant and stone. So that all but the very best maintained courts in the most affluent IL districts are their own little rural landscapes, with tufts and cracks and underground-seepage puddles being part of the lay that one plays. A court's cracks always seem to start off to the side of the service box and meander in and back toward the service line. Foliated in pockets, the black cracks, especially against the forest green that contrasts with the barn red of the space outside lines to signify fair territory, give the courts the eerie look of well-rivered sections of IL seen from back aloft.

A tennis court, 78′ × 27′, looks, from above, with its slender rectangles of doubles alleys flanking its whole length, like a cardboard carton with flaps folded back. The net, 3½-feet high at the posts, divides the court widthwise in half; the service lines divide each half again into backcourt and fore-. In the two forecourts, lines that run from the base of the net's center to the service lines divide them into 21′ × 13½′ service boxes. The sharply precise divisions and boundaries, together with the fact that—wind and your mo exotic-type spins aside—balls can be made to travel in straight lines only, make textbook tennis plane geometry. It is billiards with balls that won't hold still. It is chess on the run. It is to artillery and air strikes what football is to infantry and attrition.

Tennis-wise, I had two preternatural gifts to compensate for not much physical talent. Make that three. The first was that I always sweated so much that I stayed fairly ventilated in all ·weathers. Oversweating seems an ambivalent blessing, and it didn't exactly do wonders for my social life in high school, but it meant I could play for hours on a Turkish-bath July day and not flag a bit so long as I drank water and ate salty stuff between matches. I always looked like a drowned man by about game four, but I didn't cramp, vomit, or pass out, unlike the gleaming Peoria kids whose hair never even lost its part right up until their eyes rolled up in their heads and they pitched forward onto the shimmering concrete. A bigger asset still was that I was extremely comfortable inside straight lines. None of the odd geometric claustrophobia that turns some gifted juniors into skittish zoo animals after a while. But I found I felt best physically enwebbed in sharp angles, acute bisections, shaved corners. This was environmental. Philo, IL, is a cockeyed grid: nine north-south streets against six northeast-southwest, fifty-one gorgeous slanted-cruciform corners (the east and west intersection-angles' tangents could be evaluated integrally in terms of their secants!) around a three-intersection central town common with a tank whose nozzle pointed northwest at Urbana and a frozen native son, felled on the Salerno beachhead, whose bronze hand pointed true north. In the late morning, the Salerno guy's statue had a squat black shadow-arm against grass dense enough to putt on; in the evening the sun galvanized his left profile and cast his arm's accusing shadow out to the right, bent at the pedestal at the angle of a stick in a pond. At college it suddenly occurred to me during a quiz that the differential between the direction he pointed and the arc of his shadow's rotation was first-order. Anyway, most of my memories of childhood, whether of furrowed acreage, or a harvester's sentry duty along RR 104W, or the play of sharp shadows against the Legion Hall softball field's dusk, I could now reconstruct on demand with an edge and protractor.

I liked the sharp intercourse of straight lines more than the other 'ds I grew up with. I think this is because they were natives, I an infantile transplant from Ithaca where my dad had Ph.D.'d. So I'd known, even horizontally and semiconsciously as a baby, something different, the tall hills and serpentine one-ways of upstate NY. I'm pretty sure I kept the amorphous mush of curves and swells as a contrasting backlight somewhere down in the lizardy part of my brain, because the Philo children I fought and played with, kids who knew and had known nothing else, saw nothing stark or new-worldish in the township's planar layout, prized nothing crisp. (Except why do I think it significant that so many of them wound up in the military, performing smart right-faces in razor-creased dress blues?)

My first really detailed memory is all sharp edges. I was helping a neighbor kid help his mother till a new vegetable garden out of their backyard one April. The garden's outline was a perfect square, with five quincunx subareas, the center for hallowed zucchini, laid out in an H of popsicle sticks and twine. We little boys removed rocks and hard clods from the lady's path as she worked the Roto-tiller, a rented wheelbarrow-shaped gas-driven thing that roared and snorted and bucked and seemed to propel its mistress rather than vice versa, her feet leaving drunken prints in the earth, so that I remember remarking, knowing nothing about surveying or plumb markers, how strange it seemed that the garden's furrows were coming out straight and true as a washboard. In the middle of the tilling my friend's baby brother, maybe like four at the time and wearing some kind of fuzzy red Pooh-wear, came tear-assing out into the backyard crying, holding something really unpleasant-looking in his upturned palm. It turned out to have been a rhomboid patch of mold from some exotic corner of their damp basement. It was a sort of nasal green, black-speckled, vaguely hirsute. Worse, the patch of mold looked incomplete, gnawed on; some nauseous stuff was smeared around the little kid's mouth. "I ate this," he started crying as his mother shut down the tiller and came to him. My friend and I were grossed out as only kids can get grossed out by smaller kids' repulsive snafus. But the little kid's mother, who now that I think about it disappeared under vague medical circumstances a couple of years later, went utterly nuts:

"Help! My son ate this!" she was yelling, over and over, holding the speckled patch aloft, running around and around the garden's quadrants while my neighbor and I gaped at our first real adult hysteria, the sobbing little kid forgotten by all of us:

"Help! My son ate this! Help!" she kept yelling, running in tight complex little Leggo-shaped patterns just inside the H of string that marked the garden's quincunx; and I remember noting, and being alone in noting, how even in trauma her flight's lines were plumb, her footprints Native American—straight, her turns inside the ideogram of string crisp and martial. She ran and yelled and turned and yelled and ran. My friend's dad, who had a pipe sticking out of his face, had to go get the hose.

---

Unless you're just a mutant, a virtuoso of raw force, you'll find that competitive tennis, like money pool, requires geometric thinking, the ability to calculate not merely your own angles but the angles of response to your angles. Because the expansion of response possibilities is quadratic, you are required to think $n$ shots ahead, where $n$ is a hyperbolic function limited by the sinh of opponent's talent and the cosh of the number of shots in the rally so far (roughly). I was good at this. What made me for a while near-great was that I could also admit the differential complication of wind into my calculations; I could think and play octally. For the wind put the curves in the lines and transformed the game into 3-space. Wind did massive damage to many central Illinois junior players, particularly in the period April–July when it needed lithium badly, tending to gust without pattern, swirl and backtrack and die and rise, sometimes blowing in one direction at court level and in another altogether ten feet overhead. The precision in thinking required one to induct trends in percentage, thrust, and retaliatory angle—precision our guy and the other townships' volunteer coaches were good at abstracting about with chalk and board, attaching a pupil's leg to the fence with clothesline to restrict his arc of movement in practice, placing laundry baskets in different corners and making us sink ball after ball, taking masking tape and laying down Chinese boxes within the court's own boxes for drills and wind sprints—all this theoretical prep went out the window when sneakers hit actual court in a tournament. The best-planned, best-hit ball often just blew out of bounds, was the basic unlyrical problem. It drove some kids near-mad with the caprice and unfairness of it all, and on real windy days these kids, usually with talent out the bazoo, would have their first apoplectic racket-throwing tantrum in about the match's third game, and have lapsed into a kind of sullen coma by the end of the first set, bitterly *expecting* to get screwed over by wind, net, tape, sun. I, who was affectionately known as Slug because I was such a lazy turd in practice, located my biggest tennis asset in a weird robotic detachment from whatever unfairnesses of wind and weather I couldn't plan for. I couldn't begin to tell you how many tournament matches I won between the ages of twelve and fifteen against bigger, faster, more coordinated, and better-coached opponents simply by hitting balls unimaginatively back down the middle of the court in schizophrenic gales, letting the other kid play with more verve and panache, waiting for enough of his ambitious balls aimed near the lines to curve or slide via wind outside the green court and white stripe into the raw red territory that won me yet another ugly point. It wasn't pretty, or fun to watch, and even with the Illinois wind I never could have won whole matches this way had the opponent not eventually had his small nervous breakdown, buckling under the obvious injustice of losing to a shallow-chested "pusher" because of the shitty rural courts and rotten wind that rewarded cautious automatism instead of verve and panache. I was an unpopular player, with good reason. But to say that I did not use verve or imagination was untrue. Acceptance is its own verve, and it takes imagination for a player to like wind, and I liked wind; or rather I at least felt the wind had some basic right to be there, and found it sort of interesting, and was willing to expand my logistical territory to countenance the devastating effect a 15–30-mph stutter-breeze swirling southwest to east would have on my best calculations as to how ambitiously to respond to Joe Perfecthair's topspin drive into my backhand corner.

The IL combination of pocked courts, sickening damp, and wind required and rewarded an almost Zen-like acceptance of things they actually were, on-court. I'm pretty sure that I, as an immigrant to the township, had through contrast some unfair advantage; I could accept what drove my local opponents batty. I started to win a lot. At twelve, I began getting entry to tournaments beyond Philo and Champaign and Danville. I was driven by my parents or by the folks of Gil Antitoi, son of a Quebecois history professor from Urbana, to events like the Central Illinois Open in Decatur, a town built and owned by the A. E. Staley processing concern and so awash in the stink of roasting corn that kids would play with bandanas tied over their mouths and noses; like the Western Closed Qualifier on the ISU campus in Normal; like the McDonald's Junior Open in the serious corn town of Galesburg, way out west by the river, where in 1974 Antitoi so pummeled Norris T. Block, son of a prosperous hog farmer who was later to become the most hated man in the Midwest as Reagan's secretary of agriculture, that Norris T. Block, ranked eighth in Illinois in twelve-and-unders, was never seen on a court again; like the Prairie State Open in Pekin, insurance hub and home of Caterpillar Tractor; like the Midwest Junior Clay Courts at a chichi private club in Peoria's pale version of Scarsdale.

Over the next four summers I got to see way more of the state than is normal or healthy, albeit most of this seeing was at a blur of travel and crops, looking between nod-outs at sunrises abrupt and terribly candent over the crease between fields and sky (plus you could see any town you were aimed at the very moment it came around the earth's curve, and the only part of Proust that really moved me in school was the early description of the kid's geometric relation to the distant church spire at Combray), riding in station wagons' back seats through Saturday dawns and Sunday sunsets. I got steadily better; Antitoi, unfairly assisted by an early puberty, got radically better.

By the time we were fourteen, Gil Antitoi and I were the central IL cream of our age bracket, usually seeded one and two at area tournaments, able to beat all but a couple of even the kids from the Chicago suburbs who, together with a contingent from Grosse Pointe, MI, usually dominated the western regional rankings. That summer the best fourteen-year-old in the nation was a Chicago kid, Bruce Brescia from River Forest (whose penchant for floppy white tennis hats, low socks with bunnytails at the heel, and lurid pastel sweater vests testified to proclivities that wouldn't dawn on me for several more years), but Brescia and his henchman, Mark Mees of Zanesville, OH, never bothered to play anything but the Midwestern Clays and some indoor events in Cook County, being too busy jetting off to like the Pacific Hardcourts in Ventura and Junior Wimbledon and all that. I played Brescia just once, in the quarters of an indoor thing at the Rosemont Horizon in 1977, and the results were not pretty. Antitoi actually got a set off Mees in the National Qualifiers one year. Neither Brescia nor Mees ever turned pro; I don't know what happened to them after eighteen.

Antitoi and I ranged over the exact same competitive territory; he was my friend and foe and bane. Though I'd started playing two years before he, he was bigger, quicker, and basically better than I by about age thirteen, and I was soon losing to him in the finals of just about every tournament I played. So different were our appearances and approaches and general gestalts that we had something of a modest epic rivalry from '74 through '77. I had gotten so prescient at using stats, surface, sun, gusts, and a kind of Stoic cheer that I was regarded as a kind of physical savant, a medicine boy of wind and heat, and could play just forever, sending back moonballs baroque with ornate spins. Antitoi, uncomplicated from the getgo, hit the holy shit out of every round object that came within his ambit, aiming always for one of two backcourt corners. He was a Slugger. When he was "on," i.e., having a good day, he varnished the court with me. When he wasn't at his best (and the hours I, and David Hurst from Bloomington, and Kirk McKenzie and Steve Moe of Danville spent in meditation and seminar on what variables of diet, sleep, romance, car ride, and even sock color factored into the equation of Antitoi's mood and level day to day), he and I had great matches, real marathon wind-suckers. Of eleven finals we played in 1974, I won two.

Midwest junior tennis was my early initiation into true adult sadness. I had developed a sort of Taoistic hubris about my ability to control via noncontrol. I'd established a private religion of wind. Lord, I even liked to bike. Awfully few people in Philo bike, for obvious wind reasons, but I'd found a way to sort of tack back and forth against a stiff current, holding some wide book out at my side at about 120° to my angle of thrust—Bayne and Pugh's *The Art of* the *Engineer* and Cheiro's *Language of the Hand* proved about the best airfoils—so that through imagination and verve and Stoic cheer I could not just neutralize but use an in-your-face gale for biking. Similarly, by thirteen I'd found a way not just to accommodate but to *employ* the heavy summer winds in matches. No longer just mooning the ball down the center to allow plenty of margin for error and swerve, I was now able to use the currents kind of the way a pitcher uses spit. I could hit curves way out into crossbreezes that'd drop the ball just fair; I had a special wind-serve that had so much spin the ball turned oval in the air and curved left to right like a smart slider and then reversed its arc on the bounce. I'd developed the same sort of autonomic feel for what the wind would do to the ball that a standard-trans driver has for how to shift. As a junior tennis player, I was for a time a citizen of the concrete physical world in a way the other boys weren't, I felt. I felt betrayed at around fourteen when so many of these single-minded flailing boys became abruptly mannish and tall, with sudden sprays of hair on their thighs and wisps on their lips and ropy arteries on their forearms. My fifteenth summer, kids I'd been beating easily the year before all of a sudden seemed overpowering. I lost in two semifinals, at Pekin and Springfield in '77, of events I'd beaten Antitoi in the finals of in '76. My dad brought me to my knees after the Springfield loss to some kid from the Quad Cities when he said, trying to console me, that it had looked like a boy playing a man, out there. And the other boys sensed something up with me, too, smelled some breakdown in the odd détente I'd had with the elements: my ability to accommodate and fashion the exterior was being undercut by the muteness of some internal alarm clock I didn't understand.

I mention this mostly because so much of my Midwest's communal psychic energy was informed by growth and fertility. The agronomic angle was obvious, what with my whole township dependent for tax base on seed, dispersion, height, and yield. Something about the adults' obsessive weighing and measuring and projecting, the calculus of thrust and growth, leaked inside us children's capped and bandana'd little heads, out on the fields, diamonds, and courts of our special interests. By 1977 I was the only one of my group of ɔck friends with virginity intact. I know this for a fact, and only because these guys are now schoolteachers and commoditists and insurers with families and standings to protect will I not share with you just how I know this. I felt, as I became a later and later bloomer, alienated not just from my own recalcitrant glabrous little body, but in a way from the whole elemental exterior I'd come to see as my co-conspirator. I knew, somehow, that the call to height and hair came from outside, from whatever apart from Monsanto and Dow made the corn grow, the hogs rut, the wind soften every spring and hang with the scent of manure from the plain of beanfields north between us and Champaign. My vocation ebbed. I felt un-called. I began to experience the same resentment toward whatever children abstract as Nature that I knew Steve Moe felt when a soundly considered approach shot down the forehand line was blown out by a gust, that I knew Gil Antitoi suffered when his pretty kick-serve (he was the only top-flight kid from the slow weed-chocked township courts to play serve-and-volley from the start, which is why he had such success on the slick cement of the West Coast when he went on to play for Cal-Fullerton) was compro-mised by the sun: he was so tall, and so stubborn about adjusting his high textbook service toss for solar conditions, that serving from the court's north end in early afternoon matches always filled his eyes with violet blobs, and he'd lumber around for the rest of the point, flailing and pissed. This was back when sunglasses were unheard of, on-court.

But so the point is I began to feel what they'd felt. I began, very quietly, to resent my physical place in the great schema, and this resentment and bitterness, a kind of slow root rot, is a big reason why I never qualified for the Nationals or even Westerns again after 1978, and why I ended up in 1980 barely making the varsity of a college smaller than Urbana High while kids I had beaten and then envied played scholarship tennis for Purdue, Fuller-ton, Michigan, Pepperdine, and even, in the case of Pete Bouton, who grew half a foot and forty IQ points in 1977, for the U of I at Urbana-Champaign.

Alienation-from-Midwest-as-fertility-grid might be a little on the overmetaphysical side, not to mention self-pitying. This was the time, after all, when I discovered definite integrals and anti-derivatives and found my identity shifting from jock to math

wienie anyway. But it's also true that my whole Midwest tennis career matured and then degenerated under the aegis of the Peter
Principle. In and around my township—where the courts were
rural and budgets low and conditions so extreme that the mosquitoes sounded like trumpets and the bees like tubas and the wind
like a five-alarm fire, that we had to change shirts between games
and use our water jugs to wash blown field chaff off our arms and
necks and carry salt tablets in Pez containers—I was truly near-
great: I could Play the Whole Court; I was In My Element. But all
the more important tournaments, the events into which my rural
excellence was an easement, were played in a real different world:
the courts' surface was redone every spring at the Arlington Tennis
Center, where the National Junior Qualifier for our region was
held; the green of these courts' fair territory was so vivid as to
distract, its surface so new and rough it wrecked your feet right
through your shoes, and so bare of flaw, tilt, crack, or seam as to be
scary and disorienting. Playing on a perfect court was for me like
treading water out of sight of land: I never knew where I was out
there. The 1976 Chicago Junior Invitational was held at Lincolnshire's Yacht (?!) and Tennis Club, whose huge warren of thirty-six
courts was enclosed by these troubling green plastic tarps attached
to all the fences, with little like archer-slits in them at eye level to
afford some parody of spectation. These tarps were Wind-B-Gone
windscreens, patented by the folks over at Cyclone Fence in 1971.
They did cut down on the worst of the unfair gusts, but they also
seemed to rob the court space of new air: competing at Lincolnshire
was like playing in the bottom of a well. And blue bug-zap lights
festooned the lightposts when really major Midwest tournaments
played into the night: no clouds of midges around the head or jag-
ged shadows of moths to distinguish from balls' flights, but a real
unpleasant zotting and frying sound of bugs being decommis-
sioned just overhead; I won't pause to mention the smell. The point
is I just wasn't the same, somehow, without deformities to play
around. I'm thinking now that the wind and bugs and chuckholes
formed for me a kind of inner boundary, my own personal set of
lines. Once I hit a certain level of tournament facilities, I was dis-
abled because I was unable to accommodate the absence of dis-
abilities to accommodate. If that makes sense. Puberty-angst and

material alienation aside, my Midwest tennis career plateaued the moment I saw my first windscreen.

Still strangely eager to speak of weather, let me say that my township, in fact all of east-central IL, is a proud part of "Tornado Alley." Incidence of tornadoes all out of statistical proportion. I personally have seen two on the ground and five aloft, trying to assemble. Aloft tornadoes are green-white, more like convulsions in the thunderclouds themselves than separate or protruding from them. Ground tornadoes are black only because of the tons of soil they suck in and spin around. The grotesque frequency of tornadoes around my township is, I'm told, a function of the same variables that cause our civilian winds: we are a coordinate where fronts and air masses converge. Most days in late March–June there are Tornado Watches somewhere in our TV stations' viewing area (the stations put a little graphic at the screen's upper right, like a pair of binoculars for a Watch and the Tarot deck's Tower card for a Warning, or something). Watches mean conditions are right and so on and so forth, which, big deal. It's only the rarer Tornado Warnings, which require a confirmed sighting by somebody with reliable sobriety, that make the Civil Defense sirens go. The siren on top of the Philo Middle School was a different pitch and cycle from the one off in the south part of Urbana, and the two used to weave in and out of each other in a godawful threnody. When the sirens blew, the native families went to their canning cellars or fallout shelters (no kidding); the academic families in their bright prefab houses with new lawns and foundations of flat slab went with whatever good-luck tokens they could lay hands on to the very most central point on the ground floor after opening every single window to thwart implosion from precipitous pressure drops. For my family, the very most central point was a hallway between my dad's study and a linen closet, with a reproduction of a Flemish annunciation scene on one wall and a bronze Aztec sunburst hanging with guillotinic mass on the other; I always tried to maneuver my sister under the sunburst.

If there was an actual Warning when you were outside away from home, say at a tennis tournament in some godforsaken publi park at some city fringe zoned for sprawl, you were supposed to lie prone in the deepest depression you could locate. Since the only real depressions around most tournament sites were the irrigation and runoff ditches that bordered cultivated fields, ditches icky with conferva and mosquito spray and always heaving with what looked like conventions of copperheads and just basically places your thinking man doesn't lie prone in under any circumstances, in practice at Warned tournaments you zipped your rackets into their covers and ran to find your loved ones or even your liked ones and just all milled around trying to look like you weren't about to lose sphincter integrity. Mothers tended sometimes to wail and clutch childish heads to their bosoms (Mrs. Ayers of Pekin was particularly popular for clutching even strange kids' heads to her formidable bosom), or else to run around doing some meteorological variation of poor Mrs. Bishop's "My son ate this!"

I mention tornadoes for reasons directly related to the purpose of this essay. For one thing, they were a real part of Midwest childhood, because as a little kid I was obsessed with dread over them. My earliest nightmares, the ones that didn't feature mile-high robots from "Lost in Space" wielding huge croquet mallets (don't ask), were about shrieking sirens and dead white skies, a slender monster on the Iowa horizon, jutting less phallic than saurian from the lowering sky, whipping back and forth with such frenzy that it almost doubled on itself, trying to eat its own tail, throwing off chaff and dust and chairs; it never came any closer than the horizon; it didn't have to.

In practice, Watches and Warnings both seemed to have a kind of boy-and-wolf quality for the natives of Philo. They'd just happened too often. Watches were especially otiose, because we could always see storms coming from the west way in advance, and by the time they were over, say, Decatur you could diagnose the basic condition by the color and height of the clouds: the taller the anvil-shaped thunderheads, the better the chance for hail and Warnings; pitch-black clouds were a happier sight than gray shot with an odd nacreous white; the shorter the interval between the sight of lightning and the sound of thunder, the faster the system was moving, and the faster the system, the worse: like most things that mean you harm, severe thunderstorms are terse and businesslike.

I know why I stayed obsessed as I aged. Tornadoes, for me, were a transfiguration. Like all serious winds, they were our little stretch of plain's $z$ coordinate, a move up from the Euclidian monotone of furrow, road, axis, and grid. We studied tornadoes in junior high: a Canadian high straight-lines it southeast from the Dakotas; a moist warm mass drawls on up north from like Arkansas: the result was not a Greek $\chi$ or even a Cartesian $\vdash$, but a circling of the square, a curling of vectors, concavation of curves. It was alchemical, Leibnizian. Tornadoes were, in our part of central IL, the dimensionless point at which parallel lines met and whirled and blew up. They made no sense. Houses blew not out but in. Brothels were spared while orphanages next door bought it. Dead cattle were found three miles from their silage without a scratch on them. Tornadoes are omnipotent and obey no law. Force without law has no shape, only tendency and duration. I believe now that I knew all this without knowing it, as a kid.

The only time I ever got caught in what might have been one was in June '78 on a tennis court at Hessel Park in Champaign where I was drilling one afternoon with Gil Antitoi. Though a contemptible and despised tournament opponent, I was a coveted practice partner because I could transfer balls to wherever you wanted them with the tireless constancy of a machine. This particular day it was supposed to rain around suppertime, and a couple times we thought we'd heard the tattered edges of a couple sirens out west toward Monticello, but Antitoi and I drilled religiously every afternoon that week on the slow clayish Har-Tru of Hessel, trying to prepare for a beastly clay invitational in Chicago where it was rumored both Bruce Brescia and John Wayne (no kidding) of Crete-Monie (sixth in the nation in 1977's sixteen-and-unders) would appear. We were doing butterfly drills—my crosscourt forehand is transferred back down the line to Antitoi's backhand, he crosscourts it to my backhand, I sent it down the line to his forehand, four 45° angles, though the intersection of just his crosscourts made an $X$ that's four 90°s and also a crucifix rotated the same quarter-turn that a swastika (which involves eight 90° angles) is rotated on Hitlerian bunting. This is the sort of stuff that went through my head when I drilled. Hessel Park is scented heavily with cheese from the massive Kraft factory at Champaign's western limit, and it has wonderful expensive soft Har-Tru courts of such a deep piney color that the flights of the fluorescent balls stayed on one's visual screen for a few extra seconds, leaving trails, is also why the angles and hieroglyphs involved in butterfly drills seem important. But the crux here is that butterflies are primarily a conditioning drill: both players have to get from one side of the court to the other between each stroke, and once the initial pain and wind-sucking are over, assuming you're a kid who's in absurd shape because he spends countless mindless hours jumping rope or running laps backward or doing star-drills between the court's corners or straight sprints back and forth along the perfect furrows of early beanfields each morning, once the first pain and fatigue of butterflies are got through, if both guys are good enough so that there are few unforced errors to break up the rally, a kind of fugue-state opens up inside you where your concentration telescopes toward a still point and you lose awareness of your limbs and the soft shush of your shoe's slide (you have to slide out of a run on Har-Tru) and whatever's outside the lines of the court, and pretty much all you know then is the bright ball and the octangled butterfly outline of its trail across the billiard green of the court. We had one just endless rally and I'd left the planet in a silent swoop inside when the court and ball and butterfly trail all seemed to surge brightly and glow as the daylight just plain went out in the sky overhead. Neither of us had noticed that there'd been no wind blowing the familiar grit into our eyes for several minutes—a bad sign. There was no siren. Later they said the CD alert network had been out of order. This was June 6, 1978. The air temperature dropped so fast you could feel your hairs rise. There was no thunder and no air stirred. I could not tell you why we kept hitting. Neither of us said anything. There was no siren. It was high noon; there was nobody else on the courts. The riding mower out over east at the softball field was still going back and forth. There were no depressions except a saprogenic ditch along the field of new corn just west. What could we have done? The air always smells of mowed grass before a bad storm. I think we thought it would rain at worst and that we'd play till it rained and then go sit in Antitoi's parents' station wagon. I do remember a mental obscenity—I had gut strings in my rackets, strings everybody with a high district ranking got free for letting the Wilson sales rep spray paint a W across the racket face, so they were free, but I liked this particular string job on this racket, I liked them tight but not real tight, 62–63 p.s.i. on a Proflite stringer, and gut becomes pasta if it gets wet, but we were both in the fugue-state that exhaustion through repetition brings on, a fugue-state I've decided that my whole time playing tennis was spent chasing, a fugue-state I associated too with plowing and seeding and detasseling and spreading herbicides back and forth in sentry duty along perfect lines, up and back, or military marching on flat blacktop, hypnotic, a mental state at once flat and lush, numbing and yet exquisitely felt. We were young, we didn't know when to stop. I was mad at my body and wanted to hurt it, wear it down. Then the whole knee-high field to the west along Kirby Avenue all of a sudden flattened out in a wave coming toward us as if the field was getting steamrolled. Antitoi went wide west for a forehand cross and I saw the corn get laid down in waves and the sycamores in a copse lining the ditch point our way. There was no funnel. Either it had just materialized and come down or it wasn't a real one. The big heavy swings on the industrial swingsets took off, wrapping themselves in their chains around and around the top crossbar; the park's grass laid down the same way the field had; the whole thing happened so fast I'd seen nothing like it; recall that Bimini H-Bomb film of the shock wave visible in the sea as it comes toward the ship's film crew. This all happened very fast but in serial progression: field, trees, swings, grass, then the feel like the lift of the world's biggest mitt, the nets suddenly and sexually up and out straight as flags, and I seem to remember whacking a ball out of my hand at Antitoi to watch its radical west-east curve, and for some reason trying to run after this ball I'd just hit, but I couldn't have tried to run after a ball I had hit, but I remember the heavy gentle lift at my thighs and the ball curving back closer and my passing the ball and beating the ball in flight over the horizontal net, my feet not once touching the ground over fifty-odd feet, a cartoon, and then there was chaff and crud in the air all over and both Antitoi and I either flew or were blown pinwheeling for I swear it must have been fifty feet to the fence one court over, the easternmost fence, we hit the fence so hard we knocked it halfway down, and it stuck at 45°, Antitoi detached a retina and had to wear those funky Jabbar retina goggles for the rest of the summer, and the fence had two body-shaped indentations like in cartoons where the guy's face makes a cast in the skillet that hit him, two catcher's masks of fence, we both got deep quadrangular lines impressed on our faces, torsos, legs' fronts, from the fence, my sister said we looked like waffles, but neither of us got badly hurt, and no homes, set widely apart out near KraftCo, got whacked—either the thing just ascended again for no reason right after, they do that, they obey no rule, follow no line, hop up and down at something that might as well be will, or else it wasn't a real one. Antitoi's tennis continued to improve, after that, but mine didn't.

# ON BEING OUT OF CONTROL, OR HOW TOWNSHIPS MADE ME A PINKO

As I'm writing this, the war in the Persian Gulf, as was once predicted about the Revolution, is being televised. U.S. planes have been bombing Iraq for a week now, and all my attempts to think in depth about my misty semi-rural childhood, with its 4-H membership and Little League Baseball, are being foiled by visions of war.

I work in a two-person office, and ever since the Persian Gulf situation became a crisis, then a war, my colleague and I have been arguing over whether it's really necessary for the United States to be involved. As the bombs have continued to fall, our impasse has grown deeper, until we realized that the chasm between us is unbridgeable; the formative event of her youth in England was being bombed by the Nazis, while mine was hoping the Vietnam War would end before I reached draft age.

Like practically everyone in my generation, Vietnam forced on me an early assumption of at least partial adulthood. I wasn't actually faced with having to flee to Canada or be taken into the army, but I was old enough (seventeen in 1972, when we were carpet-bombing Hanoi and mining the harbors of Haiphong) that I already had made my decision and was ready to act. In the climate of what until a few days ago seemed a long-distant time, I was fervently pro-McGovern, my parents equally for Nixon. My generation took a long time to get beyond the war and Watergate, but eventually most of us reembraced our parents' values and got serious about making money in the 1980s, while we watched the generation younger than us skip liberalism entirely and go straight fo

the bucks with a ruthlessness and purity of spirit that both hor-
rified and amazed us.

If I seem to have failed, even to this day, to buy the wing tips,
move to the suburbs, build an IRA, and begin to say nice things
about the Reagan-Bush administration, well, I blame townships.

It was the summer of 1980, and I had just completed a master's
degree in fiction writing and was therefore broke. I was also engaged, and because my father couldn't stand watching his kids
starve right in his home town, he offered to employ my fiancée and
me as researchers and writers for his school finance consulting
firm. Our assignment was to produce, in our own loopy and pro-
crastinating way, prospectuses for possible bond buyers. These
documents included short narratives and histories of the school
district, which was usually a consolidation of two or more townships; in many cases, we were there because more townships were
consolidating to build giant high schools that, despite their amenities
such as swimming pools and auditoriums, looked more like weap-
ons factories than places where a person could get an education.

By helping in a small way to sell the bonds that raised the cash
that build such godawful prisons, I declared, my fiancée and I
would be participating in a corrupt system, and the money my father was paying us would, therefore, be tainted.

If my parents had been half as warlike as I thought they were,
they probably would have mowed me down with an M-16 for saying such things, but instead, my mother argued that my father's financial expertise actually saved taxpayers untold sums of interest,
and I accepted the job, thus beginning a voyage into the unexpect-
edly seamy underside of townships.

To acquire the information we needed for a prospectus, we'd
start by trying to get the flavor of the community. That might in-
volve a visit to the library, where invariably there'd be a heartfelt,
homemade exhibit about the importance of reading, usually constructed by Mrs. So-and-So's fifth-grade class.

There was always a solid old downtown square, the buildings
made of brick or stone, the five-and-dime still serving food, the
sporting goods store still offering a soda fountain, a drugstore, a
feed and farm store, the local barber, clothing, lots of hardware,
usually just one or two bars, a movie theater that exuded shabby
elegance, and a diner that remained the nerve center of the town.

The reality of the typical small town in Indiana in 1980 had an almost achingly sweet, bordering on smarmy quality. At any moment, we half expected to see Doris Day arm-in-arm with Jimmy Stewart.

People we'd talk to were friendly until asked about how things were going in general, and then they'd turn angry. In Paoli, they said, the Forest Service was allowing the hardwoods in Hoosier National Forest to be logged at a furious rate and replanting fast-growing, but nonnative pines in their place. This, we were told, would eventually ruin southern Indiana as a continuing source of fine-quality furniture.

In Brownstown, where my grandfather is buried, the spice-making company was on the ropes and the tomato canners were moving to California. These troubles threatened to take down the farm-and-feed-supply sector of the local economy, leaving gaping holes on that downtown square.

Warsaw, Indiana, was an exceedingly long way removed from Lech Walesa and the formation of Solidarity. Instead, the chamber of commerce director, a sharply dressed early-Yuppie woman about thirty, told me that the Chamber was trying to make sure the new industry would come into Warsaw union-free. "We don't need that kind of trouble here," she said. I listened to her heavy East Chicago accent and wondered if her dad had worked in the steel mills.

Everywhere, people were mad at what had gone wrong. The towns of Vernon and North Vernon—neighbors in southern Indiana—had found ways to restart their economies with federal money, the former to subsidize tourism, the latter to remodel the historic buildings on the square. But the gift shops were closed half the time; there were cost overruns and too little follow-up, the development director said. Too many North Vernonites were working a full day on the farm, then driving forty-five minutes to Columbus to pull the night shift at Cummins Diesel. A family of four averaged less than seventy-five hundred dollars a year farming, so the money had to come from elsewhere. North Vernon was a showcase of beautiful, empty space.

Big money—the federal government, the corporations that might or might not move the local plant to Mexico or Singapore, even the labor unions that blocked innovation—was a huge, unmanageable outside force, controlling the destiny of ordinary Hoosiers who just wanted to live like their parents and grandparents. At first glance, small-town Indiana had seemed a pastoral vision, but the empty storefronts, the surplus of "For Sale" signs, and the Victorian houses that had needed paint for too many years left little room for nostalgia or romance.

Originally, a township had been an artificial construct, a chunk of land that had once contained a one-room school to which all the kids could walk. Later, the schools got bigger and rivalries with neighboring townships developed. I knew that my father had started coaching basketball at a place called Union Township, and that he'd raised a ruckus by beating the school where he'd graduated. And I remembered talk of my grandfather serving as township trustee, but I didn't really know what that involved. Whatever it was, it didn't pay much, because he continued to drive up the road to work.

All summer in 1980, we spent hours in steamy courthouses, poring through handwritten plat books, trying to discover the names and assessed valuations of the twenty largest taxpayers. It took more time to get this information than any other portion of the prospectus, and yet my father said it was a critical page: "This is how they know where the money is," he'd say.

We'd break for lunch and take a walk around the courthouse square, usually eating in the local diner. Sometimes, we'd drive around the area, just to see what looked unique. We'd guess who the largest taxpayers were going to be. The big auto dealership that serves a fifth of the state? That locally owned furniture factory that seems to employ a few hundred people? The owners of the shopping mall? Sears? The Farm Bureau Co-op? Invariably, we'd be wrong.

Every township assessor's files told us that America's rhetoric about its classless society and reasonably fair distribution of wealth— what I'd learned in civics and social studies—was an outrageous lie, and I've never really recovered from that discovery. The Twenty Largest Taxpayers were almost always utilities, utilities, utilities. Out-of-state industry. The phone company. The gas company. In every school district, the utility companies had more wealth by themselves than virtually all the other taxpayers. Their typical assessed valuation was hundreds or even thousands of times greater than that of most familes and businesses. In addition to the property on which their lines ran, they often, seemingly pointlessly, owned vast tracts of land.

Once in a while, a bank would be high on the list, if it had done a lot of repossessing. Occasionally, a huge insurance company would appear, owning enough land for a hundred farmers. Often, the railroads were there, frequently listed as "SUSPENDED" next to their incomprehensibly huge valuations, which made me realize that to a large extent it was a thousand different bills, simultaneously due from township and county assessors, that killed the rail service in this country.

Another omnipresent force in the local economy was natural gas and oil pipeline companies. Always headquartered in Texas, these corporations were unknown to almost everyone, yet invariably owned more land than the wealthiest farmer in the township. Finally, mining companies—in Indiana, this usually meant coal, though it could be oil or gypsum—were a major force, having bought up staggering amounts of woods and fields, the timetable for exploration and/or development also a mystery.

The ultimate lesson seemed to be that in any given township, you might think you know who is important, but the wealth was concentrated in out-of-county or even out-of-state companies that not only are headquartered elsewhere but are also completely without competition. In a sense, the restaurants, car dealers across the main street from each other, even factories that make up the seeming backbone of a local economy are utter lightweights compared to the modern-day land barons, these barely regulated monopolies that really ought to be publicly owned and accountable to the people who use their services.

In the mid-1980s, Public Service Indiana, the electric company for three-fourths of Indiana, blew over four billion dollars on a nuclear power plant that was never finished and not only survived but became a hot growth stock by the latter years of the decade. That's wealth, and it's tainted wealth, too, sucked every month from the shrinking paychecks of a populace that still labors under the delusion that riches are just around the corner.

I've just about lost that fantasy, though I'm not entirely immune to throwing a dollar at a huge lottery jackpot. Though studying townships cost me my economic innocence, I've tried to retain a certain degree of idealism in the face of a truly lopsided system. Perhaps as a reaction to what seems an almost guaranteed bias against economic activity that makes sense to real people, my wife and I have toiled these last ten years solely for nonprofit organizations, where an entirely different kind of zaniness rules.

I recently had an encounter with an insurance agent that proved how little things have changed. In the wake of the bankruptcy of such once-thriving paragons of capitalism as Eastern Airlines, I asked the agent from Prudential how I could be sure my investment would be secure. "We're a very big company," she said. "We own more land than the United States government."

In Hensley Township in Johnson County, Indiana, more than thirty of my relatives live. I still visit there a couple of times a year. When I do, I see the moderately hilly, half-wooded, half-agricultural terrain as my ancestral homeland, even though there's no single place that is or was the family's original estate. I see that my grandmother's house needs paint, and I drive by my late great-grandmother's house, which my cousin sold after finally giving up on trying to remodel it. I also see the utility lines above ground and imagine the ones below, pumping the cash of the Wilkersons out of Hensley Township and off toward someplace I'll never know or see.

# IN THE FIRST PLACE

# OF MY LIFE

*It is often said that before the Almighty Creator took the red-colored clay in his cosmic hands to gently shape and mold the first human beings, he wanted to be absolutely sure these people would have a knowledgeable leader who would guide them through the suffering and beauty of earthly existence.*

*This leader, he must have felt, had to be a direct part of himself.*

*To ensure the best possible guidance for these people, in a manner similar to the extensive Preparation he had done for the anticipated arrival of these people, the Creator tore out a piece of his own heart and created O ki ma, the Sacred Chief.*

*Considering the last turbulent and painful days the Creator experienced before the jealous gods sent the Great Fire and Flood after him, it seemed appropriate that a progeny of wise decision-makers be comprised exclusively of his own sacred flesh and blood. This he did . . .*

The beginning of personal memory and history is perhaps the most important connection I have with Mamwiwanike, the young O ki ma, Sacred Chief, who founded and initiated the purchase of the Tribal Settlement in 1856:

From a distant and vague time, his grandson, Ke twe o se, my maternal grandfather, reached downward from his wooden-frame bed and called me with large outstretched arms and encouraging words. "*Ki sko, bya no yo,* come here."

He sat in the southeastern corner of the small two-room house waiting for me. Like a newborn wobbly-legged fawn taking a trial walk in a meadow of tall grass, I went to him. Attracted initially by his toothless smile and puffy, slanted eyes, I struggled past a beam of harsh sunlight and lost sight of him momentarily.

On the wooden floor beneath me I could feel the worn subtle

divisions of boards; in the brightness I could see individual specks of dust float and swirl past me and then disappear in the draft.

From the cool darkness, he lifted me upward gracefully in one swoop into his arms and placed me on his knees. The year was 1952, almost a hundred years after his own grandfather established our five thousand–acre sanctuary in central Iowa.

*As soon as the Creator made O ki ma from the flesh of his heart, the other human beings were then sculpted from the red-colored clay, and they named themselves appropriately from their very beginnings.*

*Akin to a father attending to the well-being of his children, the Creator instructed these people on the tactics and skills of hunting and fishing, and he also showed them when and where to plant seeds for gardens, as well as how to live in peace and to respect one another and the various but essential life-forms around them. He also taught them how to sing, dance, and pray. He shared with them only the good things by which to live. And they venerated him in return.*

*Yes, the Creator had meticulously prepared this earth for these people. From the claws of the muskrat who dove into the great body of water to retrieve mud, remnants of a previous earth, the Creator shaped the round earth; from the twigs and bits of grass brought by the bluejay and mourning dove, the Creator turned these into forests and prairies; and from the vulture's once-beautiful wings came the gouged-out valleys, hills, and mountains. Yes, the Creator had done much for these people.*

*All he desired was for these new people, their children, and their children's children, to remember him through the four seasons in prayers, stories, songs, and intricate ceremony. For as long as clan remembrance to his specific wishes continued, they would survive.*

In the first place of my life there is the image of my grandfather imploring me to walk to him. In the second place of my life there is my grandfather again, but in this memory he is the one who is attempting to walk:

With the door wide open to the summer night, my grandfather prepared to stumble out of the small house with the aid of three young men. It seemed the difficulty I experienced walking to him afflicted him instead. The little earth on which I once stood was now under his feet and growing smaller with hardly any room to stand. I began to feel that something terrible was wrong; he would subsequently lose balance and fall.

From the kerosene-darkened walls of the corner where he made his bed, he slowly held out his arms. The young men placed themselves under them, lifting him cautiously to the floor and then outside.

From the wooded hill above and east of the house, locusts, crickets, and tree frogs directed the start of the night songs in unison. Soon I could no longer hear the four talking men. Instead there was a buzzing sound that swiftly came and left, like the flutter of rapid wings. It brushed my face with its breeze and became still.

I later realized it was only grandfather's low voice, giving constant instructions. In soft respectful voices the young men were responding and informing each other what they were doing, where they were. The metamorphosis of arm to wing and mouth to beak . . .

In the third place of my life there is a fiery-red sunset. It is being followed by a thin, horizontal fragment of blue sky, which itself is being trailed by the ornately speckled lights of the night sky, covering the earth-island like a blanket with deliberate perforations. Starlight coming through clothes of poverty.

Three opposing parts of the day are visible as I waver on a well-trodden path of dirt and sparse grass. For clarity I try to look upward to distinguish the colors around me; I am intrigued by their variations and mysteriousness. Although I am quite a ways from my point of origin—the small unpainted house—I am not afraid or alarmed.

Somewhere on this path once, I think aloud to myself, my sick grandfather was guided to the thickets. I therefore adduce this path leads to a boundary where humans can vanish and reappear as dustlike shapes in the last faint beams of sunset. A whippoorwill, *ko ko we a*, begins to call out on the hillside.

In my plastic imitation chaps, boots, and cowboy straw hat, I am content just to stand, slightly off-balance, watching in astonishment as the three hues of earthlight follow the westward sun. As this light illuminates the forest floor nearby, I can see umbrella-shaped plants glisten like vast rippling water.

With the last of the day's warmth on my face and the cool stars coming over my shoulders, I straighten my body and rise upward, flying beyond the branchtops of the forest, and become a witness to an extraordinary renascence:

*We tti wa ba ki*, from the east, a whizzing star travels across the landscape, lighting the area briefly with a blanket of silver glare. After the fiery star passes the slow fusion of night and day, it explodes in silence and disintegrates, sending multicolored sparks over the horizon, over my inquisitiveness. By some powerful decision I believe the star has been sent for my sole benefit—to enthrall me. I gasp and tumble earthward.

In the fourth place of my life there is an irreplaceable loss. On July 23, 1954, an aged woman—the same one who had opened the door to let my grandfather and the three young men out—led me to the adjoining room of the house where a body was rolled perfectly into red and blue patterned blankets.

She pointed and then began speaking words I had little comprehension of. I was taken aback by the orderly scene of a person who slept without breathing.

"*Ma na ke ke me tto e ma i ni ke e ki tti ne ka ne na qwi be no tti ni e ya. A qwi na na tti ni ne a bi bya tti ni.* This is your grandfather; he has left us and will now go far away. He will never come back."

If he has indeed left, I asked myself, why is he still here in plain view? And where could he go if by chance this person asleep is not him? The thought of my grandfather going somewhere didn't coincide with the utter stillness of the unseen person.

There was no place one could possibly go on this little earth. Could he have gone behind the two hills? Or did he hide in the ravine by the creek?

I could not make sense of the attention his apparent departure brought. All night generous but wordless people came and left, bringing food. I could no longer hear the insects and frogs. Instead, there was a row of sitting and kneeling men with gourd rattles and a wooden barrel drum, chanting melancholic songs that put me to sleep.

The next day and for two days afterward, streams of people kept coming, but still no one knew where my grandfather was. I was sure this was the reason so many came, to assist in the search. The realization that he was the subject of much concern heightened my anxiety. Even when people congregated inside and outside the house to chat and eat, with the air filled with the aroma of corn and chicken, sweets, fruits, and frybread, his absence made me extremely lonely.

On what was perhaps the fourth and final day, we sat down on the large grassy yard to eat the cooked food. When I finished I found myself under an apple tree, looking up at a pale, hooknosed man whose reassuring voice finally told me what everything meant.

"*A qwi ke na na tti ni ne ya bi bya tti ni ke me tto e ma.* Your grandfather will *never* return," he said.

I was positive these visitors had tried to tell me that but had failed to get through. I had enclosed myself securely from all explanation. What had been so hard to understand was right in front of my face in the form of two grandfathers.

As the feast was drawing to a close—evident by clinking silverware and the scolding of impatient children by their parents—the same men who sang several nights previous came out from the protective shade of a maple tree and sat down with the barrel drum propped in front of them

A carton of Lucky Strike cigarettes was opened, and the packs were distributed to each of the singers by the same male attendants who had set out the tablecloths, dishes, cups, spoons, and kettles over the yard. With lit cigarettes in their mouths the singers quietly joked with one another; a few drank coffee, placed their heads together, and hummed in search of a tune.

The pale, hooknosed man who had enlightened me earlier stood directly in the middle of the festivity. I hadn't noticed before that he was wearing bright, sparkling clothes. He looked elegant with long swaying leaves of corn and the shimmering cottonwood trees behind him. He stood on one end of the yard where the people sat and ate. He did not speak or look around in curiosity as the others. The red fibrous wool of the blanket bound to his waist and lower torso, along with the intricate floral beadwork and yarn ties around his head and arms, reflected the fine weather.

"*Ma na ke i no ki ke me tto e ma. I ni ni a be tti i tti te e wa ni.* Here is your grandfather now. That is what you must always think," said the aged woman who opened the door, taking my hand and leading me to him.

"*Ni ne a bi ska ma ye ke me tto e ma ni.* He will take the place of your grandfather."

Finally coherent, I studied the hooknosed man and came to the conclusion he was already my grandfather; he had espied my loss and consoled me under the apple tree in a familiar voice.

As the relatives began to stand in anticipation of a dance, I listened to the instructions given him by the leader, telling him where to go and how many times this should be done. When the man with the sparkling clothes spoke, he sounded different. But my grandfather and his voice were just within him, I thought.

As soon as the attendants picked up the tablecloths and silverware, we stood in a group behind my grandfather-to-be. When the last communal drink of water was drunk and the last chewing gum opened by restless infants, the aged woman drew herself down and began to whisper.

"*Ma ni ke me me tti ne ni ke ski wi te ke ma qwi ke me tto e ma i ni a.* This is the last time we will have to dance with your (previous) grandfather."

I shielded my face with the one free hand for shade and looked upward. The aged woman held a handkerchief to her mouth and took short, sudden breaths as she cried.

Like the fierce crackling sound that precedes thunder, I was startled by the unexpected rumbling of the barrel drum by an elderly gentleman wearing sunglasses on his wide nose and a red Dutch bandana around his neck.

Although he had previously appeared tired and unimpressed by the proceedings, he, too, became someone else. From behind the old singer's sunglasses there emerged another person whose bent body combined the vocal strengths of a dozen men. He called out encouragingly to the other singers, and they joined in as a chorus with the same fervor and intensity.

Like the echo of thunder heard leaving a valley and heading through another in the distance, the song was sung by all until breath's end.

The rumbling slowed down and then stopped altogether.

The elderly man paused briefly to slosh the water inside the barrel before bringing down the wooden loop-end drumstick into a steady resonant beat over the wet cowhide.

The drum's strong vibration passed through the bodies of all those who were clustered around my new grandfather. It was as if our heartbeats were controlled by the deep, thunderous hum.

In exhilaration we huddled together and took several steps forward.

The music lifted above the crowd of dancers and stayed in place before lifting further, flying away, and then coming back to encircle us like an eagle whose powerful black and golden wingtips brushed our faces, waking us, telling us to see this dance through for my grandfather . . .

Many years after the incident with the whizzing star and my grandfather's departure, I stood in a garden which was being cleaned for plowing. I wore an impressive denim coat with short white fringes of plastic on the sleeves and shoulders, and there were tin medallions of standing horses over my chest.

Numerous fires were being set to mounds of dried cornstalks and roots. Together with two other children, I stoked the hot fires with a branch. We were amused and partially mesmerized when the thick black smoke followed us where we stood, as if to protect the fire from our intrusive branches.

Unaware that embers were dangerous, I placed a branch with an invisible flame on my shoulder and quickly caught fire. White scorching smoke shot from my coat, and my nostrils sucked up the heat. I coughed in horror and couldn't breathe. I spun in a circle, tripped, got up, and ran wildly in an effort to extinguish the body-fire.

In the mayhem, with mates chasing me and screaming, a woman grabbed and threw me violently into the clumpy garden. She rolled me like a ball over the dust until the fire went out.

In the calmness I looked up at the white clouds and blue sky, and I distinctly remember the whizzing star. I personified that very star, tumbling and sizzling with bits of my being spread out over the green foliage.

The woman who doused the fire with garden dust would become my mother, Ne tti ta, and her mother was my grandmother, Ne o ta mo qwe, the aged woman who held my hand as we danced for the last time with my grandfather. She was the earth herself . . .

When I at last became old enough to differentiate the basic rights and wrongs and apply them accordingly within family and social perimeters, my caretakers began to intensify their teachings on how to take care of myself, what to avoid, how to be friendly and respectful of others, not to lie or be mean.

To prevent even the earliest form of criticism, I was not allowed to wander anywhere by myself like an unwanted or wayward child, nor was I permitted to visit houses and the like.

This is what I was told whenever I expressed a desire to walk to a neighbor's house and play with friends my age:

"*Ka ta na ta we ne ta ka ni ne ko ta ni a ya ni. A yo ma e o wi ki ya qwi. Wa ni mo tti qwa bo se wa ni ne wo ne ki me te ne ta qwi me ko ko i ya ki ta tti me ko. A yo ki ki wi ta. 'Ne tti a be tti ki i ka ma wi ki ya bye ni' ni bi i ne ne ki me to se ne ni wa ki. Na no tti ke me ko a wi ta ke ko e ne me ko sa be me ne ko tti, ki i ne ko be na.* Do not desire to go anywhere. This is where we live. Should you traverse about, if you are seen, somebody will surely say things about you. Stay here. So people will not say, 'He is always preoccupied with houses.' His caretakers must not care for him, is what they will finally say."

The few occasions I objected to or questioned this travel restriction, comparing myself to the children given the freedom of traveling the roads by themselves, I was duly reminded of how an elderly woman, a neighbor, nearly drained the life out of my infancy to extend her own. The possibility someone could harm me by touch alone never failed to deter me.

In the mirror I would peruse my round face and see the pockmarks and long fingerlike scars on my tender skin. This was evidence of her ill-intentioned visit.

Stop and listen, I was told, before you get angry with us.

"You were asleep in the hammock the afternoon your nemesis came to welcome you. You were but a month old, a baby. She had never stopped by before for any reason. So when she made much of this visit we became suspicious. We didn't know exactly what she had done until a day or two later. Her visit was a pretext. You became very ill with convulsions accompanied by a high fever that couldn't be brought down. We then reminded one another how she had been ever so delicate with her touches on your chin and jaw. On the places her fingers came in contact, your skin broke out in blisters."

So to that end I listened and never again dared to venture beyond the natural tree, field, brush, road, and hill borders that encompassed our house. By nightfall I would peer out the windows and wonder if the green light would show up and reenact the dance of the battle, my breath or hers.

While there were many houses up and down the community's lone gravel road, I didn't know which one housed the descendants of the old woman responsible for my auspicious beginning.

# NOTES ON CONTRIBUTORS

Raymond Bial has published eleven books of photographs to date. His most recent books include *Stopping By: Portraits from Small Towns, Corn Belt Harvest,* and *From the Heart of the Country.* He lives in Urbana, Illinois, with his wife and two daughters. The photographs in this volume are drawn from a variety of his work over the past several years.

Carol Bly lives in Minnesota. Her most recent books are *The Passionate, Accurate Story,* which won the Minnesota Book Award for 1991 in nonfiction, and *The Tomcat's Wife and Other Stories.* She teaches the literature part of a three-department course in ethics at the University of Minnesota and is a board member of the Loft.

Marianne Boruch is the author of two books of poetry, *View from the Gazebo* and *Descendant.* She has won a Pushcart Prize, the Cecil Hemley Award of the Poetry Society of America, and a National Endowment for the Arts fellowship. She lives in West Lafayette, Indiana, where she directs the graduate program in creative writing at Purdue University.

Anthony Bukoski, who lives and works in Superior, Wisconsin, has advanced degrees from Brown University and the University of Iowa. His recent short stories have appeared in *Mid-American Review, New Letters,* the *Literary Review,* and the *South Carolina Review.*

Amy Clampitt was born in Providence Township, Iowa, graduated from New Providence High School and from Grinnell College, and has since lived mainly in New York City. She has been a Guggenheim fellow and has received awards from the American Academy and Institute of Arts and Letters, the Academy of American Poets, and the Lila Wallace–Reader's Digest Fund. Her books of poetry include *The Kingfisher, What the Light Was Like, Archaic Figure,* and *Westward.* She recently completed *Predecessors, Et Cetera,* a collection of essays in the University of Michigan's Poets on Poetry Series. She is currently at work on a play about the life of Dorothy Wordsworth.

Susan Dodd is the author of *Mamaw,* a novel which won the Friends of America Writers

Scott Russell Sanders, who grew up in Ohio, has been teaching at Indiana University since 1971. In that time he has published more than a dozen books, including novels, documentary narratives, and collections of stories and essays. His two most recent books appeared in 1991: *Secrets of the Universe,* personal essays, and *In Limestone Country,* narratives about stone workers and the stony landscape of southern Indiana. He is currently working on a series of stories about an urban trickster named Gordon Milk, and a series of essays about belonging to a place, for a book to be called *Ground Notes.*

Mary Swander has published two books of poetry, *Succession* and *Driving the Body Back,* in addition to individual poems, essays, non-fiction articles, and short stories in such places as the *Nation,* the *New Yorker,* and *Poetry.* Her dramatic adaptation of *Driving the Body Back* was produced by the Riverside Theatre of Iowa City in 1988. She received her MFA degree from the University of Iowa and has received numerous grants and awards, including the National Endowment for the Arts Award in literature, two Ingram Merrill grants, the Literary Arts Award from the Chicago Public Library, and the *Nation*-Discovery

Prize. A native of Iowa, an associate professor at Iowa State University, and an avid gardener, Swander is coauthor (with Jane Staw) of *Parsnips in the Snow: Talks with Midwestern Gardeners,* published by the University of Iowa Press in 1990.

David Foster Wallace is the author of *The Broom of the System, Girl with Curious Hair,* and, with Mark Costello, *Signifying Rappers.* He lives in Boston.

Michael Wilkerson has published work in *Tri-Quarterly* and the *Iowa Review* and in *Where We Live: Essays about Indiana. Can This Story Be Saved,* a chapbook of fiction, was published by Story County Books. He is director of the Ragdale Foundation, a retreat for artists, writers, and composers in Lake Forest, Illinois.

Ray A. Young Bear is a lifelong resident of the Mesquakie Tribal Settlement near Tama, Iowa. His poems are widely anthologized, and he has published two collections of his work: *Winter of the Salamander* and *The Invisible Musician.* His poetic autobiographical/ fictional book, *Black Eagle Child: The Facepaint Narratives,* will be published by the University of Iowa Press in 1992.

# BUR OAK BOOKS